MAGIC OF
THE NORTH GATE

POWERS OF THE LAND, THE STONES,
AND THE ANCIENTS

BY JOSEPHINE MCCARTHY

SECOND EDITION

TaDehent Books
Exeter

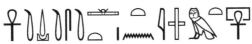

First edition published by Mandrake of Oxford, 2013

Second edition published by TaDehent Books 2020
Exeter UK

ISBN 978-1-911134-46-6

Cover image by Stuart Littlejohn
Typeset by Michael Sheppard

Dedicated to my partner Stuart Littlejohn,

and to Robert Henry, a magical brother who walked into the West
on December 25th, 2012.

Acknowledgements

Thanks to the following people who all inspire me, bully me, and keep an eye on me: Cecilia Lindley, Toni, Tony and Cat, John P, Christin, Frater Acher, and Karen McKeown. Also thank you to my daughters Leander and Cassandra for always being such inspirations. I also want to give a special thanks to my partner Stuart Littlejohn, a vastly talented man with endless patience and a wicked sense of humour.

Contents

Foreword

by Frater Acher

Before you dive into the depths of the magical teaching, techniques, and wisdom this book offers, I recommend that you ask yourself a simple question. It is so simple that it might be considered the most essential question of magical practice:

"Why use magic?"

Being truthful and honest with yourself; why you are using magic is not only important for defining your own magical path; it is maybe even more important because the first thing that any spiritual being will look at is your magical intent.

Ten years ago, if someone had asked me why I walk the path of magic, I would have answered "to gain conscious knowledge and conversation with my Holy Guardian Angel." Maybe I would have hesitated before adding: "Oh, and of course to discover my True Will!" Today, I don't think either of those two answers are relevant.

Today, I think of this essential question as a Zen Koan. It looks deceitfully simple at first glance. Yet if you were to approach your Zen teacher with your intuitive answer, there is a high chance he would smile and turn you away. So you would return to your meditation place and meditate over this most simple question again. "What possibly could have been wrong with my answer? Isn't contact with my Holy Guardian Angel a most worthy goal in life? Isn't peeling away layer after layer of ego-driven wishes and desires to finally find and fulfil my True Will what drove mages for at least... well, at least since Crowley successfully established the highly ambiguous term 'True Will' as the most successful fig leaf since the philosophy of hedonism for turning your life into a self-centred journey of narcissism...? So what is wrong with my answer?"

Well, that is exactly the question we need to ask ourselves: what can possibly be wrong with such a simple answer to such a simple question? To be honest, I spent most of the last two years searching for a better answer, one that meets with the approval of the Zen teacher we call Life.

I guess Life doesn't like this answer, because it works against a much broader horizon than I or most other humans normally do. Life simply isn't confined by the limits we often take for granted, and it doesn't need to break down its lessons by chapters, years, or decades as we do. It is free to perceive the obvious and painful challenges we encounter as essentially positive and deeply enriching, and it is never driven by angst or fear as we humans will always be to some extent.

Life, being what it is, doesn't even bother too much about my personal conditions or reasons for giving this answer. In fact, Life again might have a much broader frame of reference when asking the question 'Why use Magic?' let's use a little role play to illustrate how Life might look at this question.

For a moment let's swap roles with the spirits we tend to work with in magic. Let's assume that Life poses a similar question to these spirits, or even to our own Holy Guardian Angel: "Why use humans?" And as our Holy Guardian Angel looks completely gobsmacked, Life goes on to say: "Look, it takes years of dedicated hard work with a single human being to train them in the most basic steps, like how to deal with large amounts of energy, how to talk to us, how to be okay with not seeing us on the physical plain, etc. It takes all this effort to raise humans to a level where they can actually be helpful. Then what? How many humans have you seen who—once they reach this threshold of understanding and power—actually offer themselves up in service, who let go of their personal agenda, of their human wishes and desires, of their dreams of individual eternity, of personal remembrance by their offspring, and—worst of all—of their deeply ingrained craving to experience god-like significance?" "Well," the spirit would say, turning away from its Zen teacher in thought, "truth be told, I haven't exactly seen a lot of humans like this..." So why use humans?

My point, I guess, is quite straightforward. As long as our answer to "Why use Magic?" revolves around ourselves as the central pillar of our universe, we can't expect Life to have any specific interest in it. Because whether we fail or succeed doesn't matter to anybody but ourselves. If this is good enough for you, go right ahead. Many generations of magicians went ahead before, and I fear many more will follow.

When I draw a line under the dozens and dozens of magical training manuals I have read and practised from in my life, what remains is a few highly powerful, many average, and a lot of feeble techniques for optimizing yourself and the narrow world you call your life. Most of these books give you techniques to engineer yourself into a better version of yourself: to grow from Neophyte to Zelator to Adept to Magister; to gradually, over your lifetime, climb the eternal Hermetic Ladder of self-improvement, one rung at a time. The aim is to one day finally emerge as the master of all arcane disciplines, the stone of the wise, impersonated in a suit of flesh and bones that you can be proud to call yourself.

Don't get me wrong. I followed this path intensely for more than a decade, practising every day for hours, as many of us did—or still do. And I still believe the motivation to climb this ladder is a wonderful one for setting out on the magical path when we are young or start out completely fresh. But...there comes a time in our lives as magicians when we have climbed this ladder high enough, when we need to ask ourselves if our original motive still holds true? Is it still good enough to simply focus on ourselves, given all the things we have gained through the support of spirits and divine beings way beyond our capacities? In other words: at which point do we start repaying our debt to Life and all its forces that helped us become who we are?

If every spirit you have ever worked with was allowed to direct one wish at you, what would they ask for? How would this long list read? And how many of these wishes have you fulfilled so far? The most essential question I can think of for us as magicians to answer is "Why use Magic?" Whatever answer we come up with, it should also answer the question Life might pose to the spirits: "Why use Humans?"

How long do we give ourselves to realize that the ladder we were feverishly climbing is not only a ladder, but also a chain: the Hermetic or Golden Chain, the one that connects all beings, small and large, weak and powerful, through threads of life and power. The question I needed to ask myself was: "How long do I give myself to find my place in this chain—and when should I start working not my own agenda, but on the ones that matter beyond me?"

I don't know where you are on your magical path. But before you begin reading this book you may want to take a moment to pause and reflect. To ask yourself: "Am I still a seedling, or am I a tree? And if the latter, who has come to shelter in my shadow? Who eats from my fruits? Which nests am I ready to host in my crown?"

It doesn't mean I'll stop growing, stop following the cycles of the year, or stop refreshing myself with water and air and light every day. It simply means that even after all these intense years of work on myself, this work will continue; yet it will change from a means to its own end into a basis from which I can begin to give back.

A few more essential questions you might want to consider as you are approaching the teachings and techniques of this wonderful book could be the following:

Do I know what the stones, plants, and earth in my garden desire?

Am I aware of the needs of the faery beings and spirits who live with me in this house?

Do I have favours to return to spirits who helped me in the past?

Are any unacknowledged spirits in my personal realm—body, house, community—asking for service?

Which physical world events might have negatively impacted spirits living with me in this land? Are there ways I can help or support?

What do my dreams teach me about the jobs I can usefully do— through the tool I have turned myself into?

Even when everything goes exactly to plan, we do not necessarily move from student to teacher; often we move from student to servant.

— Frater Acher, Munich 2013.

Introduction

Many years ago as a young budding magician, I scoffed at a piece of wisdom offered to me, a true wisdom that I was too young to grasp. My mentor at that time was talking to me about the directions and the powers that flows from them. She said, "You can only really master the skills of one direction in a lifetime." Hmph. I had been working with the directions and had strong contacts in all four of them. I had passed over the threshold of all four directions and explored the inner realms filtered by them. She was wrong, I thought. And I was arrogant, as well as ignorant.

Many things she dropped in my lap in my twenties only began to dawn on me years later; and many of her wisdoms that I had swept to one side as 'quaint' or 'of their time' eventually revealed themselves to me over many years. The depth and knowledge of her insights now astounds me, and I truly wish with all my heart that she was still alive so I could go back to sit in her front room—which was heavily decorated with tons of Egyptian bling—and say, "I apologize for being a stupid, arrogant young woman."

She was right. The levels of knowledge, contact, and power that can be connected with in any one direction, plus the skills to learn how to wield that power, take a lifetime to learn. I assumed that when she talked about 'outer court' learning she meant learning Tarot, outer drama/ritual, setting up altars, astrology, etc., and that when she mentioned 'inner court' work she meant astral work. And that would be the understanding of most magicians. It was certainly my understanding for many years.

But the dawn came slowly that the 'outer court' in my understanding was not even a court, but merely the path leading towards the court. The inner visionary work in temples, Underworlds, etc. was the 'outer court' work—even though it was conducted in the Inner Worlds. The veil was slowly being pulled back to show me another layer, another 'court' of the Great Work—service to the land and Divinity—a completely other level of contact and power.

I began to work with this new layer that I had been exposed to. I didn't fully understand it, I could not form it no matter how I tried, and I found I could not express it—basically because I really did not understand it. The deeper I stepped into this newly found 'court,' the less I understood, and the more I came to realise that the work I had been doing for so long, which I considered so 'deep,' was not really even scratching the surface.

Inner Contacts tried various ways to show me how to work, how to form this power, how to connect with its levels of consciousness, but I really was not getting it. I was trying to fall back on old comforts, systems that I already knew and understood. I was being talked to in a new language, and I was trying to translate it rather than simply learn it.

Over the next five years, my connection to and contact with this new layer drifted in and out. I did not know how to consciously apply this dynamic; I didn't even have a name for it. In the end I surrendered and just let it flow naturally. The power flowed through a specific filter: a direction. And by direction I don't mean that the power only came from one place; I mean that it was filtered through a specific magical power filter: a magical elemental direction.

I had worked with this power filter for many years as part of a four-directional pattern, and all the while I thought I was learning about the powers in that direction when in fact I was only building the filter through which they could pass.

The reason I am telling you all this is to show you how magic reveals itself. When you first make contact with inner beings and power, and you have an 'experience,' you think you are the bees knees. Some people go all messiah. A decade or two down the road, once you've been knocked around a lot, you realize just how much there is to magic and how unwieldy it can be—but also how beautiful. You do rituals, visions, and initiations, and you settle in to 'being a magician.'

Then one day, a decade or two later again, slowly, silently, another veil is drawn back. It is like looking out at the universe, at the endless flow of stars, for the first time. Its magnificence and vastness overwhelm you as you realize that you have only learned the first letter of the alphabet; you have a long way to go before you can begin to write poetry.

This book is about that first, most powerful letter in the alphabet: the powers that flow from specific sources, the powers that run through our world and trigger the formation of magical and religious structures. It is viewed in this book via our work on the land, our bodies, the elements and directions, and our own mortality.

This is not a beginner's book; it is a book of techniques and methods for working magicians, priestesses, and occultists—techniques that take us deeper into magic and therefore deeper into ourselves. This book is about how that power flows, what it does, how it organizes itself, how it can develop for good or bad, and how it can all go horribly wrong.

Chapter One

The body and magic

Keeping body and soul together in the crucible of magic

The most important thing to remember, before we delve into the depths of how magic affects mind and body, is the necessity of putting this information in perspective. Yes, magic does affect mind and body once the magician starts to work in any depth, but knowing those effects and warning signs and acting accordingly ensures that any changes become part of the magician's path and not a passive consequence of their action. A magician can do many things to minimize the effects of magic on their bodies and use the power flowing through them to bring about balance within themselves. Also, having full knowledge of the possible consequences of any magical action enables the magician to make more informed choices, and to recognize the various stages of development that they are going through.

When a magician, occultist, or priestess reaches a certain level of skill and action, the power being moved around is often strong enough to have an effect on the practitioner's body. Magic is about change, and change often brings things that we find uncomfortable on many levels. As we begin working with power, the areas within our bodies and minds that are weak, unbalanced, or toxic begin to galvanize into action. Magic, among other things, is a catalyst for change, and the change comes through us before it goes out in the world. Anything imbalanced within us reacts to the energy worked with in ritual and vision, and a process of change occurs. That change can be good or bad, depending on what magical action is taken.

Whether that change will be productive or destructive is largely dependent on what energy/power you are working with and how you react to the impact of the work. If you recognize the imbalance and address it, then the interaction between the magical energy and your body is ultimately productive, however uncomfortable it may be at first.

If you resist the change brought about by the catalysing action then it will ultimately become destructive. It is akin to ignoring rising flood waters behind a dam and not directing it down safe channels. Many successful and powerful magicians and occultists that I know have gone through massive changes as a result of their magic. For example, the change can manifest as the body no longer being able to tolerate poisons or toxins: the magician may find that they can no longer get away with heavy drinking, toxic eating, etc. Their sleep changes, their dreams change, and their consciousness matures. The initial impact of this shift in how the body and mind operates can initially appear debilitating, but the magician will emerge out of that initial 'healing crisis' much stronger and better balanced.

As a former ballet dancer and coach, this process seems similar to the one I observed in dancers when shifting from being amateurs to professionals. The huge increase in workload on the body and mind is a shock to most new professionals, and it takes their bodies and minds a good six months to adjust to the new energetic, dietary, emotional, and lifestyle changes demanded of a professional dancer. And so it is with magicians once they step onto the road of serious work.

Anything we do to push our physical, intellectual, or spiritual boundaries will have an impact, for both good and bad, on our bodies. It is the reality of exploration and of working with power. The key is to work with the burdens to develop your endurance properly, like an athlete.

Magic in its depth creates boundaries of energetic opposition and tension. This is part of how power works. And along with beefing up the magician, it also protects the integrity of the Inner Worlds. If a mindless idiot is playing around with magic, when they hit such an obstruction they usually quit and move on to something else that is easier—perhaps they go back to playing with crystals and silly outfits.

Another type of idiot—I was once that idiot—would run at the obstruction with the intention of smashing it down. It tends to hurt when you do that. A sensible magician would observe the boundary, figure out what it is doing, learn how it works, why it is there, what is beyond it, what beings operate with and around it, etc. They would carefully work very close to the obstruction, then build a form of communication with it. Using that method, you learn a lot, you get stronger, and finally—gradually—the obstruction dismantles so that you can continue your path of work.

Close work with a magical obstruction (or block, or locked door) not only gives you time to learn about the obstruction, but it gives your body time to adjust to the power around it. If you body is fit and healthy, it will quickly adjust to the different power, leaving little or no ill effect. However, if you blast through an obstruction, you will either find yourself bruised and booted out of the inner worlds, or you will expose yourself to an immense amount of power that your body is not prepared to handle.

Such obstructions are part of magical learning, and a phenomenon that occurs whether you work in ritual, or vision, or both. They can manifest as total blocks in your work: a ritual pattern will suddenly not work and everything will shut down, or in vision a literal block or guardian will sling you out of wherever you were working. It has a real impact on your body and mind when you hit these walls, and it is a signal that you are on the threshold of leaping forward in your work, but also that you need to back up, slow down, and learn something first.

This was understood in ancient times, when magic was still a major part of religion, and fragments of that understanding can still be found today in some religions. Priests and priestesses of the Mystery religions were trained not only in their magical and spiritual crafts, but also in the physical disciplines necessary to maintain their strength and health while mediating and interacting with power. Often the physical training would be the first part of a young person's training to get their body into a state of peak strength and discipline.

Diet also played a major role in many Mystery disciplines: fragments of their dietary requirements are still with us today in the form of religious dietary taboos. Because so much information was lost in the West when Christianity swept through Europe, we have to piece back together as much knowledge as possible. We must regain this knowledge through direct experience, inner understanding, observation, and experimentation. Using the results of our direct experiences, we can then look at ancient texts and surviving religious/magical taboos to start to piece together a *modus operandi* for present and future magicians to work with.

So let's have a look at how magic, and the interactions with consciousness and power, can affect the body.

1.1 Basic energy principles of magic and the body

Magical energy works in tides, and these tides affect every living thing around them. The effect can alternate between good and bad depending on the action, the magician, and the ritual or vision used.

So for example, if a magician or a group of magicians (or priests) are planning to do a major working, then the energy will start to form itself from the moment the time, date, and intention is set. The initial action of focused intent is always the starting point, rather than the beginning of the ritual/visionary work. The magical pattern that is forming, from an inner point of view, begins to take up power from the egregore of the workers—hence the importance of a magical group having a properly constructed egregore, rather than thinking it is some sort of 'group mind.' (See my book *The Work of the Hierophant* for details on egregore construction.)

As the working date gets closer, the magical inner pattern takes on a more solid form which draws in energy from the inner environment around it. Magic needs fuel to work, and where the magical construct gets its power from will ultimately decide how it affects the magicians. Hence the importance of having a specific inner place/temple that the magicians intend to work within during the actual ritual: the inner pattern for the magic begins to build as soon as the inner intent and inner location is decided.

The power continues to build around and within the inner magical pattern, which has basically constructed itself. These patterns are complex weaves that will eventually act as filters for a specific magical action, and they are the result of angelic and inner contact activity triggered by an external magical intent—the magician. Hence the moral repeated in many ancient texts: 'If it is thought, then it is already done.'

How that pattern forms is largely dependent upon the skill of the magician and the strength of the inner contacts around them. It is a balancing act between not interfering too much and not letting it become totally feral: often just a conscious awareness of its existence and keeping that awareness in focus is enough. That focus allows the necessary energy to flow to the pattern and informs the inner beings around the pattern about your intent so that they can act accordingly.

As the event closes in, the need for energy builds and you get heavier. Bear in mind that the energy that flows from you for the event is not just your energy (unless you do not work with inner beings, inner connections, etc.): energy will join and mediate through you from the inner worlds, from the inner environment, and from whatever angelic, kabbalistic, or deity structure you are working within.

This buildup will translate in your life to sensations like to feeling bulky or odd, or being sleepy or hungry, or suddenly having to change how you eat, who you talk to, etc. As you get close to the day of work, the energy goes in a slingshot action: the tide of your energy goes far out, then suddenly rebounds with a bang on the day of working. This has happened to me every time I have done any major working, teaching, consecrating, etc. The week before I am very tired as my 'tide has gone out.' The day before the work I am useless, but the morning of the work I am fired up with tons of power as the tide comes back in, and that power level is maintained until the day after the work. The day after the magical work I will crawl out of bed like an old woman and just want to sleep or watch bad TV.

This is the slingshot and tide effect. The power builds from intent, and this is experienced as the tide going out. Once it has reached its critical point and it is time for action, there is a sudden release of energy: the tide comes in and you, as mediator, have that power flowing through you as you work. It is like the load on the opposing side of a seesaw is suddenly knocked off and you are catapulted upwards.

If your body is generally healthy and well looked after, then this power dynamic will not have any lasting negative effect on your health and wellbeing. If there is any weakness in your body, or slight imbalance, then it can highlight that imbalance for you and you will get stronger symptoms for a few days. That is the signal that you need to pay closer attention to your body. If you work like this with power frequently and for a long time, and you have any bodily weakness at all, then it really will begin to take its toll on you. Just as people burn out from too much work or from competing too much in sports, so the magician can burn out from working too hard with too much power too frequently. It's about using common sense.

What I have found personally is that if I do not try and control the form of the pattern in the early stages of development, and rather let nature do its magical thing, then the impact is much milder. So for example, I set the intention to gather workers together for a day of magical work in service. With the setting of the intention I book a date. Rather than look for an astrologically profound date, I just go with the flow and take a date when everyone and the venue is available. I do not filter who comes: I put out the word and whoever turns up is welcomed and worked with. The work's intent is also kept loose: rather than saying we will do a working to for some specific outcome or effect, my approach is that as the Inner Worlds have expressed a need for magical work to support the land/a disaster/the future, we will simply work in service, open the gates, mediate power, and work in ritual and vision for whatever is necessary to bring balance to the situation.

We become a link in the chain of beings working, and our bodies are supported by the long line of beings involved in the magical action. If, however, we do a magical working for a specific agenda, and for a specific outcome, then fewer beings tend to be willing to work with us, and the willing ones usually want something in return, including a bit of your energy. This way of working does have a longer- lasting drain on your system, and you need to take that into account if you wish to work that way.

Simple, focused magical intent at the start of the planning phase triggers a strong inner impulse for a pattern to form. Those patterns, which are lower octaves of fate patterns, will allow the magic to happen. How you handle that magic will decide how that pattern is fuelled, which will decide how your body is impacted.

1.2 Power on full throttle

Just before the work is about to start, the tide rushes in and the magicians are filled with power to enable them to do the job in hand. When this power is handled in a focused way and used only for the job, it will flow in an easily accessible way and maintain the magician until the work is finished. A side effect of becoming filled with this power is that any physical or spiritual issue that the magician may have (where their body is trying to adjust, as opposed to just being sick) will be catalysed. If it is an issue that the magician is aware of and is willing to address, then the power gets behind the issue as a catalyst and helps the process along.

You begin to see what a delicate balancing act this can be. If you are sick and you carry any amount of power in a magical act, then it will ultimately weaken you. If you are not sick, but are trying to get stronger or more balanced, then any action you are taking to address this situation will be helped along. The power always flows through you as a filter first, adjusting and bringing balance, before flowing from you into the magical pattern you are working on.

The feeling of being filled with such power can be heady and can easily knock a magician off balance emotionally if they are not fully aware of their emotional or spiritual weaknesses. This is why the oft-repeated maxim 'magician, know thyself' is so important. If you really know yourself and face yourself in an honest way, then when the power triggers an emotional weakness it is immediately recognized, observed, then put to one side to be worked with. The power can make you feel all-powerful, all-knowing, and all 'messiah' like. It can make you feel invincible, full of strength and vitality; but if you know that in reality it is only the power passing through you, then it will not damage your mind as it passes through.

However if you are not used to self-examination in the cold light of day, and do not fully accept yourself and your downsides, then the power will spin you out as it passes through. This can manifest itself in a number of ways, from becoming controlling of the work/knowledge, to a developing sense of evangelism. It can also divert your attention from the true path of learning, development, and evolution through experience, so that you spend all your time trying to classify, box, and control the system of magic. This is a trap that you can become caught in as you try to grab the knowledge inherent within the power.

A healthier way to interact with the knowledge and insights that flow from power is to acknowledge it, then let it go. By flowing through you, that knowledge becomes embedded within you, and it can surface when needed to work through you. If you take a major power hit and suddenly decide 'you've got it!' and begin to systematize in great detail, then you know you have taken a hit and it is expressing through the need to control.

There is a fine line between evolving from experience and passing your insights on, to playing 'Lego' with magical knowledge and power. The difference is in your perceptions, mutability, and ability to let go.

A simple wisdom that applies to managing power as it comes through is to just use it for its intended purpose, then let it go, rather than finishing the work and then taking on another physical or emotional task. When we are filled with power we feel physically strong. In simple terms, this can make us lift boxes our muscles would rather we didn't.

It can also fill us with emotions that are not real. This often manifests with sudden hormonal outbursts and with people who would not normally match up leaving the magical work and going off to have wild sex in a hotel. That often leads to embarrassing and unhealthy situations when the power wears off. So it is important for anyone leading the group of workers to be aware of this and look out for it. If the couple are still attracted to each other after the magical power has dissipated, then all is good and it is not anything to do with the group leader. But if it flares up straight after working, it is wise to find a polite way to intervene. The simplest way, and the way I handle it, is to go out for coffee with the group after working and let the dust settle. Within a couple of hours the power will wear off and common sense will return. As with all magic, it is not about the morals; it's about the reality of power and taking responsibility for that power.

1.3 The release of power after work

After the power has worn off and retreated, the magician's body and mind slumps, leaving them drooling in the corner for a while. A normal healthy body takes about two days to recover from a major magical power working. The body will need food, rest, warmth, and relaxation. The mind will need quiet, and plenty of mental 'chewing gum' to entertain but not tax it. Things start to come back online after a day or two, and any weakness in the magician's body will make itself known so it can be dealt with.

A magician who is older, has been ill, or is female and going through hormone changes will take longer to recover. Similarly, if a magician has worked powerfully for many years, then their body's coping mechanisms will start to weaken and show signs of struggle: this will manifest as a profound, prolonged weakness after their work that can last for months.

This is the sign for the magician that the time has come to shift their working method, downgrade the power levels they work with, or go into semi-retirement. This is the stage I am at: at the time of writing this I am finding it harder to recover from powerful work, my hormones are changing—I'm fifty—and the inner contacts are pushing me to work more and more in a scribe/advisor capacity rather than as a visionary worker. That may change in the future or it may not; the wisdom is knowing what is in front of you, dealing with it appropriately, and keeping an open mind regarding the future. Such a shift comes after decades of work and is akin to an athlete knowing when to hang the running shoes up and become a coach rather than a runner.

If the magical power levels worked with are not high, then these issues become irrelevant. There is much to be said for slow and steady. Many magical groups and lodges train their magicians slowly and never or rarely work with high levels of power. The upside of that approach is that there is no burnout. The downside is that it can ossify the magic and nothing really powerful every gets done: it becomes a feelgood exercise with lots of padding and no content. I guess the real balance is somewhere in the middle of the power levels. For me, I'm an extreme sports kinda gal, so moderation is a word I never really fully understood. I think different people need different approaches, and together we all make a magical whole!

1.4   Holding the reins

When you begin to work with higher levels of power in magic, interesting dynamics kick in to teach you about how power works. Once a magician works with powers beyond a certain level in ritual/vision it ceases to be an individual act. The magic becomes a collaborative act in which different orders of beings, and various threads of energy and magical patterns all come together to create a *bridge* for power to pass from unbeing into being.

For the magician, learning how to be part of that collaboration is a major learning curve. Though each situation is different, there are basic principles that underpin such work. The first principle that makes itself quickly apparent is the dynamic of *bridging* (rather than controlling). If the magician tries to overly form the filter (ritual) for the power, or tries to control it too much, then this limits the amount of power that can be bridged and they will take the full bodily impact of the power. Why is this?

When you are moving large amounts of power around and you are working collaboratively, you are one of a team: you will be expected to carry what you can, and no more. If you construct and work only with the filters that are absolutely needful, then the magical ritual pattern will not be overly formed: the inner contacts will understand what you are attempting to achieve, and the minimal filtering will allow for the bigger picture to manifest. This allows the inner beings to do their jobs without hindrance: everyone pulls their weight and the job gets done.

If the working is too controlled or filtered with complex ritual, then these dynamics do not manifest. If the ritual is unnecessarily lengthy with lots of flowery verbiage, or the vision is overly formed and psychologized, or the calling of the contacts is done with specific names (often subdivisions of bigger beings, as in a Key of Solomon working) then the filter constructed is most often too dense. The consciousness of the inner beings cannot flow back and forth through the magical pattern, and therefore the energetic burden falls on the magician. This impacts their health and strength.

On the other end of the spectrum, if the magical work is not formed enough, or is chaotic or 'free-form' then there will not be enough structure for the power to work through. Similarly, working in an *ad hoc* way without ritual structure and relevant inner contacts will result in a magical failure. The most the magician will achieve under such conditions is connections with parasitical beings who will manipulate the magician for their own ends. Usually, though, under such circumstances nothing of any relevance happens other than a bit of play-acting, wishful thinking, and the appearance of energy-hungry parasites.

If however the working was balanced then the magician will be tired after a hard day's work. They may need a day or two to recover if the work was powerful, but they will suffer no lasting damage.

Remember: magic is hard work!

1.5 Heightened sensitivity

Another bodily issue of magic is heightened sensitivity. This can be really good or really bad, or both. As inner power flows through you, it filters through your body before going off into the magical pattern to do its job. When the body has that amount of energy flowing through it, it will stimulate regeneration and rebalancing. The more that the body is exposed to this passage of power, the more things strengthen up within you as it passes through. The downside of this is that it can overly 'pump' your immune system so that you begin to react to things in your environment that are inherently imbalanced or unhealthy.

So for example, not unusual to find adepts with developed allergies to toxic things in their environment: their body is kicked into action when it comes into contact with something so unbalanced. For example, I became allergic to plastic. Great. No long conversations on the phone for me! I observed this over and over again in long-term working adepts bringing through power: while their essential organs and structure were youthful for their age and strong, they would have allergic reactions to a lot of things.

It does seem that the longer adepts work with inner power at depth, the more attuned to their environment they become, and the more psychic they become. So though the body of an adept sometimes takes hits from overwork, or doing heavy inner work and from grappling with beings—or from making stupid mistakes, like me—the underlying structure of their body, in general, is strong and regenerative. The deeper connection to the environment/land, however, will cause the magician to react to anything toxic or unhealthy.

You can assist this development of sensitivity to make it work for you rather than against you. In my twenties, my then teacher would send me off to junk shops and charity shops to handle old things to see how they felt. At that time I could feel some things, but only faintly. It took some time for me to become aware of the 'clogged energy' left on my hands from handling various discarded belongings. Once I had cleaned my hands with salt and soap, then I really felt the difference between clean hands and energetically dirty hands. I kept up the exercise, and still do to this day, of handling things to get a 'feel' of where they had been, what had been done with them, etc.

My sensitivity jumped many notches when I began working deeper in the inner realms. Some things these days I just cannot bear to handle, as they feel so disgusting. That sensitivity also expresses not just in your hands, but in how you see and feel, how you smell things, and how you sense things. It creeps up on you gradually as your body becomes more and more attuned to power, energy, and spirit. Therefore it is important that you learn to listen to your senses and what your body is trying to tell you. It is as if deeper work brings long-forgotten skills out of your DNA and wakes them back up.

It is important when developing this process not to second-guess, analyse, or try to control your developing sensitivity. Just let it develop in its own way,

and there will come a day when you really feel it in action and it saves your
ass.

Physical sensitivities that manifest as allergies in some magicians are the
body's way of telling you that you are exposing yourself to something toxic,
something counterproductive to your work or health. So again, listen to your
body and just go with it. Sometimes we can do little about it and we have to
learn how to balance living magically while in a toxic environment.

An interesting one that manifests a lot for magicians is a perfume allergy.
It took me a while to realize that a lot of our most subtle endocrine functions
centre around scents and smells. How we unconsciously communicate with
other people and the world around us is through smell. How we read people,
how we interact with beings, how we are alerted to danger—particularly in
a magical context—comes through our sense of smell. If we douse ourselves
in chemical smells, or are surrounded in our homes by chemical smells, then
we cannot access these subtle senses. The body, primed by magical power,
recognizes these chemicals as potential threats to our wellbeing and reacts
accordingly.

Magic will change your body. Working sensibly with those tides and changes
will help you strengthen in the face of heavy work. Magic takes its toll in terms
of hard work, but it also provides the energetic nourishment and strength to
maintain your magical power if you work properly. Just don't push your luck!

1.6 Knowing your body

Having an understanding of your body, how it works, and its weaknesses, forms
a major part of your magical understanding. Your body is the filter that magic
passes through: that filter must be properly maintained. Each body is different,
and that is an important point to think: when your body becomes a magical
filter, the power causes changes to your body, which changes how your body
reacts to stimuli, food, and sickness.

As you progress in magic, you may notice that one particular organ takes
the strain. This is an early warning sign that the method you are using to bring
the power through is imbalanced. It took me many years to work that detail
out, not only for myself but for other magicians around me. For me it was my
uterus: a common reactive organ in women when they are working with power.
The uterus brings life into the world, and as such is built to house a new life,
energy, and consciousness.

For myself it manifested as pain, irregular bleeding when doing heavy magic,
and eventually uterine disorders. It took a long time for me to understand that
the method of magic I was using was unbalanced: I worked almost exclusively
in vision with little externalized ritual. I am a natural visionary, and rather
than learning early to balance my use of vision with exteriorized patterns in

the form of ritual expression, I played to my strengths when I should have attended to my weaknesses.

It took many years of working with other magicians for me to realize that power needs an externalized pattern to manifest through, otherwise it will manifest powerfully through your body.

I used to keep magical diaries that plotted out what I was doing, and what magical results I was having, but it did not occur to me for a long time to keep a record of body reactions. If I had, I would have picked up on the dynamic much sooner. But I did slowly begin to realize that powerful work, when not anchored properly, affected people's minds and bodies in various ways. Once I understood that dynamic I paid more attention, kept tighter records, and adjusted my working methods accordingly.

Many of the older magical texts used by magicians have religious dogmas and cultural taboos woven into their magical systems. Many are simply irrational dogmas that developed through the Medieval mindset. Our challenge in today's magical world is to differentiate between what elements of the magical text are proper filters, contacts, etc, and what elements are useless baggage that clogs the filters. Which taboos are there to protect the body and soul of the magician, and which are simple window dressing? We are at a stage of magical development that calls for revisiting some of these archaic mindsets and reevaluating them. This requires individual observations, personal direct experience, and comparing your observations with others. That way we can truly move forward in our understanding and will be better able to tell wisdom from superstition. This cannot come from theoretical analysis, but from experimentation with an open mind.

I think the way forward, in body/mind maintenance of the magician, particularly if you are forging your path or are embarking on exploration, is simply to listen to your body and take nothing at face value. Challenge rules to find out by direct experience why they are there.

1.7 Symptoms and empathy

Another observation I made over the years on the subject of magic and the body—and one with fascinated me beyond description—is the reality of body symptoms. What do I mean by that? In the world of medicine and biological sciences, when the body manifests symptoms of disease, it is the direct result of, or the body's reaction to, an illness, infection, or malfunction. Simple. Or so I thought.

Quite early on in magic I began to notice something curious happening in two distinct areas of magic. One was healing, and the other was high-powered workings. The dynamic in healing, which is well reported even if not fully understood, involves a healer taking on the symptoms of the sick person and processing them, relieving the burden of the sick person.

The second dynamic is where a magician's symptoms, be they acute or chronic, are temporarily transferred to another person when it is imperative that the magician undertake some major magical working that must be completed.

I had been aware from quite a young age that if I was standing next to a sick person, I could 'feel' their illness, and I would sometimes unintentionally manifest their symptoms. The sick person would feel much better, and I would become sick. Usually the sickness would not last long in me and would dissipate quickly. I also found out when I was young that if someone was ill, even if they did not know it, then I would get drained and ill just being in the same room as them, whereas they would have a temporary reprieve and feel great. For years I concluded that this was just an energy drain, and sometimes it was just that.

But then I began to notice my body taking on their symptoms while their symptoms reduced. This was much more than simply energy deficits. For example, I was once working with a fellow magician who had high blood pressure and was on various medications, many of which were not really working well. He asked me to work on him and I agreed. He had a blood pressure gauge with him, so I decided to experiment. He took his blood pressure, which was high, and then took mine, which was naturally low.

After I had worked on him, I immediately got a terrible headache and felt horrible. He took his blood pressure, which had dropped significantly, and then took mine, which was through the roof! I had never had high blood pressure! His blood pressure stayed stable for months and mine dropped back to normal within hours, but this was a revelation that got me thinking. Was the healing work the cause of the spike in my blood pressure, or did I take on his symptoms?

Over the next year or so I talked to a few different healers who had trained in various traditions. They reported a similar dynamic, but their traditions had methods for working with it to protect them. Eventually a good friend of mine took me to one side and suggested I was bad material for a healer. Not because I could not heal, but because my natural ability was too feral: this could make it dangerous for me. Unless I was willing to focus all my attention on proper training for a prolonged time, doing healing would be counterproductive for me. I took the advice on board and stopped doing hands-on healing for people. I did eventually spend time studying homeopathy and cranial osteopathy, mainly for use on my children and magical colleagues, but even then I became too exposed to people's symptoms and never really learned how to shut that down.

The second dynamic—remember that one?—regarding the shifting of symptoms from one person to the next I could find little about, but I observed it a lot in magical practice. It happens when a magician has an illness or disease and has symptoms, and is called to take on a magical job where their symptoms would hinder their work. Then the person closest to the magician manifests their symptoms, the magician becomes symptom-free, and the job gets done. After the job is finished, the magician gets their symptoms back and the carrier goes back to normal. Outlandish? Yes. True? Oh yes, this has happened to me more times that I care to think about—and in both directions.

1.8 Handing over your symptoms

Like many things in my life, this had to happen a few times before I became aware of it. I had noticed before that no matter how tired or premenstrual or sick I was, if there was heavy magical work to be done, a rush of power came in and I felt great. (Remember the tides discussed earlier?)

It took a bit longer for me to notice that when I magically needed to be on top form and my symptoms vanished, someone else close to me got them. This was different from load-sharing, which happens a lot in my family, where a deficit of energy caused by a major event would be shared between family members.

The passing back and forth of symptoms I only noticed when I was in my forties. It coincided with a chronic illness that took hold of me in my mid-forties and that stayed with me for five years. In that time I did less magic and more writing, but when I was called on to do necessary magical work I would feel great and be symptom-free, whereas my partner would have my symptoms. As soon as the magical work was over, my partner would feel better and my symptoms would come back. Fascinating!

This was not something conscious or that I had tried to do; it would just happen. And this is another example of how power works when you do not try to control the magic too much: the inner tides work with you and facilitate whatever is necessary to get the job done. I asked my partner if he wanted me to find a way to block it, and he said no: it was his contribution to the work. And this is one of the dynamics that plays out in a magical group or lodge: the group works as a hive energy with burdens passing back and forth as necessary to make sure a job is done. It all balances out in the end so that no one person is left holding the can.

But a deeper question that comes up from this observation is what truly is illness, then? If visible and obvious physical symptoms can be switched on and off or moved from one body to another, then they are not what we think they are. From observing my own body through illness and also keeping a close eye on others, the only conclusion I could come to is that body symptoms are a vocabulary rooted in an energy/power deficit. Fill the deficit and the body reactions go away; move the deficit from one person to another and the symptoms move accordingly.

Which brings me to another train of thought. If it was just a matter of energy deficit, then surely when power is taken from one body and given to another, the body in deficit would show symptoms specific to the weaknesses in that specific body. But it does not happen that way. The symptoms that manifest are moved intact from one body to another and mirrored exactly in the other person. Is there some being, pattern, or consciousness that elicits particular reactions in bodies? So it would be similar in some ways to the action of something like a virus—which we also cannot see. A specific virus creates a series of reactions in a body that identifies that virus: for example, the chickenpox virus causes a distinct rash.

Is this what we are looking at? That many of these unidentifiable chronic illnesses are caused by a being or pattern that sucks energy out of the body in a specific way, thereby causing specific symptoms? Hence if you fill the energy deficit the body replenishes itself temporarily and the person donating the energy holds the 'pattern or consciousness' for a short while. If that were the case, then would that donor not also become infected? Yet that does not seem to happen.

Or is it that we are seeing a magician unconsciously holding a thread of a vast magical pattern? (Remember when you asked to be of service? Ha! You will learn to keep your mouth shut.) Could that magical pattern trigger certain responses and energy deficits within the body that become symptoms when the body's energy becomes low? I think this is the more likely scenario, and it is something I have also come across within religious patterns.

What has all this to do with magic, you ask? Everything. How we work, how our energy responds, how beings operate around us, how we can unconsciously be working on a long-term project and not realize it, and how we maintain our bodies as power filters, are all important parts of powerful magic.

This unconscious working on long-term patterns is interesting. The first aspect of this goes back, for me, to some heady days in my thirties where I under took some massive magical projects. I assumed when I had finished my part of the work that my energetic involvement with the project was over. Twenty years later I realize that I only walked away from the outer manifestation of that work: the power is still flowing, still unfolding. I am inexorably linked to that process at a deep level: the work is ongoing, and at some level my energy is still working on it. Be careful what you agree to magically.

1.9   The effects of exploration

Not every magician or priestess wishes to explore or push boundaries within the inner or outer worlds of power and magic, but some do. Many are not capable, not because they are useless, but because their skill set is in a different area. I can find things, hack into things, gain access to inner places, and communicate with random beings. Not all magicians can do that, but then there are many things that other magicians can do easily that I have to work very hard to achieve. It is about working with your strengths while building up your weaknesses. I am a curious cat: I need to know why, how, where, whom, etc. I have never taken things at face value or accepted other people's word: I need to know for myself, and to have direct experience. On the plus side this has driven me for decades in the Inner Worlds, constantly pushing boundaries, experimenting, and going where any sane person would fear to tread.

On the downside, as with all forms of exploration you hit barriers, trigger guardians, fall down holes, get stuck in places, and meet large beings who want to eat you. I have always thrived on this kind of challenge: as a late teen I did a lot of potholing and caving, pushing my physical and emotional limits and vanishing into tight dark holes in search of what was around the corner. This mentality stayed with me in adulthood and it has been a major theme of my magical practice.

Such exploration brings new understanding, a broader view, and allows breakthroughs into deeper and obscure magical places and conditions. I would say that ninety percent of what I have learned in magic over the decades has come from exploratory work. I have had to understand my results by looking over them in the context of ancient texts, teachers' feedback, etc. It is thrilling to find something obscure and odd, only to have it confirmed in some ancient writing or by an elder who says, "ah yes, I know what that is... blah..." Knowing that you are on the right track, that you are stepping through the Mysteries and finding all the staging posts, is a wonderful and exciting feeling.

It does have a major downside though: the bodily effect. If I had known about this beforehand, I would still have explored, but I would have looked after my body better and would have made a point of reaching for inner contacts to help teach me about how to handle my body through this work. Hence this part of the chapter.

When you reach in an inner place that has not had human contact for a long time, you often come across what is experienced as an energetic membrane that slowly grows across an inner place once it is no longer in regular use. Another way to describe this is as a buildup of obstruction, or a slow sealing of a place energetically. When an inner place, temple, or realm is in more or less constant use by magicians, priestesses, etc, then a path is formed that makes it easier for our consciousness to visit it. When the place stops being used, that path dies away, and the explorer has to hack through the obstructions to break back in. This takes a lot of energy, and while you do not always feel it while you are working, you most certainly do a few hours afterwards. That impact is akin to digging through a rock slide underground: you are exhausted afterwards, and your muscles ache.

The same dynamic of energy plays out when you meet an inner being/contact for the first time who has not had human contact before, or not for a long time. The energetic effort to bridge consciousness to that being is hard, and really can knock the stuffing out of you. Sometimes, if that contact or place is due to be released or opened back out into the world, then it is like popping a boil: it's easy, there is no pressure, and it feels like you have done nothing. That is because there was so much energetic buildup for the action: you were just playing your part in a bigger picture.

Sometimes when you reach deep into the Inner Worlds for an ancient contact, or one that does not usually work with humanity anymore, the energy of bridging to that contact gives you a bit of a stuffing. The contact itself—i.e. the power frequency of the contact or place—can have a massive impact on your body, as it is a power we are not really built to interact with. So sometimes deep contacts can adversely affect you without meaning to, just by the frequency of their power. It's like radiation poisoning.

Many years ago, I was working with a group of magicians and we were reaching far back in time for ancient contacts on the land. Being young and stupid, I wanted to see just how far back I could go. I did manage to reach way back in to the consciousness of the land and made contact with a being so different from me that we could not find a way to communicate. We just hung out in each others space briefly, tried various forms of contact communication and eventually gave up. Afterwards I felt weird. Two hours later my partner and I felt really weird, disorientated, nauseous, and weak. It lasted for days, and really knocked the stuffing out of me.

So how could that effect have been avoided? The impact of deep work cannot ever be completely sidestepped, as it comes with the territory; but there are ways to support your body, build up to a heavy working, and rebalance afterwards. It never occurred to me in those days that my body needed to learn how to build 'inner muscle,' to learn to slowly adapt and strengthen. I would just dive in. This is equivalent to trying to climb a high rock face with no training, no muscle development, and no tools: your arms and shoulders will hurt like shit afterwards, and you may get injuries—if you didn't fall to your death, that is. Let's look at how that can be avoided, and how we can strengthen and prepare for deep exploration.

1.10 Body matters

The best way to prepare your body and build stamina is through staging your work and learning to walk before you can run. People with natural talent for working with magic may feel able to dive in and experiment straightaway, and they can make magic work powerfully, but it often eventually ends in a burnout or crash. It is worth building a solid foundation for the body to work with so that the work continues over a longer time.

Learning to still the mind, and learning how to establish an outer ritual pattern that will then connect with inner vision anchors the work and takes some of the impact off the body in the early days. This can be achieved by working within a ritual space with an altar or altars, first reaching for an inner contact through the outer thresholds at the altars and then building up the ritual pattern in both an outer and inner sense.

The method I used was four-directional altars and an altar in the centre. I would have people first learn how to light the inner and outer candle in each direction, then progress to calling in inner contacts to the threshold of the altars from four distinct lines of power that were anchored at each altar. This first stage of working is discussed at length in *Magical Knowledge Book One: Foundations*.

Once that—or any other—basic pattern of ritual and contact is established and has been worked with for a while, it is time to begin learning and working in the Inner Worlds through well-known and well-established inner patterns— the Great Library, for example. Learning how to work in the Inner Desert, the Great Library, Death, the Underworld, the Stars, the Inner Temples, etc., not only allows you to exercise your inner muscles and get them strong, it also teaches you about how the different types of inner contact and inner realms work, what effect they have on you, what their limitations are, and what they are willing and able to do in terms of your work and theirs.

When those basics are all fully established, you will have a much stronger set of skills for beginning to explore less trodden paths and to open new ones. If you are reaching for a deep or ancient contact, then it is wise to attempt the connection in stages: do not reach right back as a first action, but attempt a series of steps back over time so that you approach the deepest contact by way of stages and other intermediary contacts.

Once you have broken through into a new or deep contact, lessen the impact on your body by externalizing the contact through ritual or image building—a deity image, for example—and learn to work with them in vision but at the threshold of your space. After a while you will learn, through action and experiment, how to completely externalize the contact and power you have connected with; and this step, of all of them, grounds the power and stops it backing up in your body.

So for example if you have been exploring and working with a ancient deity or Titan in vision, then you need to externalize that bridging. That can be done by going out on the land that is connected to them or compatible with them. Stand on the land and talk to them using your physical voice; sit on the land, commune with them, and be aware of them. This action balances the extreme inner contact by initiating extreme outer contact: it balances the energy scales.

The next step would be to work in your magical space. Light a candle in the working direction, and call them with your voice and using vision to the threshold of the altar. This is the beginning of the bridging. By this time you will have also formed an idea of what they look like to you. Don't let your imagination dress them up—yellow robe, pink hat, sparkly eyes, etc.—just focus on the key elements that they present to you. It does not matter if it is not a whole picture, as that will develop over time. This will enable you to create an externalized image or statue that can then become the focus of work.

Because you have already connected with them in the Inner Worlds, uttered to them as an outer contact, and then brought them to the threshold in ritual, they are able to cross the threshold in our world, externalizing their power without any further need of inner action from us. By externalizing the contact in this way, it grounds it so that it flows through you rather than stays within you. This took me a long time to learn, and for a while I was carrying around the burden of many contacts within me, which was like having a fifty pound weight strapped to my back. When I felt I could not carry this weight anymore, I finally listened to my old teacher when she said if you need to learn something, go to the Library. So I did.

I went in vision a few times to the Great Library and said I needed to learn how to process these burdens of contact as it was trashing my body. The knowledge was put within me—this often shows as the inner contact pushing a book into my body—and it unfolded slowly over a couple of years. The only way I can describe it is to say it was like having an invisible friend walking alongside me patiently guiding my actions, nudging me, inspiring me to go somewhere only to find myself standing out in nature wondering what the hell to do next.

It was at a visit to the ocean one day that I finally got it. I had been working in and exploring at great depth something called the Sea Temple: a series of contacts and deep 'temples' out at sea from the distant past. These were strong inner contacts, and I worked in vision with them for a long while, but the burden was beginning to take it toll.

I stood by the edge of the sea and dropped a drop of my blood into the ocean to let the contacts know who I was and who my ancestors were. I stood with my feet in the sea, just on the edge, and used my voice to acknowledge them and welcome them back to communion with humanity. It was that simple. I didn't feel anything happening, and I thought I had failed. I went home and promptly fell into a long and deep sleep.

The following day I woke up feeling groggy, but within a couple of hours I felt amazing. The burdens had gone, the contact had bridged full circle from outer element, to Inner Worlds, and back to outer element. I went back to the ocean and got an immediate response from the sea and the wind: I could talk to the contact in its deity/inner contact form, but it was grounded in nature. I visited the sea regularly from that point on until we moved inland. I would go and verbally talk to the sea and tell it what I was trying to learn or do, then I would sit in vision and connect with the inner contact either deep in the Sea Temple or on the seashore.

The bridging into nature of an ancient contact not only took the burden off me, but it also allowed me to learn about the dynamics of power in nature, and thus helped me learn about working and protecting my own body.

1.11 Elements and contacts within the human body

An important and often overlooked part of magic and the human body is the sense of connection with the different consciousnesses that make up the human body. It is easy to forget that the body is merely a vehicle for us, and that it is really a hive being.

The human body is full of different bacteria, viruses, etc., all of which have their own consciousness from a magical point of view. Beyond that is the ancient concept that key organs also have their own consciousnesses that can be communed with.

I came across this purely by accident when a healer pointed out to me that I needed to talk to my organs. I had developed a method of talking to my endocrine system by imagining my adrenals, for example, as hardworking mice on a treadmill, keeping an eye out in all directions for any potential threat. This allowed my mind to influence the performance of my adrenals, and I worked with the same method on my thyroid, hypothalamus, etc. I found I was able to 'nudge' the action of these glands by using thought and interaction. But I had never talked to an organ. I was sceptical.

I tried it, starting first with my heart and I was shocked by the result: I did not need to form a visionary/imagined interface, as a consciousness was there already, in full form, appearing as a king. I began working with him and eventually came to the understanding that certain key organs did indeed have their own form of 'consciousness.' Together they made up a collective that my spirit could operate through. I tried to get my head around this magically, biologically, and spiritually, but I eventually gave up and just went with the flow. Hey, it worked, and at the end of the day that was all that mattered.

Over time I began to see correlations between these key organs and spheres of the Tree of Life (heart/king/solar/Tiphareth...duh...) and I began to realize that some of the bodily connections with the Tree of Life were more than just the result of men wanting to make lists, put power in boxes, and find connections where there were none.

I went into the Great Library and asked for learning on this subject. Slowly that learning began to filter out into my outer life. It is still unravelling and I am still in the learning process, so there is little detail I can give of my findings other to suggest you look at this and find things out for yourself: it is fascinating and very useful.

An interesting way the knowledge that I requested in the Great Library externalized was through a book that came my way. This is often the way it happens with the Great Library: you ask for learning, and in response you are first put through certain circumstances, and then appropriate books or people are put in your path so that you can study. The book appeared just at the right time, as I had by then developed a way of talking to the organs; what I then needed was more solid information so that I did not have to reinvent the wheel.

The book was about the Classical Five Elements and Guardians system of acupuncture. I nearly did not get the hint but something made me stop and buy the book. The book talked about what I had been experiencing: the consciousness of organs, the interface between spirit and body, and how everything works together to keep body and soul together in harmony. Though the Chinese element system is different to a Western Magical System—we do not work with wood as an element, for example—the basic concepts and mechanisms are the same, and the principles of the system work. Fascinating! I am at the stage where I am still reading, learning, and experiencing, and hopefully I will be more coherent around the subject in years to come.

What it did confirm for me is something which I have worked with for a while with magic and the body: the need to balance the elements within your magical practice. Working with too much fire, for example, will put a strain on your kidneys/water system as the body tries to compensate for the overload of one element. Though the magical fire is not physical, it does trigger a physical reaction within the body, thus creating an imbalance. So be aware of that potential issue when you work with the elemental directions and powers. Keep the inner elements balanced so that the body does not take the strain and have to try and rebalance the elements physically. If you work in depth in one direction and with one element, balance the work by also being active with the other three elements.

1.12 Summary

There are more mundane practical aspects of helping your body cope with the impact of heavy magic. The basic rules are: if you are on strong medication or recreational drugs, then do not do heavy/deep inner work. Some medicines/substances will help support the body, but in general stronger drugs will make you more vulnerable. This is particularly the case with drugs that affect your endocrine system, serotonin, dopamine, and adrenaline levels. There are no hard and fast rules, as each body is different, so it pays to listen to your body and act accordingly.

If you are on antibiotics for an infection, then doing exploratory work down the Abyss is probably not the best idea. The Abyss is a fascinating but dangerous place, and the deeper you go down it the more dangerous it gets. If your body is already fighting an infection, then it cannot also fight off the energetic intrusions that some of the beings can inflict on your spirit and body. You need to be fit, healthy, and of sound mind to explore and work in such depths.

The other rule of thumb is if you are doing a lot of work down the Abyss, or in the Underworld or in Death, then you need to balance that work with work in the Inner Temples, work with angelic beings at the edge of the Abyss as they weave the future, or work out in the stars. It is also important, if you are doing deep inner work, to get out in nature as much as possible. It can be as simple as standing in a garden, standing in sunlight, or sitting under a tree. The deeper you work, the more nature responds to you. Make sure you keep your work balanced, and your body will then be able to adjust and settle itself.

Working as a magician, unless you are dense, you are going at some point in time to experience a physical reaction to a being, a place, a building, or a magical working. If you are sensitive, you may possibly experience quite severe reactions to your environment or magical actions.

The key to managing and working productively with this dynamic is knowing your body, knowing your environment, knowing what powers and beings that you are working with, and acting accordingly. If you listen to your body and observe its responses, then you will learn how you as an individual handles power. If you learn how to support your body while doing powerful work then you will develop strength and endurance. It's all about using your common sense, respecting life, and not thinking that anything magical is going to kiss your life with pink happiness and fluffy love.

Think about the outer equivalent of your work and how that would affect your body. If you are working on building Inner Temples or repairing them, then imagine what your body will feel like at the end of the day if you were working outside as a bricklayer. Your muscles would hurt and you would be tired. The same rules apply. Remember, inner work affects your outer body, just as outer work affects your inner spirit.

Chapter Two

Living magically: home and temple

Chaos behind locked doors

There comes a time in your magical life when you cease *going* to a temple, lodge, or workshop to do magic, and instead, you *live* within the magic. This is a major and an essential step in the development of the magician: the integration of magic into your life. Through books, media, and history, we perceive magic as something that happens away from our ordinary lives, something glamorous, something that happens in secret, in groups and behind locked doors. And there is a point and a truth to that, for many obvious reasons.

But there is also a way to live with magic, to have it be part of everyday life, and even part of family life. Of course, in some countries and communities there are going to be issues of persecution and potential danger with openly practising magic—and we will look at some aspects of how to be magical at home in stealth mode. In general, the approach to living magically is with the assumption that you live in a country where you will not get arrested and burned at the stake for being a magician!

I have to say that living magically in rural England in the early nineties with two young children was hard work. A couple of times, local church reverends threatened me with having my children taken from me. At that time in the UK this was a serious threat. It was one of the major driving forces behind us moving the family to the States for a few years. So I do know, only too well, how hard it can be to live your own path in public.

2.1 Temple versus home

The idea of having a temple or lodge building away from where you live, a place you only visit a few times a year to do magic, is a strange and relatively modern concept. In times past, a magician was also a priest or priestess, and worked day after day in the temple, keeping the powers balanced, keeping long-term projects going, etc. Even in tribal society, magic is lived with all the time.

Why would you live around magic all the time? Once you begin stepping towards the work of an adept, you will find that you are working magically all the time: you are never 'switched off.' If you are living in a contacted and magically supported environment, then you will cope well with being on magical call 24/7. If, however, you live in the centre of a city, in a non-magical environment, and you are carrying a long-term magical burden, then you will eventually start to really feel the strain.

People in the occult world often 'dress up' their home as part of their identity. So for example a follower of witchcraft will have brooms, skulls, herbs, pentacles, a nicely displayed altar, etc. Self-expression and expression of identity is one thing; a magically operating home is another. It is crucially important to know the difference. So for example if someone came to our home, they would not think it was an 'occult' home, but they might think that we were eccentric collectors. You can have a magically operating house that does not really appear to be anything except a little odd. So let's have a look at a magical home, what is in it, and how to balance it.

2.2 Protection

People immediately think about sealing their homes magically and frantically doing the Lesser Banishing Ritual of the Pentagram (LBRP) on a regular basis. This is totally unnecessary and will end up defeating the whole sense of magic and protection in the house. I have talked about this at length in other books, but a basic summary is that if you are balancing the house with spirits, beings, deities, etc., then the frequency of the house will filter out the unnecessary and unwelcome guests that cause problems. This also allows for various beings to come and go in the upkeep of the Work, and to reach you when they are in need of help.

Instead of ritual patterns (like the LBRP) in a magical home, guardians guard the threshold, traps draw unwanted low-level beings and keep them busy, the general frequency of the house repels unwanted magic, and the use of incense, music, and the layout of deities in the house keeps out parasites and other annoying low-level beings. The interactions between various compatible deities set up a pattern of energy in the house and daily brief work with them keeps it all tuned in. The use of specific sigils in vulnerable spots creates a filter/barrier. Most importantly, your daily interaction with the beings, ancestors and powers that flow through the land where you live together creates a living environment that is dynamic, accessible, and relatively safe.

I say relatively safe because this method will not keep everything out, and a magician should never live in a magically sealed environment: this is akin to living in a bacterially sterile environment and it will fatally weaken the magician. A totally protected space is only really needed when the magician is sick, and even then I would question its wisdom: I speak of this from direct, long-term experience. Keeping your house balanced and at a suitable magical frequency allows the beings that work within that frequency to come forward to help you, warn you, guard you, teach you, or seek you out for help. If a house is sealed with banishing rituals, that casual interaction cannot happen and the magician is left to her own devices.

A magician who lives in a banished and sealed space will find that they cannot cope with powerful inner contacts. They will be knocked easily when visiting powerful places, and they will not be able to sustain constant daily casual inner contact. Through modern teaching and popular magical trends, magical students are constantly overprotecting themselves. The net result is generations of weak, uncontacted, or faintly contacted magicians.

If, however, you work through the methods of frequencies and beings in your home and around you, then you may well take a hit now and again, but what gets through to you is a small percentage of the danger: just enough for you to deal with, learn from, and emerge stronger from. Like an immune system, it needs colds and bugs to keep it healthy.

There is also a deeper dynamic of human consciousness playing out through this issue, and that is one of an over inflated ego. A magician who feels he is protected and balanced by using banishing rituals is an idiot. It is the lone boy with his finger in the dam. Magical power, and the beings that flow through that power, are vast in some circumstances and will break through a banishing ritual in seconds. As humans we are not capable of protecting ourselves alone from such an onslaught of power, and any magician who thinks they can is an egomaniac. However if you are living in an environment populated by spirits, ancestors, and deities, then you are a small part of a wider family, most of whom are able to deal far better with incoming fire or random beings. You do your part as a physical magician, and they do theirs.

You are never totally protected from everything that could be disruptive, but things that you cannot handle are dealt with and things that would teach you are allowed through. If you are overprotected you never really learn to deal with the various 'hexes,' attacks, parasites, ghosts. etc., all of which help strengthen a magician and keep you on your toes. But anything that would seriously harm you or interfere with the work will either be kept at arm's length or you will be given a lot of help with it. Too much protection is akin to having angels sweep all humans off the road while you walk down it. So you never learn basic skills like how to identify whether someone is a potential problem or threat, how to identify someone in need of help, how to make new friends, how to bump into old friends unexpectedly, etc. The skills you use in everyday life are mirrored in magic.

Building a balanced filter in a home takes time, patience and a willingness to learn on the job. There are tons of books on magic, but at the end of the day we are all still very much in a magical dark age, and we have to relearn so many skills. They only way forward is to learn what others have discovered, but also discover things practically for yourself.

2.3 House deity

The first step to working a house magically is to establish deities or a deity to work with. The relationship is not one of religious worship; rather it is one of deep respect, honour, and responsibility. It is your responsibility to build a relationship with the deity, to make sure they have the offerings they need, and the candles, incense, gifts, and conversations that they thrive on. They become honoured members of your family.

Once their power is up and running in the house it creates a bedrock for everything else to sit on. The choice of deity to work with is important. It should either be a deity who has made themselves known to you repeatedly, or a deity that you have a deep resonance with. Do not choose a deity from some current occult fashion trend (Hecate is the current 'in' deity) nor is it wise to choose a modern constructed deity like Baphomet or Babalon. To work well with you, and for you to learn magic in depth, you need a deity who is ancient, stable and compatible with the land around you. Some deities are specific to a culture or a landmass, and others have a much wider reach. Some are compatible with magic and family, and some are not.

It is worth taking the time, if a deity or a small group of deities make themselves apparent to you, to find out about them and discover if their power has been subdivided in antiquity, or if they still have opposing powers flowing through them. Ancient powers will have a destructive and creative side to them. Subdivided powers, where the deity has been ritually fragmented in two, will bring an unbalanced power to the house.

The deity who was the foundation for my home made herself known to me in my early twenties. People kept giving me gifts of her picture and statues of her. It took me a while to figure out that she wanted me to work with her. She is an ancient power and has both creative and destructive sides: a perfect balance.

Once you are sure that you have found the right deity for you, your family, and your home, then you need to create a window for them to reach through. Just getting a picture or a statue is not enough: their image has to be enlivened for it to work in our world. This enables the power of the deity to flow back and forth into the space and to interact with you. The statue is not the deity itself; it is merely a window that acts as a communication and access point.

There are various ways enlivening can be done: I have discussed various methods in my other books. One way, which I have not discussed previously, is to take a direct transmission and transplant it into the statue at home. This only works with a limited number of deities simply because only a small number of enlivened deity statues are still functioning and accessible. The action itself can be a major learning curve, as it needs various skills and abilities, as well as access to an enlivened deity statue.

The first step is finding a statue of your chosen deity that is enlivened and still operating. It is worth bearing in mind that by Greco-Roman times, the skills to enliven a deity statue were fragmenting and ebbing away. The same is true now of many Indian deity statues, which are no longer enlivened but 'blessed', which is something different. So it is worth trying to find a deity statue dating from ancient Egypt or Mesopotamia, pre-British India, or early Greek, Roman, or Etruscan times.

Old deities can be full of power, but where little knowledge remains about them things can get a bit risky. For example Belinos, a solar deity from pre-Roman Britain, is much used within Wiccan circles, but we know little about this deity and the power he brought through. A whole modern construct of revival paganism has created a mythos to work with him, and that work happens within a 'worship' context. Now that's fine in such a setting and the fact that no one actually knows what is coming through that deity pattern is also okay; the relationship is still at arm's length and not a working relationship. However if that deity was brought into a magical household and worked with in great depth, it might be a different matter.

Belinos has not been consistently worked with as an active deity: the revival in the last hundred years is not remotely long enough to count, in deity terms. So his power could be unstable or parasited, or he could be a destructive deity: there is no way of telling. And because there has been such a break in 'work'—not worship—with this power, it would be a major risk to use his power as a foundation for magical work in a home setting. So unless you are a total bomb-head adventurer with no kids in the house, stick with powers who have had a lot of work done with them, are stable, and can be easily identified.

Once you have chosen your deity, then you need to find a source for direct transmission. This could be a museum, a temple at home or abroad, or a private collection. What you need is a statue that was at one point in a working temple, a statue that was ritually enlivened and is still functioning. You can tell which ones are enlivened and which ones are not, but it does take patience and practice.

When trying to find the enlivened statue—and not every statue in a museum is enlivened—the first step is to go still internally, which is not easy in a busy museum. Find a place to sit, be still, and work with a Void/stillness meditation with your eyes open. Once you are still and tuned in, begin to walk around the statues that you are trying to connect with. Some will feel like nothing, some you will feel a resistance to, like a field of energy around them, and some may jump out at you by talking to you or appearing in your inner vision.

The ones that reach out in communication or make themselves apparent are the enlivened ones. The ones with a feeling of energy around them are not fully enlivened, but they are tuned. If a deity really makes themselves known, remember that the last time they were properly talked to was probably in a temple by priests and priestesses who worshipped them as well as worked magically with them. They will expect to be honoured and respected, which is how it should be: the blind worship of deities by priests comes towards the end of a temple's life cycle. Every temple has a life span, and when the priesthood degenerates from balanced respect and magical interaction into blind worship then you have the end of a true temple. Honour the deity by acknowledging them in your mind, then find a place near them where you can sit.

Close your eyes and work in vision. Go into vision and stand or kneel before the deity. Tell them who you are, what you do, and what you are trying to achieve. Ask if they wish to come home with you to live in a sanctuary there and be worked with. If they agree then it is time to do the transmission. If they refuse, ask them if there is anything you can do for them, and if there is something you can do, then do it. They may come home with you another time; this is not something you can force.

When the deity agrees, open your eyes and go to stand by them. It is important that the transmission be physical: only a small number of people are capable of taking on the burden of a deity without touch, so it is important to make physical contact with the statue. This can get you in a lot of trouble, as most museums will freak out if you touch their statues. But if the place is busy or the guard is distracted, just look as if you are trying to see something close up on the statue or down the side of it. As you get close, ask the deity in your mind and utter it under your breath for them to come into you, to reside within you until you can transfer them into a statue. By asking, you give permission for the deity to pass into you; if you don't ask, it will not happen.

The actual physical contact does not need to take long: a brief touch is often enough. Make sure your hands are clean and have no oil or any other residue: it is also important to protect the physical integrity of an ancient artefact. When I did this for the deity I work with, I briefly touched her feet while pretending to tie my shoelace. It was enough. I had asked her to come into me, and she had announced she wanted to be working with me. It all came together swiftly and powerfully.

Bear in mind that what passes in you is not the deity in its entirety; it is more like a 'signature' frequency that, almost like a GPS, allows the deity power access: you can then implant this frequency into the statue at home.

It can be difficult to get our heads around such an idea as a deity transfer, as we are used to ourselves being single units. The idea that a deity power can flow through multiple units at once can be difficult for some to understand. So think of a statue as a plugged-in telephone. The transmission into you is a telephone number, which you then take home and 'program' into the statue.

Carrying this transmission can be a bit of a burden on your body. When I have carried such transmissions, I want to eat like a horse, sleep like the dead, and I feel very weak and tired. The reason for this is it takes a lot of energy to carry such a transmission, so the sooner you can transfer it to a statue the better.

2.4 Transferring the transmission into the statue

This part of the work is fairly simple, but you need to have a proper vessel to receive the transmission. Your statue of the deity needs to be a traditional one, not a New Age one, and it should not be covered in trinkets, crystals, and so forth. You will need a statue, two candles, an altar or work surface, a small cup of honey, and a small cup of fresh, clean water.

Put the statue on the altar or surface where it will live and light two candles on either side of it. Place your hands on the statue, one at the head and one at the feet, and close your eyes. Go into stillness until your mind is uncluttered and silent. The key is to not form an image in vision, but to be an open door that allows the power to flow through. You will feel the energy in your hands, or somewhere in your body, as the passage begins. This will not take long, and once you feel the power pass from you into the statue, pick it up and place your lips to the lips of the statue and breathe in it, finishing the breath with the utterance of the deity's name.

Now the visionary work starts. Standing before the altar and statue, close your eyes and see the altar in vision. See the statue and see the power in it. See the two candles creating a doorway and see the mists beyond/behind the statue. Call out in vision for a priest or priestess of the god or goddess to come and work with you, to teach and guide you. Slowly, a shape will appear out of the mists beyond the altar and a priest or priestess will appear. Tell them what you are trying to do and ask for their help.

You may notice other people in a line behind the priest, each one standing behind the other while placing a hand on the priest in front of them. This is the line of succession in the priesthood that the power of the deity will filter through: the human inner contacts form a bridge that allows the power of the deity to flow from the depths of the Inner Temple and connect with the powers of the deity from the outer temple. The two meet in the statue and it 'comes to life.'

Once you see the bright union in the statue, which can appear as brightness, or as a bright pattern, welcome the deity into the statue and offer them the cups of honey and water, doing this in vision and physically at the same time. Place them at the feet of the deity and quietly open your eyes. Light a small candle or tealight before them, and offer them incense resin on charcoal—not incense sticks, which tend to be artificial and low quality. Frankincense is good to use, but it is worth finding out what your particular deity likes. Modern websites connect all sorts of colours, resins etc to particular deities. These are all modern inventions and have no value in this work. Look to ancient texts, myths, and stories; and if all else fails, just ask them what they like.

The final step is anointing the statue with oil. I use a mixture of frankincense, opoponax, and vetiver that I consecrate for such use. Anoint the forehead, lips, heart, and feet of the deity, then leave the room with the candles going. I call this the cooking time: a time when the inner contacts are still working in the room but you are no longer needed. You will feel when it is time to go back in.

The working I just described is the 'opening of the door' for contact with the deity. The actual god or goddess contact/power will now start to trickle through, and the more you work with the contact, the stronger it will become. Do not clutter their space with decorations, magical toys, etc.: remember it is not a shop display or an artistic presentation; it is a working altar. They will need their candles, an incense burner, and two little bowls for gifts, food, and drink, and any tools that they specifically work with. The tools will be acquired over time, or they will ask for them. Anything else will only muddy the filter of the altar and fragment the power.

It should be simple, working, and not obviously an altar. Our living room has a series of working altars in the room and no one has ever noticed: it is that simple and basic. There is no showing off, no drama, no window dressing, just the work. Make sure that all candles, incense, food, drink, and gifts are good quality. And never take shortcuts: electric light bulbs and a living flame are not the same thing. A deity needs a living element to work with, not a light bulb.

Each day light their candles, make sure they have what they need, and spend just a few minutes in meditation or communion with them. Talk to them, involve them in your daily life, and sit with them as you work in vision. This is your foundation deity: they need to be at the heart of your life at home, and that can only happen if you build a relationship with them. Your transmission work will have ensured that only the deity or the deity filter/priest can come through that statue, so you do not have to worry about opening doors to random beings. Build the relationship and once it is established, you can start to work together.

2.5 Other deities

Once you have established a foundation deity you will find that others come in your orbit over time. Don't go running out to stores to buy lots of different deity statues; let them find their way to you, as often the ones that you think should fit together do not. These days we have become narrow-minded as a culture and we like to make things fit together neatly in boxes, but power unfortunately is not that accommodating.

Often the combination of deities that find their way to working with you seems random, but on closer inspection you will find that they are very connected, not through their attributes, but by geography or cross-cultural connections from the times when they were at their height of power. So you may find old Egyptian, Canaanite, Sumerian, and Anatolian deities working together; but they will not work with younger generation deities from their own pantheon.

Don't fall for the 'all goddesses are one goddess' trap: it is not true. Deities are akin to humans. All humans are humans, all women are women, but we are all different and work in different ways.

Some of the deities that move in with you will settle in a specific room. you will need to make sure that they will work in harmony with any other deities, ancestors, etc. in that room. The deeper you go in magic, the more your sensitivity to power will increase; and if you introduce a power into the wrong space then you will most certainly know about it. You will either have nightmares, 'bad feelings,' or the house will begin to feel out of balance. If there is imbalance, then things will get disruptive in the house, with statues falling over, pictures falling off the walls, or small fires starting: deities can really get into pissing contests with each other.

There are two ways that work to deal with this issue. One is to introduce a new deity or magical object by walking around the house, going into each room, and standing quietly with the object or statue and seeing how it feels. The nudge can often be like a faint whisper, but most of the time I get a defined 'no, not in here.'

Another way to check is through using Tarot. I use the Tree of Life spread for this and look at the last card. I ask a question like 'what would the balance of the house powers, spirits and deities be like if I bring X in this room?' Notice I ask about the effect the newcomer would have, not 'does this power belong here?' The reason for this is that you need a clear answer about how something will affect you directly.

It may be the right room for the deity, but if it does not work for you and causes disruption, then it is the wrong choice. You have to be able to work together, and the deity has to be able to cooperate with all the house's other occupants. You will also find that the dynamics within the house and between all the powers are almost unique to you: the variables are what sex you are, the power of the land beneath you, what bloodlines flow through you, what ancestors are around you, what animals are in the house, and what longer-term inner path you are walking (often without realizing). So you can see there are no hard and fast rules.

When people say things like 'this deity must work with that deity and must be housed in this direction because that was how it was in the days of the great temples and that is what their attributes were,' they are missing a major magical point. Your house is most unlikely to be on the same landmass as the original temple of your working deity, and it is not in the same culture, time, or setting. Nor do you have a whole priesthood keeping all the energetic plates spinning. The dynamic is different, and you need to be mutable to flex and bend with the intricate nuances of power. So reading books on a specific deity and their likes and dislikes will tell you little of value: a direct relationship with the deity will slowly build your understanding about their power and how it works. Sure you will make mistakes, we all do, but that is part of the process.

One thing to be acutely aware of: if you move house to a new land or a totally new area, then you may find that some deities change how they behave. The very old, primal deities—usually the foundation deities of a pantheon like Sekhmet, Mut, Enlil, Magna Mater, and Shu—are manifestations of vast powers and tend not to change much from landmass to landmass. But other deities, usually the children of foundation deities, which are really powers that were subdivided in antiquity by priesthoods or are localised powers, tend to be more fluid in how their powers work. This means that they may work in one country, but not in another. Its not about them being on their 'own' land; rather it is about whether they are on top of a land power that they can connect with or are compatible with.

I have moved many times in my life, across continents and oceans, and I have found that as I wander around the world, some of the deities I take with me fall asleep in some countries and become inactive, only to awaken when I move again. Other deities become more powerful, more verbal, and express previously unknown attributes and powers when they move onto a new land. Again, all this is unknown magical territory, and you will have to learn on the hoof. The key is being sensitive to a deity's shifts in power, and that comes from regular work with them.

The basic outer rules are:

1. Let the deity find what area of the house works for them. They will want to go in a specific direction for a specific reason, so don't, for example, stick a destroying goddess in the north because that is where all the books say she belongs. She may want to work from another direction for a specific reason, or that direction may bring out an aspect of her that you were unaware of.

2. Don't clutter their space with New Age tat. There will be specific things they need, so make sure they get them, but don't fall for the altar display routine. It's not a storefront or something to show off.

3. Remember, you do not have to have altars and all the dressings. For the most part deities will blend into your home happily: they will wish to live among you and work with you, not turn your home into a temple. Most of the working deities in our house would be easily missed: they are fitted in among our books and herbs, not on altars. Well, except for one goddess, who needs the full deal. Sigh.

4. Most importantly, this is your living space and your life. Deities are working powers that you work with, not worship. Sure they deserve

respect and honour, but make your working boundaries clear. Your life is not theirs.

2.6 Spirits, ghosts, guardians, and ancestors

Once you have built up a working network of deity power in the house, you will come across other potential occupants looking for a home. Again this builds over time and cannot be set up like flat pack furniture. The frequency generated in your house by deities will attract certain types of spirits, and will repel those who have no part or purpose in what you are trying to achieve.

Smaller land spirits, faery beings for example, can be attracted like cats: leave food out, and one will turn up. If you make a point of tending the land around you, talking to the elements, the land, the weather, the plants, then this will get the attention of various beings inhabiting the land around you. Some people build outside shrines, others have a gift patch. Whatever you do will have some effect and will draw inner beings to your home.

If you have mountains, odd hills, ancient trees, or anything of natural power around you, then connect with them by visiting them both in person and in vision. Introduce yourself and ask the spirits of that place if they need anything. This good-mannered approach will catch their attention, and soon you will have beings turning up needing things, offering things, or moving in with you. If one offers to be a guardian for your home in return for shelter, food, or song, then all is well. Just make sure that the guardian knows to allow beings—usually ancestors from the area, or from your family, or ghosts—to enter the house when they need access to you.

Slowly, through trial and error—and there will be errors—you will acquire a family of spirits who live and work with you. This method is the greatest teacher of all: you will find out about inner beings by living among them. In my book *The Exorcist's Handbook*, you will find greater in-depth descriptions of various types of beings and how to work with them, what they do, and how they act.

2.7 Balancing the home environment

When you live in a home with working deities and spirits, certain considerations must be taken into account on an almost daily basis. The frequency of the house will become so finely tuned that when something is introduced to the house that is unbalanced or unhealthy, the house will react. This will affect the magician in various ways, depending on their level of sensitivity.

Again this is a matter of experimentation and of being aware of the subtle shifts in the house energy. In the past I have brought in statues which I assumed were simple ornaments, but the temple frequency of the house activated them in the strangest of ways, which wreaked havoc. I have had the deities of the

35

house react to certain music, foods, people, movies...it is important to put such reactivity in perspective and not to become neurotic about it. It is all about finding balance and operating within that balance.

I think the bottom line is to use one's common sense. Generally, treat a magically working house as a temple. Remember that certain high levels of power are flowing through the space daily, and be mindful of what you introduce to the house. Just as you are careful of what you expose your children to, so care has to be taken with house spirits.

The guardians who accompany the deities will also be very active: this can be good thing and a bad thing. On the plus side, a working house of such magical frequency tends never to get broken into: the guardians do a good job. On the down side, any visitor that you have who is unbalanced, has bad intent, is using drugs in a destructive way, or is parasited or mentally ill, will basically get run out of the house pretty quickly. They will feel uncomfortable, and you will feel drained.

Another thing to note is that the balance of the powers in the house will shift and change. Sometimes this happens in line with the seasons, sometimes it seems random and is hard to understand why. But the power will ebb and flow, with occasional sudden upsurges of immense power, which is usually a signal that you should be working and everything is lining up ready.

Working this way will not suit those who need a simple rule book with easy steps to follow; nor will it suit those who are nervous, paranoid, and self-obsessed. It takes a lot of mutability, a willingness to learn, to flex, to experiment, and the ability to feel shifts of power. However working within this structure will also teach you so much about how deities interact, how powers work together, and how guardians operate—and the lessons can be funny, crazy and sometimes terrifying.

When children are added into the mixture they learn about power by proxy. You do not have to teach them anything, and they should not be particularly involved with the magical side of living in the house. But being passively exposed to these powers will help them learn at a deep level about how power works. When my kids were growing up I never mentioned anything to them about magic or the statues around the house, but they were individually drawn to specific ones that they would chat to and sometimes ask for help. The house guardians also watched over them and would warn me if the children were taken sick through the night, or if they needed help. They would also warn me of impending danger around the children.

I have two settings of reaction that I go by. One is sudden adrenal response, and the other is fatigue. If there is something dangerous in the house that is a potential threat, magical or otherwise, then I will get an immediate adrenal response. If there is something out of balance or unhealthy in the house, then I will become suddenly overwhelmed with fatigue. The first response is my body's reaction to the guardians reacting; the second is my inner energy being drained off, which triggers a bodily response. Other people react differently: it is important to learn your own signals and reactions. If there is severe danger, usually you will get a physical warning, like something literally being thrown at you or a voice shouting at you to wake up.

Here are some examples. Many years ago, my then-partner was being stalked by his ex, who had many problems with her mental instability. One night I was in the house alone except for my two small children. I was asleep and dreaming happily, when I thought I heard my name called. I was tired so I just turned over and went back to sleep. A few minutes later I was shouted at in my dream to 'wake up or die' and in my dream I saw fire coming through the letter box (letter boxes are built into the front doors in the UK). I woke up and had an instant adrenal hit. It was 4 a.m. and quiet.

I went downstairs to find my cat sat staring at the front door and growling. I looked out of the curtains and saw my partner's ex with a petrol can coming down the path to the house: she was intending to pour the petrol through the letter box and set fire to the house, with the children in it.

I switched the lights on, pulled the curtains back, and stood in full view of her, staring at her. It was enough to frighten her, and she ran. If the guardians had not woken me up, we would likely have all burned to death in our sleep.

Another example, though less dramatic, was a box of occult and history books I brought home after finding them in a thrift store. Within minutes of getting home I felt sick and disorientated. I could not figure out what was causing it: it did not occur to me that books could have such an effect. I did a reading to see what was going on, as the feeling was strong. It turned out to be the books. It was not what was in the books; it was rather *where* they had been for a long time: they had absorbed something very unbalanced that had become imprinted on them. The solution was simple: I magically stripped and cleaned the books, and peace was restored within an hour.

A comical example was when a magician was trying to attack me—a total waste of someone's time and energy. A house spirit suddenly made himself known to me, so I went in vision to talk with him. The house spirit told me that a magician was attacking me and that the magician had sent a being to carry out the attack. The house spirit had the being held at arm's length and asked me what I wanted done with it. I asked the spirit to hold the being while I observed it, so I could see if it was a thought form created by man, or a faery/land being, etc. It was a land being who had been trapped into service. So I freed the being of his servitude and released him out to the moorlands, thinking that would be the end of it.

However, the house spirit told me that the fire magic of the attack that had been carried by the being was still in the house; it just had no available 'out' as the being was the aim mechanism. I asked about lighting a fire and feeding it through the fire so it would literally burn itself out. No, not a good idea, was the answer. So I asked for suggestions. The house spirit said it could direct the fire magic through the electricity and burn it out that way. So I turned off my computer for the day and unplugged any sensitive electrical equipment, just in time for a light switch to blow and catch fire. I put the fire out immediately, and that was the end of that.

Later I tried to figure out why putting the fire magic in the fire was a bad idea, as every encounter with magic is a learning curve. I did some readings to see what would have happened. It showed that instead of it consuming the magic and burning it away safely, as I was expecting, it would have amplified the magic like throwing petrol on a fire. The end result would have been a major house fire. The electrical system was sideways enough from the pure element of fire for it to channel the magic and cause a small fire that was harmless. I learned a lot that day. And it was also a perfect example of the dynamic with certain forms of magical attack. Once set in motion, an attack cannot always be disengaged and dismantled; it must be safely 'ousted' or allowed to manifest so it can run its course harmlessly. Some magic can be taken apart and composted, but certain forms of powerful and complex magic have to run a course. The trick is finding a safe and harmless diversion course for them to run.

2.8   Down times

The other magical dynamic you will discover is the sudden magical silences that occur, often out of the blue. If you try to logically assess how this dynamic works—if it flows, for example, from lunar cycles or seasonal cycles—you will simply waste a lot of time. Working in this magical way with deities means you need to learn to be fluid with your thinking and approach.

There will be times where the deities suddenly become active, and other times when the silence from them will be deafening. I have found that when the powers in the house suddenly become silent, it is not because they have all gone away or shut off. It is more that they are suddenly working on a different frequency that we (or I) cannot operate at. Although sometimes it feels like they are sleeping. They will not want interaction, candles, offerings, or conversation: it will be as though they do not exist. There will be no discernible power flowing around the house, and it will feel strangely silent once you have become used to all the background chatter they normally exude. I learned eventually that this is a kind of stealth mode, and it often happens when they are working hard but in a way that most humans cannot pick up.

I started to keep a record of this 'stealth mode' and found that it often occurred either when a major incident was about to happen out in the world, or there was a major incoming attack—one of the down sides of being a visible magician in print is that everyone feels they have to right to take a pot shot at you for speaking out. The reasons for the stealth mode would often become apparent a week later. I learned to respect this stealth mode, keep my antenna up, and trust their judgement.

What I found curious was how this would happen before certain major incidents in the world, but not others. I have not got to the bottom of why this should be, that a disaster halfway around the world will elicit a response but one nearer home or somewhere else will not. There is just so much I do not understand about power dynamics, and the older I get, the more I realize how little we actually know about how energy and power work.

A lesser octave of this crushing silence is when a deity suddenly 'goes to sleep.' They withdraw their powers, and you begin to get a sense that you should not be working with them. Again I have learned to just respect the ebb and flow of their power. For example, in spring 2012, my image of the Goddess Tefnut suddenly wanted putting away out of sight. I was dumbfounded because we were still in the midst of a drought—she brings moisture. A week later the rain started to fall. 2012 turned out to be one of the wettest years on record. She was not needed: in fact her presence and any magical interaction with her would have possibly made a bad situation worse.

If such a silence occurs in your home and/or your magical work, flow with it but keep an eye on it and an eye on world events. I use Tarot to track if a silence is the result of an attack or of world events: if it is world events then I will go in vision and ask if I am needed in service somehow. Usually the answer is no, but occasionally they will give me a job to do.

2.9 Magic and relationships; bringing a new partner into the house

This is another aspect of working in a home temple or magical household. It is often overlooked, and it can bring chaos into the home. If a new person is coming to live or even stay in your home, then it is a good idea to let the spirits of the house and the deities know there is going to be a new addition to the family, either permanent or simply visiting.

It can be that simple: just tell the house, the spirits, and the deities, and keep an eye on the newcomer for a week or so. Failing to do this—as I have more than once—in an active, working magical house, can have strange consequences such as the newcomer feeling uncomfortable and sleeping badly, being attacked in their sleep, or constantly getting sick. The other annoying thing that can happen, if you forget to tell the house guardians that you have a friend staying, is a night of being 'tapped' on the shoulder while you are deeply asleep. You find yourself being woken up by a guardian telling you there is a stranger in the house. Annoying. . . but they are just doing their job.

It will not be not a major issue unless the newcomer is sensitive, and it is just good manners and common sense. These are the little details that we

2. Living magically: home and temple

have lost over the millennia, and such details can make a major difference in a magical life.

2.10 Summary

Living in a temple house, for me at least, is infinitely preferable to having a separation of working space and home. Through decades of living with deities and spirits I have learned to work closely with them without pomp and ceremony, involving them in my daily life and work. This allows a deeper understanding of their powers, needs, wants, abilities, and tides. It is a harder way to work, as it keeps you on your toes, and you have to maintain integrity in all that you do. There is no off switch, no 'time out,' but you do learn a lot and get strong!

Chapter Three

The magic of the land

Ground zero: the environment and its powers

The magical inner powers that flow through the land have fascinated humanity since the dawn of time. Power spots became sacred places, and people constructed groves, stone circles, and temples. Some power places were avoided at all costs. This interrelationship between humanity and the power that flows from the land is still a major part of cultures, religions, and magical systems to this day.

In this chapter we will look at some different tides of power that flow through the land, to gain a deeper understanding of what we are working with. First we will look at how the process of magically connecting and learning evolves: understanding how we operate is a major step towards developing a working practice.

3.1 Learning approaches and understanding how we operate

As magicians I think we have all, at some point in our lives, worked our magic in total isolation, often locked away in a room, ignoring the land and beings around us. This is encouraged by certain streams of magic in which a temple is constructed indoors, banishing is done, magical circles are set to exclude all except the one spirit to be called, and then we work magic from within that protective bubble. Often the streams of magic worked with have little or nothing in common with the powers that flow from the surrounding land, and the magic is totally disconnected from the tides of power, knowledge, and contact that flow through the land around us.

For magicians using specific magical methods for specific results—i.e. results magic—such isolation works. However, if the magician wishes to expand beyond that paradigm and reach deeper into magic, both for practical work and for a better understanding of power, then we have to start to take in account our environment. We need to start asking questions like what power, contact, wisdom and magical pattern is already here in the land? Why is it here? *Who* is here? What affect are they having on my work? What effect is my work having on the land, the spirits? Can they be part of my work? And so on.

There are two distinct ways of approaching this. One is to explore the landscape and inner population of a land area through a spiritual or religious format; the other is to explore without the religious and cultural interface, but with more of an attitude of exploring what power is present. How does it work, and how do I interact with it? Both are extremely valid, both have upsides and downsides, and both have their own difficulties. How a magician approaches this would probably depend on what stream of magic they were working with, and how they personally approach magic.

It also depends on the development of focus that the magician has acquired over the years. When we first start out in magic, we are like blank pages that take everything in but absorb only a bit. As we progress and begin to specialise with a specific focus of study and work, we begin to narrow our field of understanding so that we become more and more able to see the fine details or undercurrents of a specific section of magic. The downside of that specialisation is that it becomes much harder to process patterns outside your field of understanding: you start to see the world around you in a narrower but more focused way.

That level of specialisation makes for some interesting understandings once we realize that what we are seeing and processing in fine detail is not an ultimate 'truth,' but merely a specific pattern. This progression is an emotional, psychological, and philosophical process that is an integral part of our magical development.

When we first begin to see the fine detail, the 'machinery' of magic in action, we think we have stumbled on the truth. Our specialisation makes it so much harder to see the same power in action through a different pattern, so we feel that 'our' view is the best or the real one. This is a higher octave of the messiah trap where the magician begins to think they discovered the 'real' path. But when you get a few experienced magicians together all from different disciplines, and they begin to discuss the dynamics behind the magical act, something wonderful happens: you begin to realize that you are all talking about the same thing, just approaching it in a different way and using different language.

Which language we gravitate to is the one that is most accessible to our mentality. Once the language is well learned and successfully used, it becomes easier to talk to someone who speaks a different language but is working at the same level: the commonalities become obvious. The other side of this coin is the ability to see bullshit even when it is well dressed: the commonality of power signatures in different paths is obvious—and so too is the lack of such power.

Discovering the common thread of power signatures was a major facepalm moment for me. It made me step right back and really look at various magical practices, where they came from, and why, how, and where they were going. It also highlighted something to me about human nature, which is that the more we look in a specific way at certain phenomena, the more we rewire our brains to interpret what we are looking at in order to obtain the information we need. We become specialized interpreters. The more we specialize in one area, the less accessible other interpretations become.

This understanding made me go back and look at the outer court training of basic magic and question why certain elements are there. If we have a basic understanding of the wider options/expressions of magic, even when we specialize in a particular field, we retain some basis of understanding of the other paths, as basic neural pathways relating to them have been established. If we only walk down a specific path from day one, we quickly become specialized but lose our ability to see the similar methods operating in other paths.

This led to an internal discussion with myself (I talk to myself a lot, except around anyone working in mental health!) about why paths develop a certain way, how they develop out of the needs and wants of a population, and how we as modern magicians extract the relevant and discard the irrelevant or dogma. Magic grew out of a religious and spiritual conversation that humanity had with its environment, both physical and non-physical, about everyone's demands, wants, and needs. Keeping that in mind helps us to look at our methods and adjust them to help them evolve.

So, back to working with your environment and the powers that flow through the land. Working in isolation from our surroundings eventually becomes limiting and often self-defeating. So what do we do? Often the spiritual connection with our own land has been broken by incoming religions, cultures, and modern agendas, and it can be a struggle to reconnect with what is there.

The first instinct is to revert to early religious patterns and try to recreate them. We see this with neo-paganism, neo-druidism, neo-shamanism, and the revival of the Saxon religions in Europe. While this is not a bad thing in many ways, it can end up recreating the same dogmatic patterns that are no longer applicable to our land or culture, and it can quickly devolve into dressing up and role playing with an extra side of psychology.

It also puts us back into the mode of repeating religious patterns rather than evolving a more mature conversation with the powers around us. But throwing away all the accumulated knowledge and wisdom in these older religions is also counterproductive, as many of them originally developed as a result of experience and experiment. So it becomes a matter of looking at the religious/cultural patterns with new eyes: the eyes of magical enquiry rather than worship or the wish for belonging.

It is also a dynamic that requires something that we humans are not comfortable with: taking responsibility. While ever we feel there is a paternal— or maternal—deity to oversee us, protect us and feed us, we are happy to look no further and place our welfare in 'their hands.' In magic, when this reliance on a parent god is enacted, it quickly falls apart, as magical power will only work with that dynamic to a point. It also does not take into account that many deities—and particularly local ones—are not all-knowing, all-wise, or all-powerful. So it all goes wrong and we blame the deity, or we ask if we did not sacrifice enough goats to them (an action which also tends to piss off your neighbours).

If, however, we approach the local powers and deities in a slightly different way, i.e. being willing to respect and interact with them but taking responsibility for ourselves, then an interesting dynamic emerges. Through taking self-responsibility in a magical relationship with land powers, what tends to happen is that things that you are really capable of handling are left for you to do, anything you are not capable of doing and really need is handled for you. So in a way you do end up with a protective deity, but with a subtle difference: you are not in a parent/child situation; you are in a chain of action where you become one of a team. Like all teams, you learn to watch each others' backs while not babysitting each other.

3.2 Researching your land

So let's get down to practicalities. Unless you are living on land that has only recently been settled by humans—in which case you are screwed—there will be various resources you can draw on. One major resource is the local myths, legends, and faery tales. These stories are the result of longstanding oral traditions, and they often include ancient wisdom, knowledge, and experiential learning that was passed down from generation to generation. These stories, if you know how to look at them, will give you clues to the local powers, deities, ancestors, land qualities, etc., and will indicate how to live and deal with them.

There are many elements that affect magic and the magician, for example the geographic makeup of the land. The type of rock, semiprecious stones, and metals in the land beneath and all around you can have an effect on your magical work, depending on what you are doing. Many magicians use certain metals and stones in their ritual tools, yet do not think about the minerals under their feet. So for example, some ritual work will be affected if you are sat (like I am) on massive outcrops of granite with the added ingredients of lead, copper, tin, and silver: a powerful alchemical mix.

The landscape is also important. Is it Desert? Is it flat forest or mountains, or on a fault line? What are the local power herbs and plants? All these aspects can affect your work depending on what you are trying to work with and why. Then we get to the inner beings of the land. The first and most obvious contacts are the ancestors who are buried in the land, and the ancient ritual Sleeper burials: people who actively stay as an inner contact within the land, usually for the good of the local tribe.

Then there are local land spirits/faery beings, deities, elemental beings within the land, the local animal groups, and planetary alignments, key stars, etc.. There are so many ingredients that make up a magical landscape, and taking the time to connect, work with, and become acquainted with them can make a major difference in your long-term magical projects.

I have lived on different continents and on different landscapes, and as such I have learned how to connect, interact, and leave certain powers. I saw how some similar landscapes had similar power flows and how some land beings did not take well to people living in certain areas. I came across other instances in which land beings did not want a person to leave, and the powers would try to make them stay.

So where do you start? Firstly get as much information as you can about local legends, myths, and tales. Read them carefully, and look for the main spirit characters, the main land features, who is a 'goodie,' and who is a 'baddie.' Look at the local faery tales to see what types of beings are described, and keep an open mind. You may have to pull back from a human-centred view and moralizing that often gets inserted at a later date.

These tales will sometimes tell you about the responsibility humans have within the land collective of beings. These can appear at first to be moral lessons, but on closer inspection they will show some of the ancient dynamics between the land, the beings and humanity, and outline what is expected from humans in return for cooperation. They can also hold clues about how we can work at a very deep level with the land—but such a relationship is finely balanced and dependent on the human living up to their side of the bargain.

Be careful not to simply discard any myths that seem irrelevant. If you do not find them particularly useful, then just file them away, as they may become really useful in the future. It is also good to find out what layers of cultural ancestors are on and in the land, and to find out, for good or bad, what they are about. Not all layers of ancestors are nice or wise: some are stupid or bloodthirsty, so be ready to give them a wide berth if needed.

Geologically, find out what you are sat on and look up, from an alchemical point of view, how those layers or rock, metals, and stone interact with any minerals you use in your rituals. It also helps if you find out whether there was ever any destructive mining around you. If there was, you may end up having to give a fragment of whatever was mined back, or bury some in your garden. There is an interesting dynamic between metals and stones like gold or quartz in the land, and how the land is affected when they are taken out.

You may find that certain elements under your house do not respond well to elements within your ritual tools. It really is a matter of 'experiment and see,' but stay mindful that many things in your environment will affect how you work.

3.3 Working with beings

There can be many vast levels of beings around you that can affect how you work, both for good or bad. Doing banishing rituals before you do magic, unless you are doing simple results magic, defeats most of the magical dynamic. Magic does not happen in a vacuum, and if a human is the only being involved in the magical patterning, the chances are it will be a piss-poor performance.

Magic of any real power is a combination of patterns, energies, and beings all interacting at a certain frequency. Together a great deal can be achieved, as you are operating as just one link in a long and powerful chain. You learn how to work as a team, how to understand your limitations, and how to trust other beings to do their job. This of course has to be done carefully, so that you do not open yourself up to every Tom, Dick, and Samael who happens to be passing through.

This is achieved by 'tuning' a working space—or even your living space—to a certain frequency so that you are operating at a different speed/frequency to lowlife beings: you effectively 'vanish' from their radar. This is discussed in further detail in chapter 2, so I do not want to repeat myself, but working in combination with different specific beings, powers, inner contacts, and ritual actions will make sure that your space and house is always tuned so that you do not become dinner for a hungry local energetic vampire or bottom feeder.

I have also learned through trial and error to develop a good friendship with local spirits and do whatever I see necessary to help them and the land. I rarely ask for anything, but when I do, usually in a a time of great need, it is immediately there for me. I have also learned from this dynamic that if I am respectful and helpful, they will often offer help before I have realized that I need it.

Moving on, let's have a look at some of the bigger waves of power that work through the land.

3.4 The tides of destruction

Over the years I have observed some interesting phenomena in the various landscapes where I have lived and visited. It took some time for me to realize what I was actually observing from a magical point of view, and even longer to see the various patterns that seem to emerge in similar ways on the land.

My first real encounter with such phenomena—or at least my first awareness of it—was in Milwaukee Wisconsin. The area around the great lakes from Chicago up to Milwaukee and across to Madison is littered with ancient burial mounds, and when I first discussed this with a Native American whose tribe comes from that area, he told me that this area was considered an area of death.

The place where I lived was badly haunted, as were areas of the land on the outskirts of Milwaukee. There was a heavy energy to the city that seemed to come and go in waves, and at that time I assumed it had something to do with the modern city sat on top of burial grounds. While visiting a burial mound out in the countryside towards Madison, a being appeared and asked if my daughter and I would release something that had been blocked and was building up like a pressure cooker. We agreed, and off we went.

My daughter did the contact work, and what was released was a wave of female spirits, warriorlike, who spread out across the land. Neither of us was quite sure what to make of it, but the moment we finished the work we were told it was time for us to leave that area. Within two months fate moved the chess pieces, and we did indeed move out of state.

At that time I had no idea what had happened or why, only that it was necessary for the land there. I started to do some research in the history of the state and found that the area was renowned for mass murders: Milwaukee had produced more mass murderers that any other single city in its history. I did wonder about how that power mixed with the Sicilian community and it's penchant for gang-related violence, in the form of the mafia, in the region's history. Did one feed the other?

Once I moved out of Wisconsin and in Montana I did not give Wisconsin much thought: the place had affected me badly and I was just glad to get out. If I knew then what I know now, then I would have stayed longer and worked in more depth to observe, record, and discover what natural force was flowing through the land and how the Indians in history would have worked with that force. And as I am writing this, I have just been informed that the river that flowed naturally into the lake at Chicago was reversed by civil engineering in the late nineteenth century to flow out into the Mississippi basin. Rivers and aquifers play an important role in keeping a land in balance and moderating the powers that flow back and forth. Could this have contributed to the unsettled power in that whole area? We will never know, but it is a point worth considering. An inspired question would be to ask the link between the warrior women/spirits and the water? In the UK and Northern Europe there are powerful links between springs, rivers, wells, and female warrior spirits.

Once I settled in the Mission Valley, West Montana, I slowly became aware of a strange force that blew through the land regularly. It would come on the tail coats of a storm or a strange wind that would blow through the valley. It felt different to the power in Milwaukee, but it was a tide of destruction that would occasionally blast through the land and leave a string of accidents and deaths in its wake.

It did not occur to me at the time, as I can be incredibly dense sometimes, that this tide of destruction was more feral: it felt more natural simply because that area had only been settled and colonised in the last hundred years, and what civilization was there was basic and low impact. It was a small population, mainly Indian, with little towns and settlements.

I began to seriously observe this power. When the tide was about to come, there would be a brief blast of turbulent high wind, often only lasting an hour before it settled. Then a strange energy would descend on the land that I experienced as a heavy 'lead boots' feeling, mingled with a sense of fear. The power would build to become heavy and adrenal over a a few days: people would begin to argue, feel ill, and become disorientated. Then something odd would happen: owls would begin to congregate in quite large numbers. One night I sat out on my deck listening to trees full of owls calling back and forth.

Sure enough, a morning or two later when the energy lifted, there would be news of 'crops' of death in the area. Youngsters killing themselves by driving into trees, into other cars, or off roads, drug overdoses, suicides, heart attacks, traffic collisions, shootings. . . you name it. The longhouse would have a busy procession of wakes before it would all fall quiet until the next storm of destruction barrelled through.

I talked to various tribal members about the phenomenon to see if there were stories, legends, or medicine methods that dealt with or at least talked about this occurrence. Elders were quietly consulted, and the answer came back as a no: there were no stories or myths about tides of destruction, but the valley was never considered a place for settled living by the tribes. They had been herded into the valley by government forces and it had become their reservation. The tribes had been marched into the Mission valley from their home in the Bitterroot valley. Shortly after that the Jesuits arrived, and the tribe was 'converted': tribal activity was squashed immediately and aggressively.

The tribe has only been living in the valley for about a hundred years at most as a settled tribe: before that it was a valley visited for fruit and root picking, hunting, and major ceremonies. People in the past camped briefly, then moved on: there had never been a settled community there long enough to develop any relationship with this power and learn how to live alongside it.

So over the years that I lived there, I watched this pattern of destruction roll in, scoop up a handful of people and animals, then barrel out to leave us in peace. At first I used to hunker down and shield myself magically as it passed over, but eventually I learned to commune with the power as it passed through, flowing with it and breathing across the land. In vision, I would fly with the wind and see the wind look for 'lights' of life that were fading or which somehow looked 'wrong': the wind would scoop up those souls and carry them off.

It would be easy to psychologize or try to theorize about exactly what was happening, but in truth I learned with such natural expressions to simply take them as I found them and work with them instinctively. That way, my preconceptions, cultural overlay, and intellect did not get in the way. I approached these experiences with the mentality of a child who will play, interact, and accept without having to analyse, explain, and conceptualize. I found that this approach stopped me getting in the way of the experience, and it allowed my imagination to create an interface through which I could experience without prejudice what was a perfectly natural phenomenon.

3.5 Natural tides of death and ritual patterns

After my experiences in Montana, I became far more observant with the powers that flowed through the land and the tides of death that seemed to roll in and out of particular landscapes. I moved to Nashville where the tides were often linked to the spring storms and tornadoes, but the city and community there was too large for me to discern exactly what impact these tides were having on the local population.

In Montana, the local community where I lived was only six hundred people, so sudden crops of deaths were easy to observe. However in Nashville the city was far too large for me to rationally come to any conclusions. I was also immersed in jobs, kids, and general life: too many distractions for any real magical observations!

It was not until I returned to live in the UK and moved out to Dartmoor National Park that I was able to really look closely at this occurrence and work with it magically. Dartmoor is in the southwest of England and is a wild moorland surrounded by sea coasts on its north and south sides. The land itself holds a bigger collection of Bronze Age settlements, stone alignments, and burial cairns than any other place in England. It is also a land relatively free from Roman ritual overlays: the area where I live has never been touched by the Romans.

Over time I learned which ritual stone alignments seemed to work with death, fertility and sacrifice, and which ones worked with weather patterns. While exploring these stone circles and alignments near my house, I became acutely aware of how the energy of the land and the beings that presented themselves responded and interacted both with tides of death and the weather.

To my west, going into Cornwall, I came across an inner contact who seemed connected to or residing in a vortex on the land. This was a place where the trees all leaned into each other in a swirl, their limbs twisting towards the centre of what appeared—and also felt—like an energy vortex. I sat in the centre and reached carefully into the land in vision to see what was there. I was tentative in my approach, as though the land here does not have the major power punch that America has, it is still potentially dangerous in these wild areas.

I came across a being who presented themselves as a giant who carried a small, childlike being. My immediate thought was the image of Saint Christopher, and I wondered if I had hit a layer of early Christian consciousness in the land. It quickly became obvious that it was far older, and was a natural expression of a being in the land who had slowly taken up human form after millennia of interactions with the local community.

The giant was constantly feeding the child, and it asked me if I had anything to give the child to eat. The giant acted nervously at the prospect of not having food for this little being, and I offered some snacks that I had in my pocket. The child munched happily, and the giant breathed a sigh of relief. I was intrigued. I asked the giant what happened when the child did not have food. The giant told me that if the child was not fed, then it began to scream. If the child screamed, storms would gather from the west and kill who were all at sea.

This area has strong fishing communities along the Devon and Cornwall coast, and a sudden storm could indeed do serious damage to the local fishing boats and their occupants. I mentioned this to a local magician who lived by the coast and whose family had lived in that area for generations. He recounted tales of legends of the screaming winds. Some storms would barrel in from the west and would whip up winds that sounded like a screaming child as they flowed from the sea onto the cliffs and around the steep narrow valleys. In times past local fishing families would say that if the storm screamed, the boats out at sea would be sunk and lives would be lost. Hmm... interesting.

I could not find any legends of feeding the child to keep the storms at bay, in the form of offerings to the land or sea, but probably through generations of interacting with the local powers the inner image of a giant and child developed, and the screaming sound would signal a particular kind of storm. We could hypothesize until the cows come home, but in the end you deal with what is in front of you and how it interacts with you. I found it fascinating, and when I went back to my part of Dartmoor, I began to keep notes on the different types of storms that frequently hit the area. The giant contact did not appear on my part of the moor, and I didn't experience a screaming storm, but I did come across something far more interesting.

3.6 Death and weather: talking to the storm

Once I had settled in my home in Dartmoor, I noticed over the months that the weather patterns for the specific valley I was living in were different to those on the rest of the moor. I mentioned it to the locals, and they agreed that the steep little valley had a microclimate all its own. They had learned to read the signs of the weather over the generations, and would use those clues in the running of their farms and livestock. I did not see anything particularly magical about it, it was more a matter of the layout of the land in relation to the sea, and the shape of the valley itself.

After a couple of years I began to notice that some storms were different from others. Some storms came in with a feeling of cleaning the land, cleaning the air, etc., and others felt heavy, oppressive, and sometimes dangerous. I also realized that when the heavy, oppressive storms came in, I would feel drained, tired, and disorientated. One day the feeling of oppression became too much for me, and I decided to do some readings to see what inner dynamic was playing out with these storms.

The results of the readings were strange, and I was not sure how to interpret them. The readings seemed to show that the storm had a specific consciousness and it was angry. It certainly did feel that way, but I wondered if I was reading too much into the situation and if I had missed rational explanations.

Then a really nasty storm came in and hung over the village for days and days. I went to check on some elderly neighbours, as the heavy constant rain and wind had trapped them in their houses. All of them, without exception, as well as other neighbours I talked to, complained of feeling drained and agitated, and they were having nightmares. They also mentioned that when these nasty storms came in and hung around, people would die in the village, usually the pensioners. That really peaked my curiosity, as I had assumed the bad feeling was just me, but it seemed that the connections with storms and death were making themselves known again.

So I went back to the cards and asked how I should actively work to bring balance. Cards can be used not only for divination but also as a vocabulary and as a form of communication with spirits. The answer was simple: go and talk to the storm, and let your instincts take over.

Off I went, out into the rain and the wind. I stood on the hill where my house is, and stilled myself. I felt an anger and rage in the storm; a hostility to all the people of the village. I reached out in my mind to the storm to get its attention. I was going to talk to the storm in my mind, but got a really strong instinct to actually use my voice—the power of utterance. I told the storm how beautiful he was, how wild, how nourishing. The feeling I got back was surprise: the storm thought that humans hated it, hated the land, and were totally hostile to nature in general.

I spoke out loud, telling the storm how much I loved the land, the trees, the rain, the sun, how I loved tending to the creatures, land beings and plants, and how I honoured the wind and all it brought to us. I'm glad no one was standing nearby, as I felt like an idiot: I would have probably been hauled off for being a nutcase.

I got no response from the storm, so I felt I had failed and had got the whole thing totally wrong. I went back inside, dripping wet, and got changed. Twenty minutes later, my husband Stuart nodded towards the window and told me that whatever I did, it had worked. I went outside in total awe. The wind had ceased, the rain had stopped, and the sun had come out. And it stayed out. The storm had withdrawn, and the heavy aggressive feeling had left the valley.

I was really not sure what to make of this. Though I am a visionary magician, I am also a rational being—no, really! For any such incident I feel

51

there is usually a logical explanation as well as a magical one: it is just a matter of vocabulary. But I could think of no rational explanation about why a storm would move on just because I had made friends with it: that left only magical explanations. The next time a nasty storm came in I did the same thing. This time, I also sang to the storm. The same thing happened again: the aggressive storm moved swiftly on. I learned to feel the difference between ordinary weather patterns—weather that was coming from imbalance in the climate—and weather that appeared to have consciousness.

The lesson in all of this, for me and for you, is that magic is far more than robes and rituals and systems: it is about learning how to interact and be in harmony with the forces around us. It is about learning how energy and consciousness flows back and forth—and to do that, you have to approach new learning experiences like a child with an open mind and be willing to make a fool of yourself. The rationalizing can come after the experience. I truly feel that science, particularly physics, will eventually find logical patterns in all this: the universe is logical and harmonic in its chaos. Magicians use one language, and science uses another. The problem occurs when religion and dogmatic belief on either side come into play.

My experiences communing with storms led me on a path of historical research which took me into the realms of ancient history (Enlil *et al.*) I was beginning to truly understand how humanity first made connections and relationships with storm deities. First would come the communion, then the deity image would develop in the human consciousness as an interface and highway for energy. Keeping it at that level works well. If you take things further and try to control the filter of the deity by manipulating it, then you begin to cause imbalance—but that is another chapter of its own.

3.7 The land and accidents

Going back to my time in Montana, there was another thing I came across in the land, but that I did not understand fully at the time. For two years I commuted back and forth to a job in Missoula around fifty miles from my home. The road I would take, Highway 93, is a dangerous road, so my antenna had to be in full operation every time I drove. I noticed that there were certain areas on the road where the energy was heavy, dangerous, and aggressive. The areas that had this energy were also parts of the road that were particularly dangerous because of the narrowing of the road, the position, cliff faces, etc.: they were also hotspots for accidents and deaths.

I assumed the horrible feelings at these points were because there had been so many accidents and deaths there over the years. I did toy with the idea that they were bad energy hotspots, but I dismissed that thought and went instead for the idea that they had developed as a result of the deaths there, not been the cause of them.

As I moved around the States, I encountered a few of these accident hotspots, or areas where the energy was really nasty, and I would narrowly miss a bad accident or come to one that had just happened. So again, I thought that what I was picking up was a *result* of accidents, not the cause.

It was not until I returned to the UK and was driving a lot that I began to realize that something more interesting was happening. I was often driving up and down the M5 between Dartmoor and Bristol, and would pass an area that I began to call the Black Hole. It was an area on the motorway that felt destructive and horrible. The more I drove through that patch, the stronger the feeling became. After a year of this, a newsflash broke about a massive pileup on the M5 in fog, and an accident that had caused many deaths and injuries. The horrific accident was right in the centre of the Black Hole. I had to drive through it again a week later, and I was unsettled as to what danger I would be putting myself in.

To my surprise, when I drove through that patch of road, the energy was clear and healthy. Something had built up and dispersed through the accident: the road was now clear. This was not what I had expected. I had thought the patch of road to be an unhealthy land energy that was a part of the land. Instead, it seemed like a vortex or energy patch that had built up and resolved itself with the energy of the crash and subsequent deaths. This was a new experience for me, and it caused me to look at how land energy, tides of life and death, and the consciousness of the land worked.

Is this what the ancients were working to avoid by tuning the land, interacting with land deities, and performing energy exchanges with the power forces? Was that vortex of destruction a purely natural occurrence, or was it a result of the road being there and the heavy buildup of humanity trucking back and forth? I don't know, but it has led me to look far more closely at the forces that flow through us, through the land, and through the worlds.

3.8 Tides of weather; the heralding of storms

Just as I discovered buildups of death and accident patterns on the land, I also experienced a curious thing regarding big storms. I had experienced various weather patterns across the land when I lived in the US, and buildups of power on the land as discussed earlier. I had also experienced being warned and protected by local land beings in dangerous situations, particularly in respect of tornadoes—but that contact was usually immediate, often only an hour before the actual event.

A curious thing happened that pointed me in the direction of exploring and learning about the long-term buildup patterns of dangerous and damaging storms. While I was living in Montana, I had been invited to Nashville to work with a magical group of people. It was the end of term at the school where I was working, and so that June (2005), off I went to Nashville. While we were in the midst of the magical work, something curious happened.

We were working in a magical pattern of the four directions in vision and ritual, and at one point in the day we were taking turns in walking around the directions and stopping to commune with the contacts in each direction. When my turn came and I got a particular direction—I cannot remember which one—the being I was attempting to communicate with became distracted and stepped to one side, indicating that I needed to pay attention to something deeper in the direction itself. So I focused beyond the being and became aware of a vast force of wind. It was destructive, powerful, and focused, but without emotion. It was so intense that it worried me, as I felt we were in imminent danger.

I asked the people gathered if hurricanes came through Nashville and I was told that Nashville tended to get the remnants of hurricanes but not really the full-on hits: this was more tornado country. I explained what I saw but that I could not ascertain whether it was just a natural force in that direction in the land, or whether it was something about to happen: I just could not tell. I could say that a massive force of wind was building up and it was dangerous enough to take many lives.

A few weeks later, hurricane Katrina slammed into the US doing terrible damage and taking many lives. It also had a profound impact on the nation, the land, and the people. I do not know if such an early warning or buildup happens for every hurricane, or if it was only noticeable because of the intense inner power of destruction that flowed through that storm. What it did tell me was that such storms gather first as an inner impetus before they express as an outer storm. If we had been properly tuned into the land and powers, and understood the vocabulary of the buildup, we could have warned people—if we lived in a community open to such warnings. We see fragments of this in tribal cultures: sometimes tribes pre-empt a natural disaster by moving out of harm's way.

Maybe this is something that people in the distant past worked with and were in tune with. It also began to dawn on me that when someone does a Tarot reading, they are not necessarily 'seeing' the future; rather they are reading the vocabulary of the current inner buildup for an outer event to manifest in the future.

3.9 Summary

It does seem that major natural events, weather, death tides, and accident hotspots build slowly from an inner perspective and gather inner energetic momentum weeks or sometimes months before they express out in the physical world. This is something that I am sure ancestral people long ago were aware of, and worked with, and we have lost that skill through becoming civilised.

This is something, however, than can be rediscovered, learned about, and understood. A willingness to be open, curious, and attentive will develop that long-broken bond with the lands around us. We have to relearn all that has been lost and pass on what we learn for future generations to build upon and develop.

Chapter Four

Working with land powers

The Gardens and the Groves

In the last chapter we looked at some of the power manifestations that flow naturally on and within the land. In this chapter we will look at practical ways a magician can work directly with land powers, and how a magical relationship between the land and the magician can be forged.

There are various ways that a magician can work with land powers. What methods you use depends on what your magical practice is, what you are trying to achieve, and what level of power you are willing to immerse yourself in. Working with the land can range from simple interactions with the environment, to, at the other extreme, a sacrificial upholding of the land through the body until death—and then possibly becoming a Sleeper.

In between those two extremes are many layers of magic that can be worked with and put into action. It all depends on what you are trying to achieve, and why. This type of work tends to move away from ritual magic and becomes more shamanic or faery-orientated, just by nature of the powers you are working with and the environment around you.

Lets look at different magical dynamics for working with the land, from personal magical interaction all the way through to long-term generational magical service.

4.1 Nurturing the land

Our cultural attitude towards the land has been heavily influenced by a passage in the Pentateuch, Genesis 1:26:

> Then God said, "Let us make man in our image, after our likeness. And let them have dominion over the fish of the sea and over the birds of the heavens and over the livestock and over all the earth and over every creeping thing that creeps on the earth."

That one word, dominion, has had terrible far-reaching consequences in our relationship with nature and the land around us. We have raped and pillaged our environment and all the creatures that exist around us in a selfish orgy of resources. But if we change that one word 'dominion' for 'stewardship,' then a different story can be told.

We are unique as a species in that we can reach beyond our everyday consciousness and manipulate power, energy, and inner contact to build, destroy, or simply commune with the invisible Divine forces around us: the act of magic. It is time to evolve beyond a mindless stripping and controlling of everything around us, and instead move towards a more mutually respectful, beneficial relationship with the world around us.

There is a movement within neo-shamanism and revival pagan groups that calls for the non-interference with nature. This is a noble idea, but it is not realistic and certainly not balanced. We have enclosed land, killed predators, and fostered beneficial plants and edible animals over inedible ones. We have built highways, cities, etc.: this is the reality that we live in, and we have to work within that reality. This can be done in practical ways and in magical ways.

The revival of nature worship and neo-shamanism by people who really are civilized, well resourced, and generally out of touch with the harsh reality of nature has coloured magical practice today in various subtle and not-so-subtle ways. A simple example is one regarding land management. A couple of years ago I met someone who had just finished an environmental degree, moved from London into the country, and bought a few acres of forest. He wanted to live as naturally as possible on the land with his family and planned on building a house in the woods and letting the land govern itself. He felt that the faery beings within the land would keep the land in balance: a quaint idea and totally devoid of understanding of how nature worked.

I went to visit him and his family after a year. He bemoaned the fact that though the land was covered in trees, no herbs or plants grew, and the house they had built was damp, dark, and difficult to live in. I pointed out to him that though his heart was in the right place, he needed to step back and look at how the land would have been if the house, fences, dogs, and nearby town were not there. He did not understand what I was talking about.

If that patch of land was completely natural, then it would have had deer to keep the saplings in check and to strip bark from some trees to slow their growth, letting sunlight get to the ground. The boar would have grazed the forest floor which would also have kept brush down and allowed plants to grow, wolves would have kept the deer in check, fires would have burned up the brush and stimulated new growth, and the local river would have flooded across that patch of land—it had been diverted and the area was an old flood plain—to replenish the soil and again keep certain growth in check. The list was endless. Instead, the fenced acreage and lack of land management resulted in the overgrowth of the forest, and a brush buildup on the forest floor which suppressed plants, turning the land bitter. The land was slowly killing itself.

The trees were densely packed and were all dying. His house got no light, and the family were generally miserable.

We have to work with what we have in reality, and we have to compensate for the changes our presence makes. This can make for interesting living, and can be as simple or as magically complicated as we wish to make it if you use your common sense. The first trick is to stand outside mainstream thinking and the comfortable 'cuteness' that an abundance of resources has allowed us. We can be all compassionate and loving to trees, birds, and animals when we have full bellies and a roof over our heads. But that is not true nature. When resources are low, then the fight for survival resumes. Keep that in mind when you plan your magical action. Are you looking at the land with a true perspective, or through the lens of the 'Disney channel'?

4.2 Magical gardening

The simplest way of working with the land is often the most profound teacher, though it is not very glamorous. This is the most basic way to work with the land, but it also the most powerful. Once you have done deep inner work with the weather tides, the land beings etc., returning to this method brings a new level of depth and awareness of land power through a simple, almost non-magical action.

It can be a small part of magical practice, or it can be the only magical action a person wishes to take on the land. Either way it will teach you a great deal about how the land, the plants, and the animals all jostle in a fight for survival. That battle for survival is like base camp for magical gardening, but it can step beyond that into much deeper magical and power dynamics.

The first step of magical work with the land is to tend a garden. Most of us these days think of gardens as lawn, herb, and flower patches with few if any weeds, raised beds, garden ornaments, etc.. A lot of gardens like that quickly become sterile: they are inner wastelands. A lawn is a sterile environment and serves no purpose other than sitting on. A heavily weeded garden is out of balance and is akin to having to a room full of uptight people with nothing in common with each other. Also bear in mind that a lot of flower species are now heavily genetically modified and have little, if any, natural functions left in them: they are beautiful, but it is like looking at a beautiful caged bird.

On a practical level, first find out what plants would have grown naturally in your area. Find out which native species attracts bees, birds, insects, butterflies, and so forth. Look at what are the poisons, what are the medicines, and what are the functional weeds that strengthen the soil and the other plants around them. We have an odd mentality as humans in that when we grow herbs or food, we tend to grow them in a line, all the same plant in one big patch, and weed around them furiously. It really is the worst thing you can do.

My mother was an amazing gardener and could grow just about anything. One of her rules was to scatter things around, find out which plants make friends and support the delicate ones, watch to see which ones are the bullies, and finally sing to your garden. It worked, and I began to apply her reasoning to the work I was doing. I had wonderful results. I also learned a great deal about the consciousness of plants by observing, listening, and watching inner interactions between them. It truly is fascinating, and rather shocking. I knew plants had some form of consciousness, I just had not realized quite how much and how sophisticated it was.

My garden looks like a patch of chaos, but it is healthy, pest resistant, and fertile. I got rid of ornamental bushes, grass, and invasive species, planted native plants, medicinal and magical herbs and poisons, and let the dandelions, chickweed etc grow between them. My mother taught me that weeds, when kept in balance, help protect delicate plants by providing strength and 'buddy' immunity from pests. It worked! So my garden looks rather overgrown and unkempt—and it pisses of the neighbours—but in reality it is as healthy and as balanced as I can get it.

The next step—the first magical step—is the power of intent. When you train up in visionary or ritual magic, the power of focus of intent becomes honed to a fine point. You can cast your power of thought in a focused, direct line and let power flow down that line. When I go out in the garden, I go out with the magical intent of tending the surrounding landscape and all who live there.

A plant that is young, delicate, or not quite established, but that has great magical and/or medicinal potential must be fostered and cared for. A plant that grows out of control and is swamping all the others must be cut back. But when that action is done magically, done with the intent that the power of the action is magically mirrored across the land. The harvesting of herbs is done carefully, and at the right time, to make sure of the healthy survival of the plant while you take some of it, but not all. It is like working with homeopathic magical intent: what you do in the garden from an inner point of view spreads a corresponding potential for action across the land. This is the simplest and most basic of inner dynamics.

4.3 Tapping into hotspots

This is where real earth magic begins, and where the magician can really begin to develop skills, while at the same time learning how to tune an area of land to work with it magically. This would be the introductory foundational action for building a temple or a sacred grove, or working to effect balance on the land, species, or weather; or to elicit protection in times of great danger, etc. Temples, stone alignments, and groves do not become magical or powerful due to their building, but by finding a power spot on the land, tuning that land, contacting the powers there, and opening the gates of that power spot.

Most temples and stone circles in the ancient past were positioned with great care, as they were mediators of the power that flowed through a specific landmass or power spot. A degenerate or reverse form of this wisdom can be observed in the early Christian church: they positioned churches on sacred pagan places, power spots, burials, and former temples in an attempt to suppress what was underneath.

The following methods can be used both for 'virgin' powers spots, i.e. places with no previous ritual workings or construction, and for land with no particularly known power point, but which is to be fostered and used for a magical purpose.

The first step is identifying a hotspot or power spot on the land. There are more about than we often realize, and some turn up in the strangest of places. If you are psychically sensitive then you will find yourself drawn to power spots, and will either be drawn in or repelled by the power: either reaction is good, and can be worked with. Dowsing is also a good way to identify power spots, and for those who are not psychic and not dowsers, looking into local legends, myths, and stories regarding the land area will often give you clues.

Usually though, if you are a magician working with the inner contacts and the land, you will be dragged kicking and screaming at some point to a hotspot and told to work with it: the key is to listen carefully to faint voices that try to nudge you to visit a particular area.

The second step is to ascertain what sort of power is running through that hotspot. Again, this can be easy or really hard, depending on the magician's level of inner sight, instinct, connectedness, and stillness. The best and easiest way is to go and lie on the land. Still yourself internally until you are deep in the Void, in stillness, and slowly bring your consciousness back to your body and the land. As you do that, be acutely aware of tiny changes in how your mind and body react to the land, then how your emotions change.

How you react should tell you a great deal about what type of site it is. If you feel a rush of excitement, or an expansion of energy, or a sense of being taller than you are, then chances are the land power at that spot is about energy *output*, i.e. regeneration, healing, fertility, or growth—or a pressure point for the weather. If you feel sleepy, drained, on alert, and in danger, then most likely it is an energy *input* site, i.e. pulling energy from the beings, people and creatures around it. In such cases it is more likely to be a power spot for death, storms, disease, or an entrance to the Underworld. If it is an input site, don't necessarily shy away from it: you can learn a great deal of important magical knowledge from Underworld, death, disease, and storm power points. They are part of existence: creation and destruction are powers that should be worked with equally across the lifetime of a magician.

The third step is figuring out what type of pattern would be appropriate to develop over the power spot. That depends on the power, the land around you, and your agenda or intent. One important rule to remember if you are going to develop a magical pattern to tune a hotspot (which could last for a long time): if you build it, you are responsible for it. If you create chaos, you are responsible, and you may 'carry the energetic can.' With that in mind, if you are not intending to work with the site for a long time—years or decades—but just for a few months or weeks, then the pattern you establish magically must reflect that. You should use a simple construction for short-term use, clean it up afterwards, and disperse its power when you have finished. If you are planning long-term work, then the construction must be built to last and have the potential to hold vast amounts of power—you never know...

let's look at a simple short-term construction first. This would be a construction lightly built for making contact with local powers, dealing with a specific job, then closing down.

4.4 Short-term Construction

The first point of construction is the anchor point, the area which acts as a gate for the construction, grounds the guardian position, and literally anchors the construction to the land. To establish this, first work in vision while sitting on the land. This is a simple action. Sit and go into stillness/silence. When you are still, be aware of the land around you. See yourself in vision standing up and walking around the four directions of the land you are working on, and be aware of the subtle feel of the energies in each direction. Hold the intention of trying to find the 'gateway' direction: the direction where power flows freely into the area where you are working.

It can be a subtle sense, almost like a whisper, or it can be a strong force that makes itself known. Having established the 'power in' gateway, you then need to find the 'power out' gate. Which direction does the power flow out of? Notice I have not included the directions 'down' or 'up.' This is deliberate. In a construction, you use down or up as *fuel* points for the pattern you are constructing: if the pattern is for the future, then you draw down power from above. If the pattern is about ancestors and invigorating them, or about death or the past, then 'down' is where you draw power from.

Once you have established the 'in' and 'out' gate directions, you need to start building up the pattern itself. This is easy, but can be time consuming. The keys are mental focus of intent and stillness: do not let your mind wander, but keep a clear mind as you work. Starting in whatever direction the 'in power' gate is in, stand before the gate and 'see' a gate or two standing stones that create a doorway. Imagine in your mind the power flowing into the circle through the gate. Then move on to the next direction, working clockwise, and imagine a stone or pillar or stone altar marking the direction. Make sure that you build the 'power out' gate in whatever direction it made itself known to you. Continue this method until you are back at the 'in' gate and go around again, repeating the process.

This action builds an inner template using the imagination; and because you work magically with intent, the imagined template begins to form an energetic impression on the land. This informs the spirits and powers within the land what your intentions are, and what you are trying to achieve. The pattern you establish on the land becomes a vehicle for action, and the power becomes the fuel. You are the driver.

Depending on the response from the land, you may have to repeat this simple exercise repeatedly over the span of days or weeks to build it up, or it may power up and pull into focus straightaway. Personally I have found that if what you are planning to do is necessary for the land/people/creatures/weather etc., the power comes into focus almost immediately and the whole thing is finished over a day or two.

When the pattern is established and you can feel it on the land as you walk around the directions, then it is time to get to work. Position yourself in the centre with your back to the 'in' gate. Stand, don't sit, and go in vision into stillness, into the Void, to quieten your mind and body. When you are still, focus on your task and see in your imagination the gate behind you, the gate before you, the direction to your right, and the direction to your left. Be aware of the ancestors beneath your feet and the powers of the stars above you. Draw your attention to your centre, and see your centre as a light: an almost formless light that allows things to pass through it.

With that focus, using your inner vision, see the power flow in the working area through the 'in gate'; channel it through you, through your centre. See energy also flowing into you from below or above, and see the directions on either side of you as strong boundaries upholding you. When all the threads of power have been brought together within you, focus them like a beam and see that beam flowing through the 'out gate.'

As the power flows out of the out gate, 'see' where the power is to be sent beyond the gate, and utter your intent and direction for the power, for example, "I send you out in the world to bring about whatever change is necessary for the balance of X, the protection of X," etc. Notice that the utterance does not specify what the change should be: you are only asking for what is necessary. So if this is about protecting someone or a place, then you ask for whatever is necessary to achieve that.

This open-ended way of working allows the power to find the weak spot in the situation and fill it to bring about change. After that it will work at its own pace and in its own way, but the final result will be achieved. This way of working is simple but also difficult: it uses no beings, no inner contacts, no tools, and no weaving of rituals beyond establishing gates. You become the pontiff of power, the bridge that gathers energy and focuses it in a specific way for a specific purpose. If you have done little or no visionary magic, then chances are your mind will not yet be focused enough and you will not be connected enough, from an inner contact point of view, to gather the power and send it. But if you have established a working practice in visionary magic then this way of working can be powerful. It uses no additional workers or spirits: it is just you, the land, and power.

Once the work has been done, then the pattern needs breaking up and dispersing. This enables the land to go back to its natural flow and also make sure that no one else can stumble across your work and tap into it. The best way I have found is not to go back and manually dismantle the gates in the directions, but to use a dispersal pattern that is natural to the weather and the land. This make sure the patterns and powers are broken up naturally and can flow back into their natural channels.

It is a simple method, but very effective. Stand in the centre of the pattern and begin to turn. It does not matter which way you turn: your body will have a natural inclination to go one way or the other. As you turn, outstretch your arms. Imagine that your arms extend far beyond you and are knocking over the gates and gathering the power up, a bit like a tornado or whirlwind. Begin to turn faster. See the power and the pattern break up and become sucked up in a column of wind that you are the centre of. Once everything is in the column, stop and immediately begin to turn in the opposite direction. Let the power flow out through your hands, spreading it out across the land at random. It may also flow up to the sky or down into the earth through you. When you feel it has all gone, stop. It's that simple.

This method draws on flows of power and energy that are natural and part of the land. It leaves no echo, does no damage, and achieves its goal while working with the land.

Note: If you are naturally psychic and wish to work as naturally as possible, then once a power spot has been identified, simply make friends with spirits and powers in the land. Walk around the directions and make friends with those spirits and ancestors drawn to you, tell them what you are trying to achieve, and ask for their help. Follow their lead and simply hold the intent of action while standing on the land. Just be clear in your intent and what help you need. The rest will happen organically and use no magical patterns. It is a simple, powerful way to work in union with all the beings on the land, but it only really works if you can easily connect with different beings and if your intent fits what they are willing to work with.

4.5 Longer-term construction: building a sacred grove

This technique can be used when you are trying to develop a sacred working or temple space from scratch on the land. It is only used when the type of space you are trying to build will be dedicated to working with the powers of nature, so it would not be suitable if you were trying to establish a new ritual temple or deity working space that uses ritual or temple magic. This is more of a method for building spaces that would operate similarly to stone circles, medicine wheels, sacred groves, etc.: spaces that work with the land powers, the weather, and the ancestors.

The methods for identifying the space and establishing the entrance 'gate' are the same as the techniques described in the 'tapping into hotspots' section above. After that the technique diverges slightly. Building a sacred working space on the land establishes a focused working space that should withstand the ravages of time. It will not be as long-lasting as the Neolithic and Bronze age sacred sites scattered across the world, but it should at least last for your lifetime and will continue as long as it is worked with.

Establishing a sacred space requires identifying a power spot, tuning it to a working pattern, bringing in land spirits, ancestors, and elemental powers, and weaving them all together in a balanced and harmonic pattern. How you construct the site's inner and outer aspects, the beings you work with, and the actual work you do in the space, will decide how successful the site will become. It is all a matter of keeping balance, working respectfully with the spirits, and cooperating rather than commanding.

Once the gate and basic directions are established, it is time to call in spirits and beings to assist with both the construction and the work itself. Working in a clockwise fashion, go to the first direction past the gate—so if the gate is in the north, start in the east. Stand in that direction and first work in vision. See a directional threshold in the form of a stone, and see beyond the threshold out into the inner landscape of the land. Using the power of utterance, using your breath with magical intent, call out for a spirit of the land to join you, one who is willing to work with you in establishing this sacred place. See in your imagination a being appear in the distance and come walking towards you.

When the being reaches you, tell them who you are, who your family is, what land you were born on, where you live now, and what you are trying to achieve. Tell them what work you want to establish on the land, and why. If the being agrees with what you are trying to do, they will agree to stay and work with you. They may indicate to you what type of being they are, what skills they have, and what they may want in return.

If no being appears in your mind, do not force it. Not every direction on every patch of land has a being who will be forthcoming. Remember, your imagination is only an interface: it sends out signals that spirits can decipher, and creates a window in your consciousness through which beings can interface with you. Your imagination is not the creator or controller: that is just psychology, and not what we are working with here. If you try to control your imagination and force an image or happening, then the contact will shut down. It is a delicate balancing act to create an imaginary interface without allowing your imagination full control.

Once contact is established—or not—move clockwise onto the next direction. Repeat the same exercise in each direction until you come back to the gate. The only difference with the gate is that you put out a call for two beings to act as guardians and threshold keepers. Again, do not try to form what they are, or what they look like; just allow them to commune with you through your imagination and show you what they look like. Another way for them to reflect through your imagination is to show you an image from your mind that tells you what their powers and abilities are.

Now that the inner contacts are established, it is time to ritually build the space. This action implants a physical pattern onto the space and anchors it to the land so that power can flow from inner to outer and outer to inner. Each direction will need a stone to act as a directional marker/link, and the gate will need two stones to act as the gateposts. Getting the right stone is important, as some stones can bring a strong presence or resonance into the space. To find the right stone, go and stand in the first direction. Remember the contact of that direction, and ask them to guide you to the stone needed for that direction. Cross over the threshold and physically walk in that direction while trying to keep an awareness of the land around you.

Let your instincts and the contact guide you as you walk around the land until you find the right stone. You will be drawn to an area and eventually discover the right stone. If you handle it or touch it, it will feel different energetically to all the other stones around you. If the necessary stone is far away, which sometimes happens, then you will get a strange compulsion to set off in your car, or on foot, to some specific spot.

When you have found the stone—and it does not matter how big or small it is, only that it is the right one—tell the stone what you will do. This is important: often smaller land beings —faeries—inhabit stones and you do not want to anger them by being disrespectful. It is worth taking time with this part of the work. Commune with the stone to ascertain if beings are inhabiting it, and if they are, talk to them. Ask them if they want to join you, and if not, ask if they need anything from you before you take the stone.

When all negotiations are suitably finished, take the stone to the site and put it in the right direction. Make sure you enter the space always from the direction of the 'in' gate, even if no marker stones are there yet: you establish the flow within the space with the regularity of your actions. Walk a full circle, and come to rest in front of the direction the stone belongs in. Place the stone on the ground and stand or kneel before it, placing your hands on the stone.

In your inner vision call out to, or see, the spirit/contact of that direction. They come towards you, pass through you, and go into stone. They are not trapped there and will not be always there: what you are doing is establishing a physical anchor in the site for that being. You will use the stone in future to make energetic physical contact with the being, and the being will leave a thread of themselves in the stone so that they can flow back and forth to the site.

Having said that, it has happened to me that the spirit goes right into the stone and stays there, living in the stone. If that happens, then that is just how that being prefers to work, and they will establish their energies within the structure of the site. You do come across this sort of thing occasionally in stone alignments where the stones are still housing spirits asleep within their stones.

You need to repeat this action in each direction, and for the two gate stones at the entrance. This can take some time, and can be muscular work if the stones that the spirits want are big. It might be a good idea to have others working with you to lessen the load and to assist in the construction. If you are a group of experienced magical workers, then each of you can do a direction: this makes life a lot easier and less sweaty.

Once the stones are in place and the contacts/spirits are all connected to the stones, then the threshold needs to be sealed. This is simply but powerfully done. Stand at the gate on the threshold and be aware of the beings on either side of you. This part is all physical and not visionary, as it seals the place into the physical realm. Call out to the wind:

> "I have built this sacred temple of the land with the rocks of the earth, with the spirits of the land, and by the will of my heart. I ask that you—wind that blows through the land, wind that brings weather, wind that brings life—bear witness to this sealing. I ask the sun and stars above, the sun that brings warmth and strength to us, and the stars that seed the future of all things, to witness this sealing, I ask the great Mother beneath my feet—She who gives of Her stones, She who birthed me, She who holds all the ancestors in Her rich earth—I ask the Great Mother to witness this sealing. This is the threshold of the sacred grove, and I ask the guardians to uphold this space. None who have destructive or unbalanced intent may enter, but those who love the land and wish to serve shall be upheld within this space."

When you have spoken, prick or cut your finger and drip your blood in a line between the two guardians. This informs the guardians of the ground rules you are establishing, and your blood connects you to the site. If anything powerful is happening in the grove, you will get an energetic 'pull' to visit the site.

4.6 Starting work

To operate the grove you will need a central element to work with, to draw the power in and to act as an access route for the land spirits around the grove.

This can be a flame in a fire bowl (to protect the land from the fire) or a bowl of water. Sometimes in the past a person was used; they would be ritually slain and buried in the centre of the grove or at the threshold to act as an intermediary. These days, killing your granny and burying her in the grove is not socially acceptable, so fire or water is a better and more modern approach.

To begin work, start in the centre with the element. Still yourself before the element, until your mind is completely silent (going into the Void). Using inner vision, see yourself get up and go (clockwise) to the first direction after the gate, and stand before the stone. Call out for the contact of that direction to come to the stone and establish the visionary contact. Greet them and ask them to work with you. Repeat the action in the other directions until you get to the gateway. Acknowledge the guardians and ask that they allow the deity power—say a local land goddess or a storm god—to flow freely in and out of the gate.

Then it is time, once the contacts are all primed, to begin work. Start at the first direction again, this time working ritually. Stand before the first directional stone and call out, using your voice, your intent to work, and what you ask of the powers in that direction. Keep your request simple, and be aware that the more you try and condition the action and outcome, the more restricted the magic will be.

So for example if you were trying to work with a recent disaster on the land, then you would state that you wished to work to achieve whatever is necessary to bring balance to that situation and the beings and powers involved. So for example if there had been a mass shooting, murder, or terrible accident, then you would work with the directional contacts to bring balance. That may entail gathering up the souls of the dead and providing a path in which they souls can flow into the grove, through you, and into the fire. This would direct them into the Void so that they could begin their death journey: often people killed in such circumstances become stuck on the land. This can often be directly experienced by visiting a disaster area and feeling the energetic impact and the trapped, unhealthy energy.

If you were doing such a task, then you and the directional contacts would create a circle, the guardians would hold the gates open for the dead, and you would stand between the gates and the fire, allowing the souls to bridge through you in the fire.

On the other hand if you were aware of the disaster area being imbalanced and lots of unhealthy beings/spirits being drawn to that area, then you would work with the contacts and a local deity to restore the order of the land, which would happen either by beings of an opposing power being drawn from the directions onto the affected land, or the re-establishing of the deity power on the land.

The possible techniques are endless, and you need to develop a working method that spans vision, ritual, and utterance that works for you. The key is intent, focus, and building up the energy pattern in the grove by constantly walking around the directions and communing with the contacts in each direction in vision. This establishes a simple working pattern that takes on its own frequency which shuts out parasitical and unhealthy beings.

If you work with this method on the land then you will find that the grove slowly takes on a life of its own. The more you work around the directions, the more you 'tune' it, and the stronger the contacts will become. Over the years you will find that the grove starts to work with you through dreams, through everyday life, and that it powers up the moment you stand within it.

Just don't make the mistake of trying to dress the grove with New Age trinkets, crystals, incense, etc. You are working with pure nature, so keep it that way. Often the beings within the stones like simple food offerings such as bread, nuts, fruit, things that would not harm the local creatures or birds, or olive oil or wine poured over them—the Romans were really into that.

We are at the stage of magical development in our time where we are trying to relearn what was lost. What is needed is a fluid, organic way of working as opposed to grimoire-based and heavily crafted rituals. Such an excessively organized way of working often works in conflict to the land and spirits rather than in union with them. Let the grove and its spirits teach you how to work successfully.

After a working session, go back around the directions to thank the contacts and ask if they need anything doing. It is important that you establish a two-way system of work. The grove work is not all about you and your agenda: it is a working interface between you and the land. The land spirits will at times ask you to do things for them, and you may find that over time the grove will develop as an interface of constant magical flow between you and the land. It becomes your work station in service to the land.

Always, at the end of a session, leave a gift for the grove spirits. This might take the form of honey, tobacco, bread, or mead: things that degrade, that have a strong energy, and that will not kill or damage local creatures. Either leave your gift in the centre or distribute it between the directions. Always acknowledge the guardians every time you walk in and out of the grove, and place your hand on their stones and let them take some energy from you.

It is also good practice to build a friendship relationship with the grove and the spirits there. This is done by simply going there to hang out. Be in the space while you read or sleep, or just sit and be still. Take bread and/or honey gifts, and if a land deity has established themselves in the grove, go to honour them and just be with them. Do not be overly formal with a grove: though it is a magical space it is also a natural space. The relationship between the magician and the space is informal, often intense, and will develop organically into a closely bonded relationship. Listen to the grove; listen to the spirits and the deity. They will talk to you through your thoughts, instincts, dreams, and through the animals and birds. And do not try to own the grove. It is a sacred land space, and at some point it will call to others to come and work. If you find inappropriate gifts and things left there, just quietly take them away and dispose of them. Leave any gifts that are appropriate. (For instance you would take out plastic ribbons and candles, but leave food and bones.)

To finish, I will give you an example of a sacred grove that called to me. I think I have talked about this a little bit in a previous book, but it is pertinent to this chapter, and it will save you from having to sift through my books to find it.

4.7   The story of Medicine Wheel

When I lived in Montana I used to run errands for tribal elders. One weekend I was asked to take some supplies in my truck to a powwow on the Crow Agency Indian Reservation which sits on the border between Montana and Wyoming. When I looked on a map for the best route, I noticed a mountain called Medicine Mountain that was nearby. I made plans to go back home through Yellowstone Park so I could visit this mountain, which seemed to be pulling at me for some reason. I mentioned it to one of the tribal elders and he told me about Medicine Wheel, a sacred site up on the mountain. He asked if I intended to go there and I said yes, unless he felt there was a reason I should not.

He said it would be fine and I could do him a favour. Would I be willing to take a prayer bag there from his family and pray for them? I felt honoured just to be asked, and of course I agreed. By the time the hour arrived for the trip, I had three medicine bags to take there as gifts for the sacred site, some sage, and 'husks'—a local sacred root—as gifts for the site, along with a beautifully crafted medicine wheel given to me by one of the elders to hang in the truck, to protect me. So what started as a casual idea rapidly turned into something of a pilgrimage.

I dropped off the supplies at the Crow Agency and set off up Medicine Mountain. As my truck struggled with the steep mountain roads, I watched with foreboding as the bright warm summer sunshine slowly turned to dark clouds and cold. As it was summer I was dressed in T-shirt and jeans, but the higher my truck inched up the steep mountain road, the colder it became, until I was seeing snow at the sides of the road. Uh oh.

I finally arrived at the place where I could park the truck, as the rest of the journey had to be done on foot. I groaned outwardly when I saw other trucks there: I had hoped to do this alone, undisturbed. A faint voice in my head told me to wait. To park up, roll a cigarette and just wait. So I did. Within minutes the dark clouds really gathered and snow began falling—in summer! I was at nine thousand feet, and it had not occurred to me that the weather might have been colder—duh. I had just finished my cigarette when I saw people running down the mountain path to the trucks, trying to get out of the blizzard that was slowly building. Within fifteen minutes I was alone—and cold.

Luckily I had some Indian blankets in the truck with me, a habit I had gotten into after being caught by cold weather in the Montana wilderness before. I gathered the gifts into a backpack, threw two blankets over myself, and began the hike up the mountain to the wheel.

I could barely see where I was going for the snow, but every step I took, voices challenged me and were all around me asking me who I was, why I was going there, and what were my intentions. The voices got stronger and stronger, so I answered. I told them out loud who my family was, and that I was not Indian and did not want to be. I told them about the medicine bags I was carrying with prayers from the Salish elders, about my own gifts and prayers, and that I intended to honour the site.

When I finally arrived at the top of the trail, the medicine wheel was laid out on a ledge. At nearly ten thousand feet, it felt like the edge of the world. I asked the wheel guardians' permission to enter and realized that they could well say no, in which case I would have to say the prayers where I standing, leave the bags by its perimeter, and go. Thankfully they said yes. I cautiously climbed into the centre of the wheel, being careful not to dislodge the ritual pattern laid out in the stones, and sat down. I laid the medicine bags from the elders in front of me and began prayers for them, and for an ancestor of mine who was buried on the reservation. I had wrapped one blanket around myself and had one draped over my head like a veil, so that I would be warm but still able to see. After the prayers, I closed my eyes and went into vision.

I had a long and detailed visionary interaction with an elderly woman, some of which I did not at that time understand, but it was vivid enough that I would remember. It did not seem to take that much time, and thankfully the snow was easing up a bit. When I finished I left a gift of tobacco and husks, and hung the medicine bags on the posts nearby. I got a strong urge to sing, which is most unusual for me, as I sing like a strangled cat; but the urge was strong as if it was something the spirits wanted. So I sang the spirits a song from my childhood: a Sean Nos song. The Sean Nos songs are old Irish ballads, myths, and poems sung without instrument in a highly stylized way that reaches far back in time. I was not sure what reaction a foreign song would get, but they did seem to like it. I got a feeling of benevolence, almost like an adult smiling at a child who is saying all the wrong things but has the right intent.

I set off in the snow and worked my way back down to the truck. I did not feel too cold, and I realized I had not felt the cold at all while I had been sitting in the snow. The shock came when I got back in the truck. On firing up the engine, I saw that I had been sitting on the mountain in the snow for three hours! I thought I had only been there for about ten minutes, with half an hour to get up there and same coming back down.

My experience with the old woman in the wheel triggered things that changed my life and my magic most profoundly. The wheel itself was powerful and ancient: it had been built to last over millennia and its pulse still beat loudly enough for anyone listening to hear it. This is a perfect example of a constructed grove site that does not exclude those who need to touch base with its power, or to pass by and offer work, or to go to honour the land. It was well guarded and tuned, and was willing to work with me despite my being from a foreign land. And that is another important point to remember with these ancient powers and places: they do not see race, colour, creed, or culture.

But they do see respect and integrity. When that particular wheel was built, there were no issues with invaders, colonizers, or New Agers co-opting others' traditions. There was issue with good intent and bad intent, with respect and disrespect. The guardians of that place had grilled me on who my ancestors were—one of whom is buried on the Flathead Reservation—and on the place and people where I currently lived. They saw I was approaching the wheel in the right way and for the right reasons: I was going as myself, and with the deepest respect for the land and ancestors there. I was not trying to slot into an Indian role or co-opt a tradition. Anyone approaching that kind of power spot in an unbalanced way will either not get there, or experience nothing. It is that simple.

If you work to develop a sacred space, it will more or less operate in the same way. It will grow beyond you and your wishes: it will become its own place that takes a position in the larger pattern of the land. It will draw or repel people according to their agenda.

4.8 Summary

Working magically on the land often takes on a life of its own. You will find yourself pulled into a pattern and tide that is much bigger than you, and that reaches far beyond your time. This is not a bad thing, but it can be a scary thing. Learn how to work on the land, learn how to create gates and work with them. Read the local mythology, the local legends and tales. Learn about the mythical creatures in that area. All these things will give you clues about what it is you are working with. Most stories are heavily overlaid with morals and later added dogmas, but often they have grains of magical truth within them. The key is learning how to separate out what is the pertinent information and what is not.

Keep an open mind and be a curious cat: curiosity and an open mind creates explorers, and exploring is the best way to learn magically.

Chapter Five

Shrines on the land

Land spirits, faeries, deities; having friends around for tea

Part of the work of a magician is the building of shrines. This is done in various ways for lots of reasons, but the biggest reason is to create a point of contact and place to exchange energies. How and where you build the shrine depends largely on what types of beings you are trying to work with, where you are working, and why.

If you live in an area that is a strong faery/land spirit area, then it makes sense to work with those beings and use a shrine as a place of exchange. If you are working more in a place where deities are flowing back and forth, then a shrine to work with the local deity would be productive. It also really depends on what work you are trying to achieve.

It is also important to understand that as we change and develop, so the beings we work with and the work we attempt also changes. Everything has a time and place, and it is wise to bend and flex with that change. So for example you may find yourself working for a span of time with nature/faery beings only to find the work evolving to a point where it needs the input of deities or larger powers. There are vast bodies of work, however, that do not require shrines and such a physical level of contact: it is all about using the right tools, the right contacts, and the right approach for what you are trying to achieve.

5.1 Faery/Land spirit work

Shrines for land spirits/faery beings are good bridge builders for friendship and working relationships with the land and the elements.

If you are trying to clean up the land, balance out the impact of civilization/buildings/pollution, learn about plants and their power, work with animals, and generally learn about the land/beings where you live, then a faery/spirit shrine would be useful. They are also good allies when it comes to healing and protection, and for developing an early warning system and your inner sight. The work they ask for in return is usually simple in human terms, and consists of moving things from one place to another, fostering certain plants, cleaning up the land, offering food, and generally being social with them.

In such a case the shrine would be used to make contact and develop a relationship and a place for work. You and the spirits that inhabit or pass through the shrine will slowly build a method of interaction and exchanging energy, and eventually friendships will develop.

When working with land spirits/faery beings it is important to understand that they can be unpredictable. They do not think the same way that you do, and they are partial to practical jokes. They anger easily, but they are also generous when they see clear and good intent. If you wish to work with such beings, then it will pay great dividends to do your homework. Find out about the local faery beings through local legends and stories. Research stories and myths of other countries in the same hemisphere, as you will find the same stories repeat across many different countries. Many key elements are the same, and will teach you operating methods of working with these beings.

Before you start to build the shrine, step out of your normal way of thinking and assess each step of practically building it. And think about how it will impact the local environment. This is a important magical step: think about the construction in terms of the beings that will use it, not your own convenience and satisfaction. For example, shrines are becoming a major fashion at the moment thanks to an interest in Voodoo and similar traditions. People are furiously building shrines and filling them with plastic images, toxic substances, and ornaments. If this is in your home, at least you can do no damage. But if you do that out in nature then you will get a hostile response or no response at all. Why? Because these materials poison the land and are meaningless or useless to the land spirits. Really such shrine-building is more about a grown up playing at 'doll house': something done for their entertainment and enjoyment rather than to help build a working relationship with land spirits.

Faery/spirit shrines out in nature need to be compatible with nature. They need to be focal points of land energy for creatures and spirits, so their contents need to enhance that, not inhibit or detract from it. So their structure needs to be made of wood or woven sticks, stone, or earth: things that are of nature and cannot poison the land. Stay away from plastic and nylon, or anything that is chemical-based and does not degrade. The shrine *needs* to degrade slowly through time, as it should not be permanent. Also veer away from metal: various metals have specific, usually blocking influences around land spirits.

If you wish to work with herbs in the shrine, then dried herbs will cut no ice, as they have no life left in them. But planting herbs around the shrine will be well received, so long as they are herbs that grow naturally on that land. Let weeds grow around them, but keep them in check: don't let anything overgrow the shrine. I work with a shrine by my house: it is a simple large stone with a flat stone before it that receives the offerings. Flowers and herbs have sprung up around it, and local birds visit it frequently to partake of the offerings.

Unlike a deity shrine, it is unnecessary—unhelpful, even—when trying to attract land/faery spirits, to have an image or statue in the shrine. As any image or statue can be walked into by a land spirit if the statue is not tuned to a deity, you may end up with a bit of a problem if you get a bully: once they have a face and a humanoid form to play with, things can get a bit tricky. Faery beings are best worked with, and are more stable, when they are themselves and are not given access to a humanoid interface. It takes longer to learn how to interface with spirits if you have no point of reference like a statue, but perseverance really pays off. Once the spirits have figured out how to communicate with you, then the contact becomes much deeper than the type of contact you get when it is filtered through a statue.

Use the shrine to leave food and offerings. Sweet foods like honey, breads, milk, fruit and nuts are generally good: you will slowly get a feel for what the spirits like and do not like. The more powerful the substance you leave, the more they can draw on its energy and use it for good or bad. One way to operate is to regularly take out food offerings, but when there is some powerful work to be done, give them power substances like coffee and alcohol. Just make sure these substances cannot be accessed by birds or animals, and take them away after a day. Do not give them power substances on a daily basis, or you may end up with a caffeine-crazed land spirit that wants to mate with you or move into your house and take over—this is also a good reason why it is best not to have a faery shrine in your house.

The work would go a little like this: build a shrine out of wood, bark, stones, etc., and have a large stone for the beings to reside in. Every day take out food and drink—the local creatures may eat this up, which is not a problem—and sit with the shrine. Talk to the shrine as if the being was there—this action starts an inner calling process—and tell them what you are trying to achieve and why. Do this every day for a full cycle of the moon so that the contact has a chance to build up slowly. After you have been feeding the shrine for a month, on your next visit, sit in silence/meditate in stillness, and when you come out of that, take note of what is around you. What creatures are appearing nearby; how does the shrine 'feel,' how do you 'feel'? If you have developed your inner senses, then just listen to see if anything is trying to reach out to you. If you have problems with such sensitivity, or if it is not normal for you, then you need to develop an inner form of communication which is done in vision using the imagination.

To do this, simply be still. Once you are still, then use your imagination to see yourself stepping out and standing next to your body. Imagine the shrine before you, and look at it through your imagination. See what looks different, see what seems to shine and what does not. Then look at the area around the shrine. See the bushes, trees, water, etc. nearby. If any inner beings have been attracted to the shrine, then they will begin to understand that you are using your imagination as an interface: they will start to develop ways to contact you through your visionary action as well as through dreams and nature cues. At first it will be difficult to tell what is simply your imagination, and what is a real contact. The key to overcoming this is to treat *everything* as if it were real unless it is obvious that it is not—like Mickey Mouse appearing, or cute butterfly wing faeries.

This will strengthen the interface and stop you second-guessing yourself. There will come a crossover point where it becomes obvious what is real and what is not. You will see something strange, something you had not expected, and you will question yourself. But then you will pick up a book on spirits or local legends, a book that you have not read before, and you will see a description of exactly what you experienced. This is because it is an image interface they have used before with other humans who have then gone on to describe it.

After establishing contact, you will be able to interface with the spirits through vision, dreams, and through instinct and outer happenings. You will notice simple things like a certain bird or creature always appearing when things are getting powerful. The same creature will start to appear in your dreams, or away from the shrine. This is where the contact is starting to strengthen, and they are beginning to work with you.

Working at this level with faeries and land spirits is evocative, imaginative, and just plain odd. For a magician who is used to more ordered work and contact it can take some getting used to, but it is rewarding and interesting work. It does have its limits, though. Local beings tend to be active only in a certain area and have certain skills. They do not have the reach and power that a land deity would have, but if you are searching for a more down-to-earth coworker, they are great to work with.

I worked in this way when my children were little and had illnesses. I worked with local land beings, and had a gift area—but not a shrine—where I left things for them and I would sit and talk to them. If my daughter became sick then I would ask for their help and advice, which would be given. In return they would ask me to plant certain things, move certain things off the land, or pick up trash: all simple stuff for a physical body to do, but hard for a spirit to do. They would provide a protective barrier around the children and help their energetic bodies when they were ill. They would also warn me if there was a problem with one of the children, or if there was danger around.

Here is a solid example of a not particularly good way of doing shrine work. Unfortunately this was retrospective work: work to rebalance a wrong done on an area of land. A few years ago I was asked to help a family. The grandmother was ill, but the doctors could find no reason for her pain. I went along and found that the old lady had chopped down a bush at the back of the property which had angered some local spirits. This was a wild part of the country in Montana where the spirits were strong and still not used to human interaction. They had launched an attack on her to punish her for cutting down one of their 'houses.'

I managed to negotiate a truce with them. Another bush in the garden would be allowed to grow wild, and sweet foods would be placed at the base of the tree every week. They also wanted a gift from her to be buried in the base of the bush. She gave a little medicine wheel she had made, and the children buried it for her at the base of the bush. Food was left out and the bush was not touched. Her pains stopped immediately and she started to get better. I called each week for a month and all was going well.

Six months later I got a call from the family. It had all started up again. I visited the grandmother and she was in pain again. I asked about the routine with the bush, and I was told that some flowers had been cut from the bush to put in the house, and they had stopped putting out food as they felt it attracted bears. She had broken her agreement. The family asked if I could renegotiate for them. The spirits in the bush were angry and refused to make any other agreement: the flowers had been cut from the bush, which to them was a crime, and the food had stopped which was a breaking of the bond. They felt the family could not be trusted, and had not kept up their bargain.

I explained all this to the family. I asked why they had cut flowers from that bush where there were tons of flowers on the other bushes which they could have cut with no harm done. The daughter replied that the special bush gave off the best flowers. They did not understand that the best flowers, for whatever reason, were to be protected for the land spirits and were not for humans to touch. That had been the deal: there was to be no cutting of that bush in any way.

As for the food, the shrine was far enough away from the house for it to not be a major bear problem, and bears were part of the pattern of nature there. Bears came through all the yards in that area anyhow: we were sat right on the edge of the wilderness. I asked if the food had drawn bears into their yard and they said no and admitted they just got lazy and didn't want to go out in the cold to put the food out.

There was nothing I could do. I had set up a way for the humans and spirits to coexist, but the humans had not kept up their side of the bargain. Land spirits don't do 'sorry': if you break a promise then the deal is off. Sad to say the grandmother then suffered pain constantly from that time on, and there was nothing anyone could do about it. It was a harsh lesson for her, and a major lesson for me also. It taught me a lot about working with land spirits and what they can do, but it also taught me a great deal about personal responsibility and acting as a mediator. You can only set up the conditions, but the people themselves have to keep their side of the bargain, and often they do not. They wanted me to fix it again, but magic does not work like that: a major component of magic is responsibility and keeping your word.

I felt really bad about walking away knowing that an old lady was in constant pain, but she had had the power in her own hands to fix that, and she chose not to. A harsh lesson was learned by all concerned.

This situation does illustrate how shrines can be used, and the dangers involved when dealing with strong land spirits. Always keep your word and keep up your end of the bargain. Land/faery beings will do something for you, but for a price—and you must be able and willing to pay that price. Before you agree to do something with a shrine, make sure you can keep up your end of the agreement. If necessary, give a time limit of what you are able to do. Think carefully about what you are willing to undertake, and stick to it.

A shrine to land spirits brings the contact in sharp focus, which in turn intensifies the contact and the work. This can allow you to achieve and learn a great deal, but it is a responsibility that needs thinking about before you undertake it. When I had faery gift areas on my land, I always agreed to uphold it for as long as I lived in that place, and when I moved on I would stop working with it. That was part of the agreement I made. It's just a matter of stating your boundaries and them stating theirs.

5.2 Deity shrines

Working with deities on the land can be powerful and a good source of great learning. There are two main ways to approach it: one is to work with a known deity and the other is to reach out to a deity that is still within or on the land but has fallen into obscurity.

Working with a known deity involves a bit of background research. It is important to know if that deity is compatible with the land and community, and to know what power the deity mediates. In some countries like the UK, deities were brought in from other countries to protect and assist invaders, immigrants, etc. Some blended well, and some did not. It is wise to question your motives in setting up work with a specific deity: is it because you wish to work with and learn from a particular power, or are you simply following a current occult fashion?

Working with a deity who is not directly involved with nature is pointless in an outside shrine. For example Athena, a goddess who was fashionable for a time, is a power that works in temples, in cities, and with male warriors. It is pointless having a nature shrine out in the countryside and putting an urban goddess in there. Whereas a deity connected to creatures or the fertility of the land would be ideal.

Are you wishing to work with a deity, or worship them? If it is the latter, then it is better to work within a religious setting rather than a purely magical one. I work with deities magically but not religiously, so my techniques will not be best for someone wishing to become a devotee of a particular deity. There is a clear distinction between the two approaches, and they have different outcomes.

5.3 Known deity shrines

If you are wishing to build a shrine to a deity out on the land, first make sure they would be happy to be worked with out on the land. Ensure that the land spirits would be compatible with the deity so that you do not inadvertently create conflict in an area.

Correct choice of deity pays great dividends. If the god or goddess is from another land, use vision or readings to see how your land would react to them. It is also a good idea to see what elements or powers would balance the deity so that you do not end up working with a lopsided power. If you research well, which is easy these days with the internet, then look into what companions, what tools, and what spirits are depicted with a particular deity. Instead of just working with text, let your instincts contribute as well. It can be a interesting learning experience.

The first step, once the deity is chosen—or they have chosen you—is to build the outer shrine on a chosen patch of land like in a garden or yard. Again, care needs to be taken with what materials you use to make sure that you do not put the local wildlife or land at risk. Natural materials are good; bits of plastic are bad.

Take care to build according to what the deity needs and the tools you wish to work with, as opposed to building in a way that simply looks good. A shrine is not a New Age display: it is a working space and needs to be constructed with that in mind. Once the construction is in place, introduce the image of the deity to the shrine so that the interface is ready for activation.

The next step is the inner opening of the shrine. This work is done in vision. It allows the inner flow of power across the land to integrate with the shrine and the intermediary powers of the deity to flow into the image. A simple way of doing this is to sit before the shrine and still yourself. Using meditation, still yourself until your mind has settled, and slowly become aware of your surroundings in vision. With your eyes closed, see the space around you and see yourself walking around the land space. You may notice that your home or building does not appear on the land: this is normal if it is a modern building. Buildings, unless they are consecrated spaces or temples, tend to take hundreds of years to fully appear in the inner landscape of the land.

When you have a clear vision of the land around you, slowly imagine the shrine building up on the land until it clearly appears on the inner landscape. It may take more than one session to build the inner image strongly enough for it to stay. The building of the shrine is done only through physical construction and then imaginary imprint. This is different from constructing a temple, which involves many different beings and working with visionary magical construction. Building a shrine is akin to setting up a telephone line to a deity as opposed to a fully constructed work space like a temple.

When the shrine is clear in your mind on the inner landscape, then it is time to 'open the doors' to call the deity in. Sometimes this happens naturally with shrines, and the deity power will almost immediately begin communicating with you. Other times you need to open the door. This is done by lighting a candle in front of, or within, the shrine—when it is windy, putting a tea light in a glass jar works well—and working the shrine like an altar. 'See' the flame with your inner vision, and see the shrine as a gateway. Using inner vision, call through the gateway for a priest or priestess of the deity to work with you as an inner contact to activate and guide you in the work of the shrine. A figure will be drawn to the shrine and will appear to you in vision. Talk with them and ask them to work with you and guide you.

That is all that is needed from a visionary magic point of view. The key is to try and maintain contact with the priest or priestess in the way that works best for you, either through vision, dreams, or instinct. The inner contact will act as a slow door-opener and mediator for the deity power to flow into the shrine, a bit like an interpreter. Working regularly with the shrine, working with it as an altar and a place of offerings, will slowly open the door wider, and allow a natural interaction to develop.

Take note of how the animals, birds, and plants respond to the shrine. If the power is unbalanced then it will negatively affect the wildlife around it. If it is positive then you will notice that plants flourish, more birds visit, and the wildlife becomes more noticeable. The shrine will become a working point of focus that can be used for all manner of nature work in conjunction with the deity. Often shrines take on a life of their own and teach you how to work with and for them.

5.4   Local deities and ancient powers

The actual construction method of the shrine would be the same as the method above, but there are unlikely to be images available of the local deity: most ancient gods and goddesses in Europe, for example, were overlaid and forgotten. If this is the case then your detective work has to be mainly in vision.

Take your time when working in vision and repeatedly walk through the inner landscape: this will enable you to connect with any ancient deities that are still accessible on or within the land. For example in one place where I lived, I wanted to know who and what the local deity powers were. I lit a candle, sat down, and went into vision, seeing myself walking out of my house, down the road, and into the fields and the forest. I did this a few times and slowly got used to the land I had moved to. I also became aware of local spirits, ancestors, and a large burial mound with guardians that appeared in the inner landscape but not in the outer landscape. There was no burial mound anywhere nearby that I was aware of.

The next time I went in vision, I talked to the guardians who told me that the Mother of this land was sleeping in the mound and had been trapped there for a long time by human magic from another land. I went to the doorway of the mound that the guardians showed me: the door had a crucifix on it and behind that, lots of script and strange-looking symbols. The guardians told me that people had locked the goddess in the mound a long time ago, and though they still guarded her, they could not set her free: only a human could undo what a human had done.

I decided to take the job on and spent time repeatedly going in vision to clear things off the door before slowly dismantling the door/blockage step by step. Eventually I managed to get the door open and go inside. A goddess was sleeping on the ground, surrounded by black dogs. One of the dogs woke up and barked, which woke her up. She was angry, not at being woken, but at humans magically sealing her in the mound.

I apologized for how she had been treated in the past, and I agreed to help her leave. In retrospect, this was not such a good idea. She was angry, very angry, and she wanted revenge. It took a lot of negotiating to calm her down. One of the terms of our treaty included a shrine, offerings, and adjustments to the surrounding land and to how I lived on it. She is really a warrior goddess, specific to a small area—really only the village and surrounding land—and she has a very fixed idea about how humans should interact with her.

Such local deities can be difficult to work with, and they seem to be a combination of deity, ancestral consciousness, and land spirits. As a result of my experience with this goddess, nowadays I am wary of this level of deity, as they are so unpredictable and difficult to work with. But such work is not impossible if you work with a bit more care than I did, and find out a lot more about the local deities before interacting with them. In retrospect I should have consulted with local ancestors, inner contacts, and land spirits to learn more about the deity power before deciding to hack down a magical barrier. That way I would have been better prepared to interact with her and would have been better able to counter any danger posed by opening an ancient contact of power.

If you do decide to build a shrine to a local deity, keep it simple and use it as a point of contact and offerings. The more you work with it, the more they will get the idea that it is a place to meet and work, and they will keep their interactions with you confined to that shrine: there is nothing worse than having a local spirit, ancestor, or deity tramping through your home at all hours of the day and night. Which brings me to another point: this method of outdoor shrine building can also be used as a meeting place of contact for local ancestors: really a shrine is a magical meeting point for you to connect with local spirits/beings. It is the intent that counts: the slow building, both in vision and in ritual action, will tune the shrine and get it in focus.

When you have come to the end of working with a shrine, or you are going to move, you should bury any deity image (unless you are taking it with you), break up the shrine, and let it go back to nature. Leave a last gift and tell the spirits that you are going, why you are going, and where you are going. If they are long-range beings, they may be waiting for you in your new home, whether you like it or not. Putting down boundaries at the beginning of the relationship ("I will only work with you here") can be a good idea!

5.5 Befriending local spirits and ancestors, and having them live with you

This is an interesting way of working should you cross paths with local ancestors in the area where you live. If you live in a city, you are more likely to get confused ghosts that find you and seek refuge with you: magic switches all the lights on and draws them in. In such instance they will either want help passing in and through death, or they will want a place to hide and rest.

If you do end up with a resident ghost that is not ready to move on, then living with them can be simple: just state your boundaries and give them a safe corner of the house to 'reside' in. As long as they do not cause problems and do not drain energy from you—in which case a parasite is masquerading through a ghost shell—then they will live happily in an area of the house and will leave when they are ready.

Under these circumstances it is not a good idea to work magically with them or interact too much. Remember, this is a stranger who is unbalanced or needy: giving them shelter is enough. Much more than that can cause problems for the living and the dead. Often they will suddenly vanish in a magical working: the gates open and they will be pulled through into death.

When my cousin died after a long and terrible illness, he hung out with my partner and I for a while. He would not cause problems other than blowing the light bulbs on a nearly daily basis: he was terrified of death, and in his terror he latched onto our home and hid there. Slowly he began to relax as he realized that he still existed, and I was not going to attempt to move him on. For a dead person, coming to understand their new state and form of existence is a major shift of awareness, and if they can make that shift themselves it will be a major part of their learning and evolution as a soul. So let them have some time to get used to the idea of their being dead.

After a while we were due to go and work with a magical group in Bath so off we went, and my cousin came too. He sat in the back of the car, which felt a bit odd, came with us to the working, and sat in a chair as we opened the gates. He sat through a couple of the magical workings and was picked up on by one of the magicians ("I can smell alcohol," said one worker: my cousin was an alcoholic.) The major working of the day was underway when suddenly he just vanished through the gates. That was it. He had overcome his fear, seen where he was supposed to be and not supposed to be, and had moved on of his own accord, with his own understanding.

This is a bit different to moving in a house that has a resident ghost. Usually this is someone who is trapped, or is a parasite, or is an echo. These must be dealt with in a specific way: see my book *The Exorcist's Handbook*.

A different type of ancestral work is where you cross paths with an ancient ancestor who is purposely staying in our world for a specific reason. They will find you, often through strange routes. It tends to happen more frequently out in the country where there is less 'civilized psychic noise.' Because we know so little of the culture and beliefs of our ancient ancestors, you really have to play this by ear.

As I have discussed in my books before, when I move into an area, I go to the local burial ground or cemetery and make friends with the people buried there. I show respect and honour those who have lived on the land before me. Often that is enough, but on one occasion something interesting happened.

I slowly began to make friends in the local village where I was living and my neighbour began to understand that I was a little bit, well, odd. Her family had lived in that area as farmers for at least a thousand years that they knew of, and they were closely connected to the land. One day she came to me with a bundle and sat down to tell me a story about her grandfather. He was a local farmer and had begun to expand his farm decades ago, by ploughing rough land that they owned but had never touched.

The ploughing dug up a body, an old skeleton from one of the mounds in the rough field. His friend who was a doctor looked at the body and said it was old, not a recent one. The grandfather took the skull, which was the best preserved part of the remains, and gave it a home in his house, where it lived quietly in the corner for decades. When he and then his son died, his granddaughter was clearing the house out and came across the skull. She remembered the story of it from when she was a little girl. She did not want to throw it away or pass it on to historians who would not respect it. So she brought it to me, after having a strong instinct that I would look after it.

After she left, I placed the skull on the table and tentatively felt around it for any presence. Many remains do not have any connection to their original owners, but some do. I was also aware of something my first teacher told me, which was that when you work magic, things happen for a reason. Things find their way to you for a reason, and one must find out what that reason is. She was clear about this and saw reason in everything. I was not that convinced, and I still feel it is important to differentiate between everyday happenings and magical jobs and events... but never take anything for granted either way.

So I felt around the skull and yes, there was a faint something, like a whisper. I went in vision with my hands on the skull and came across a young girl, young, maybe twelve or thirteen years old. She was strong, present, and was showing me birds. She tried to convey to me that she worked with birds, in what we would call a magical way, though to her it was normal. I told her I too had worked with birds and she nodded, saying that was why she wanted to come and live with me.

I questioned myself: I was not sure how much of this was just my own imagination, as it was a slightly different way of working to what I am used to and I was on uncertain ground. I found her a place in the house to live, on a shelf with my birds, feathers, etc. that I had collected. She seemed happy enough.

Over time I began to learn a lot from her about local birds: how to call them in, how to 'fly' with them in my mind, and how the local winds worked. A friend came to visit me who is an archaeologist, and he took a look at the skull. Without doing tests he said it was difficult to confirm, but his opinion was a child aged somewhere between 12 to 14, and it was *old*. Hmmm.

So I worked with her for a couple of years, then one day she wanted to go to sleep. I did not quite understand what she meant, and it took me a week or two to figure it out. In the meantime she was getting frustrated and was beginning to get disruptive. Things were flying off the shelf and birds were hitting the window or pecking at the window: it was the Inner Worlds crying out for attention.

Eventually I figured it out and got her a casket. I put the skull in the casket and did a reading to find out where she wanted to be buried. She did not want burying; she wanted to sleep where I slept. So she was moved into the bedroom, still in her casket, and was placed beneath a bit of furniture so she was hidden. She sleeps for certain lengths of time but occasionally she will wake up and ask to come back out among the living for a time.

I do not know why she does not want burying, or even how her spirit had managed to hold onto her skull for so long. It is all part of an ongoing learning experience for me, and we are in such a magical dark age that we need to find our own way through the dark and figure it out as we go along.

I have learned a great deal from her, and she has found sanctuary: a good trade! I began to think about how magicians use skulls, often without respect and without care for the person to whom the skull belonged. There seems to be little emphasis on trying to find out if the skull is still connected to a spirit and what that spirit may need. It has become a fashion to have a skull along with a glamorous grimoire, and it makes me wonder what effect this is having on the magicians and the ancestors that are still connected to those skulls.

I certainly learned to be far more conscious and compassionate towards body remains, and I learned that there is a lot more to working with skulls than meets the eye: sometimes those skulls might not want to work, they may want to sleep.

So if some remains come your way, particularly unexpectedly, and you are a magician, then step back before including the skull in your work. Take time to try and find out who they are and what they need. Why did they come to you? Find out what you can do for them before asking what they can do for you.

5.6 Summary

Working with the land and the powers that flow through the land is ideally a natural, instinctive interaction with everything around you: no dressing, no shrines, just you and nature. This works immediately for some and not for others. For those who find such formless work a bit overwhelming or difficult to penetrate, then working with shrines, offering areas, and key places on the land is an intermediary step towards building up a relationship with the powers around you.

I still work with an outside offering area that houses a large stone, not only to keep in touch with the land beings, but also to feed the birds and creatures in winter. Building up a relationship with the land involves connecting to the land spirits and deity powers, as well as the local creatures, birds, waterways, springs, hills, and rocks.

Differentiating between temple-based deities and land spirits/ancient deities of nature is important: know who you are working with and why. Temple based deities work best with you through temple spaces, altars and other interfaces, and usually have heavily formed rituals. Nature deities connect with you through the elements, the creatures, and the land. They connect directly with you, and they can certainly pack a punch!

Working in such a way is an interesting and good training exercise for a magician: we can get too locked into a system and end up shutting out all the powers around us. It is better to learn different ways of working, different types of contacts, etc., as it is all part of the bigger picture and creates a well-rounded magician. We are in a culture of specialization and magic can get sucked into that mentality too.

Learn the basic structures through one path, then branch out and learn in as many directions as possible so that you gain experience and allow for the right skill set to find you. After many years you will find that you naturally start to specialize, once you have learned many different skills. That specialization 'wires' you to a focus point so that you become 'adept' in a certain area. But specializing too much too early has the opposite effect. Let it happen naturally and in the meantime, if you are a heavily ritualized magician, get out on the land. If you are more shamanic in your practice, learn how to work within a temple setting. The learning never stops!

Chapter Six

Working with the magical elements

Knowing which way is up

In Western Magic we work with the directions and the elements as an integral part of our magical practice. This manifests itself in the use of directional altars, magical tools connected to elements—sword, wand, cup and shield/stone— and the elements placed with the directions; east/air, south/fire, west/water, north/earth. There is some variations of this pattern within certain traditions, but on the whole it is a consistent pattern that runs through Western magic. It also pops up in various religions in a number of ways, and when you recognize this, it will help you see what the 'builders' of that religion or magical tradition were reaching for.

When looking at the magical elements and directions of a tradition, there are two things to be aware of. The first is that some recently formed traditions have aligned their use of the magical directions in accordance with psychology and poetic expression. That is more relevant for a religious pattern, like Wicca for example, but not so useful for magic, particularly magic that reaches deep into the Inner Worlds. The psychologized use of the directions and elements works only to the threshold of the human psyche and not beyond, and is therefore limited in deeper magic.

The second is that some magical and Pagan traditions have developed their use of magical directions in direct relationship to the land they were on. This is a layer of magic that works directly with the land on which you are standing and the beings that inhabit that land. When those traditions are moved to a different land, it is important to be aware that more surface directional patterns may not work. So for example some Western Mystery paths put the mountains in the north and the sea in the west. That will not work in a lot of places. If you are working in conjunction with the land and the beings that inhabit that land, then you have to go back to the drawing board and work with what is is actually there on the land.

Some directional powers go much deeper than the land and are not about the physical direction but the magical direction. The magical direction is where the power of a particular element has been worked with over millennia and has formed through a certain orientation and a certain group of deities, and has been developed through a temple or ritual system. This can be worked with in ritual and vision on many levels from basic workings, to conditional magical group workings, and beyond.

The ultimate expression of power that flows out of the magical direction gives the magician a connection to the deepest and most beautiful patterns of creation and destruction: the universe in action. At this level the power cannot be controlled, and any attempt to control or particularly form the power will cause it to degenerate before it shuts down and withdraws. The deepest expression of power that flows from the magical directions is there to be experienced and mediated, often without form and most certainly without and beyond human understanding. You become a part of something much bigger than yourself and by engaging in such powerful service, the power flows through you, changing you as it flows out in the world. You undergo personal change without focus on the self but with focus on service, on a selfless act.

To get to that level of work takes time and much learning. It is best to start at the bottom of the ladder and work up. Learn how the elemental directions, contacts, and powers work; learn about the magical tools, about how the conditional form of power works as it flows from a direction. Learn about the magical structures, Inner Temples, and inner realms accessed through the directions; learn about how the elements of air, fire, water and earth can be worked with magically. Once you have pulled all those threads of learning together, then it is time to throw all the structure away and stand in the midst of power. Only by learning the form can you step beyond it: one must learn the outer forms of magic, and work within those structures to gain knowledge and experience, to develop a working practice and most importantly to prepare the mind and body for the greater levels of power that come with deeper work.

Once you can work at a level beyond the appearance of the structures i.e. the temples, beings, tools etc, then you can really begin to mediate the true elemental powers that flow through and out of the elemental directions. Reaching that stage of connection with raw powers allows the force and nature of those powers to truly begin to affect change in your body, mind, and soul.

The deeper gifts of self empowerment, development and maturation that we seek through magic begin to develop through our actions and reactions to the adversity of power. The power will fill whatever is happening in our daily lives and will confront us with a deeper gnosis of the nature of events that will challenge us as we grow and mature.

The power will also fill our bodies, finding the consciousness in our organs and interacting at a deep level to bring about change. How that change will manifest in our bodies depends on how we let go and allow that change to happen, and how we consciously interact with both the power and the spirits that reside as mediators within our organs. We are made up of many different forms of consciousness and working with the elemental powers that interact with those forms of consciousness brings about change and regeneration.

The following section breaks down some of the details about the directions, the elements, and the deeper contacts within the directions. Chapter 6 of *Magical Knowledge Book One* provides details regarding the magical tools and the basic working practice to open the elemental four directions to make contacts, so I will not repeat them here. It is important to learn about these factors in magic not just by reading about them, but by actually practising, experimenting, and engaging with the powers to do active work.

6.1 The powers and qualities of the elemental directions

East: Element of Air, powers of justice, the sword/blade, warrior virgin goddesses/gods, sacred utterance, sacred alphabets, sacred writings, knowledge keepers, sigil formation, working with the weather, the whirlwind.

South: Element of Fire, powers of healing and poisons/disease, the wand/staff, solar deities and the power of the sun, the Golden City, kingships, war and cleansing by fire, volcanic magic, firestorm.

West: Element of Water, powers of generation/genetics/humanity, the cup/chalice/cauldron, deities of the sea, rivers, wells, midwife of life and death, divination, the second sight, the threshold of death, the ocean.

North: Element of Earth, depths of death and the dawn of regeneration, the shield, the Underworld/Dark Goddess, Earth Goddess, the Abyss, Divinity within substance, the stone/mountain/cave.

Centre: The Void; a state of potential where there is stillness and silence: the intake of breath before the universe is breathed out into existence.

To truly begin working in the directions, an element of practice is needed so that you can familiarize yourself with the energetic feel of each direction. This is far more important than memorizing attributes. It is better to go out in the garden and experience the flowers in real life than it is to sit in a house and learn their names, colours, and smells.

The directions have many layers and depths to them, and bear in mind that the information is this chapter is just one perception of the directions. The directions do not really change according to belief structures—they are what they are—but how each culture perceives them and approaches them is different.

It is also important to understand that they differ according to how you approach them: the layers reveal themselves to you depending on what your focus of intent is. Approaching the directions from the point of view of wishing to connect with the elemental powers will give you a different experience from approaching them from the point of view of connecting with the inner priest/priesthoods, which would take you to the inner temples of the directions.

Intending to connect with the powers of Divinity in the directions will give you a different experience again. It is all down to frequencies and therefore intent: the more you work in the directions with the elements, the more aware you will become of the different levels, frequencies, and vibrations that the elements/powers express themselves through. The different levels manifest for us as different presentations from deep vision, to inner contact, and to outer enlivened tools.

What method you use will also give you a different experience. The main two methods used in magic are ritual (ceremonial) and visionary. In ritual you bring the powers of the elements, deities, and inner contacts into your physical world by way of a pattern, an utterance, and the use of sigils. The power can be tied into substance and used. Ritual can also open doors for powers to pass through, and the conditional extent of the ritual will decide what that power will do.

Most magicians get themselves in messes at one point or other in their ritual lives through the conditional manifestation of power. But there are many safeguards in place to stop a novice from treading where they shouldn't. The biggest safeguard is that if you don't know what you are doing from an inner point of view, then the outer pattern will either not work or will only trigger a minor effect.

Here is a breakdown of the directional elements in more depth:

6.2 East: the power of utterance and swords

If ever a magical direction was a reflection of an epoch of humanity, I would say that the age we are currently living in is the age of the east. I say east in a magical sense, not a topographical sense. Yes you would work magically with the power of the east at an east-facing altar, but that is just a surface land expression: the power of the east is so much more than that as a magical direction. The magical east is a threshold for a specific quality of power that flows into our world, and its element is air. Let's look at some of the manifestations of this power that flows out of the magical east, and how we can work with it.

6.3 Utterance: 'In the beginning was the Word'

The use of utterance—the use of the voice and the breath—is the most basic and powerful form of magic that flows from the magical east. Everything else flows from that basic expression, that bridging of a magical power that we breathe in, convert, then mediate out as a magical pattern. The use of breath was, and is, the most fundamental magical tool we have at our disposal. Curses, bindings, blessings, invocations, calling the wind, breathing the weather, bridging sacred utterance in substance... the list is endless. These are uses of the element of air that we see in most religions today, and in all magical paths.

There are two basic principles that work with the power of utterance. One is contacted/mediated utterance, and the other is uncontacted utterance within a preexisting power pattern. Contacted utterance is where the magician acts as a bridge between an inner world consciousness and the outer world. This can mean anything from releasing a wind power from the Inner Worlds out into the air (a weather working), to reciting a magical pattern as a chant or tone that is a sound which brings about magical change as in a contacted ritual, to breathing life into substance.

The uncontacted utterance is the recitation of words, songs, or chants that were originally mediated from the inner to the outer world, and are learned by rote to be recited or performed at key times of the year or within specific conditions. Uttering exactly the same words in the exact same way triggers the original magical ritual and intent that brought about the creation of the song, chant, or recitation. So for example, in the Catholic Mass, the recitation of the mass unchanged in Latin over centuries created a ritual pattern that power could flow through. If you change the pattern drastically then it will no longer mediate the power, and it becomes meaningless.

Songs and chants are interesting ones. Sound frequencies and pitch have a interesting effect on substance and energy. Depending on whether it is a high pitch or low pitch, it will repel or attract certain orders of beings. The use of instruments like bells, gongs, horns, and cymbals in sacred chant and music is part of this use of sound to affect substance. Certain recitations and songs, when constructed ritually, affect the substance of the building and the land on which it stands over time; which is why they are used in so many religions and magical traditions. Often it is not the actual words, but the pitch, frequency, and rhythm that effect the change. Having said that, in certain languages that are used magically and religiously as well as for everyday communication—for example Hebrew—the use of specific letters does create particular magical effects.

For the longest time I did not buy into the idea of a letter and word being a sacred expression within itself, simply because I had no direct experience of it. I tend to be a major sceptic until proven otherwise. But then I was taught about the sacred use of letters, utterances, and words, and I began to work with them. And work they did, in the most powerful and extraordinary way: I gained a whole new respect for the sacred use of language.

The use of breath to mediate the utterance of Divinity—the breath of life—is a major element of magic. It can be the deepest magical act anyone can ever do. Methods for working with this power in magical forms are discussed in *Magical Knowledge Book Three.*

To experiment practically with this concept, the best way to work is not to use a script or have already formed patterns of ritual, but to stand at the altar of the east and work in vision and ritual at the same time. Work in vision with a specific contact that mediates the power of utterance while mediating that power through ritual and speech, breathing out power and directing it or writing at the altar.

This is one of those things that you need to play around with to see what form of mediation you are best able to perform. For me it was simply breathing out while bridging power. That breath was either released out into the world, or it was placed within substance to enliven it.

6.4 South: the power of the sun and fire

Fire is the other magical element still used widely in magic and religious mystical practice. This can express itself from the simple use of a candle flame to tune in a direction or power, to using the power of the Black Sun to destroy a nation. In between, thankfully, there are many stages of fire/solar power that can be worked with in various ways, some of which I have mentioned in other books and therefore do not need to repeat here. These are some of the things not covered in the other books:

6.5 Fires: sending power: curses and seething

Flames, like candle flames and fires, can be used to move power from A to B. Such action can be done by working with focused intent and ritual action, or by utterance. What you do and how you do it will largely depend on what you are trying to achieve.

A candle flame is a useful tool for dispatching patterns of magic, for example in the case of a Kabbalistic curse or highly patterned ritual attack. When such an attack is ritually constructed, it acquires a specific pattern or shape that can be seen from an inner visionary point of view. Even if the attack was constructed using lettering, sigils, utterance, etc., it will still have an inner shape expression which appears to us as a three-dimensional pattern.

If it cannot be dismantled using visionary techniques for whatever reason, and it is not a major construction, then it can be dispatched and dismantled using a candle flame. This method requires a highly developed mental focus, one of the prerequisites of more powerful magic. The basic technique is to light the flame, then focus on the flame. Imagine the shape of the pattern appearing in the flame. Capture the 'feeling' of the pattern, and your body's awareness of the pattern—each attack has a specific 'feel' to it. Let that image and awareness build in the flame until it is stable. Once you can hold that image in the flame, utter your intent into the flame: "I reject you and cast you into the Void," for example. Then blow the flame out with the intent that your breath will send it to wherever you are directing it. This action often has to be repeated in intervals over a few days to break the pattern down.

This method is effective with certain levels of magic, though it will not address really nasty and well-crafted attacks. It can be used to construct and magically send things in both positive and negative ways, but regardless of your good or bad intent behind it, if you are instigating an action, rather then responding to one, you must be fully aware of the unfolding of the pattern, its effect on you, whether it draws power from you, etc. before you act. Often magicians throw power around when they are angry, enraged, or depressed: this is an infantile thing to do. It is also self-defeating: initiating a magical act that directly and conditionally affects another human being will place you in an energetic relationship with that person. That can take a lot of getting out of, and will end up being more bother than it is worth.

However, when in a hostile situation and magic has been thrown at you, sticking it in the flame and putting it in the Void will not affect you, but it will drain the sender, because all their hard work and energy will be flowing down a dark hole.

Another way of using fire ritually in the south is to make a large fire and ritually build power around it. When the power is at breaking point, the intent is cast in the fire. This is usually a more emotive way of working, rather than controlled or focused. It seen most often in folk magic, and is potent in its effects. For this reason it is important for the magician to be aware of it and its effects, so that if you are confronted with it you will know what it is, how it works, and what to do with it.

Where I grew up in Yorkshire, this folk method was known as 'seething'; probably an overlap from our Viking past. It was not viewed as a specific thing that was done; rather a woman—it was usually women—who was enraged at a person's actions would build her anger and stand before the fire shouting and uttering curses into it, with her curses aimed at a specific person. The woman would be full of rage, and would sometimes cut her finger and cast blood into the fire as she cursed. Whether or not this is directly connected to the Nordic tradition of seething I don't know, but the area where I grew up had a rich Viking past.

I have been around a woman seething, and I tell you, I would not want to be on the receiving end of that. It's feral, powerful, and destructive. But if someone is on the receiving end of a seething, then as with the candle method described above, directing the power through a fire and into the Void—rather than sending it back to whoever sent it—is a good way of disengaging from it. The reason it should not be sent back to the person is to avoid ending up in a game of magical ping pong, with the power batted back and forth until someone buckles. Better just to stick their power straight in the Void and let them wear themselves out.

6.6 Working with the Sun Temple

The contacts in the south come from various different lines. The most common worked one being the Sun Temple. This is a generic or 'root' contact from which flow the world's many solar religions. Their work is tied in with civilizations, empires, and kingships, and when it is in balance, it is a powerful but compassionate force that flows through great nations. When it is out of balance it mediates greed and lust for power, and causes bloodthirsty battles for resources and supremacy.

In a magical setting, the power of the sun is formed and mediated in patterns that we interact with in the form of priesthoods who work with fate. Often this appears in myths and ancient stories as a board game where the fate of nations, family lines, and individuals is manipulated to bring change. These powers do not create fate or oversee fate; rather they change and interfere with fate. The best way to learn about these priesthood lines is to work in vision at the altar in the south before the flames or before a large fire, and reach for an inner contact of that line.

The deeper aspect of the solar power in the south is the power of fire in the pattern of creation on the Tree of Life. Part of the element of the angelic patterning for creation is fire, and it is an inner power that brings light and life to the pattern/ritual being worked. Learning to work with fire in vision—for example in the Desert of the Tree of Life—will teach you all you need to know about how fire works in magic. Working with the fire, communing with it, interacting with it, and learning how to work with the angelic beings that oversee it, will teaches the magician a great deal. You would not work with a 'named' angel; rather you would reach into fire in vision to find the angelic contact that is the mediator of that power.

6.7 West: the power of genetics and water

Working in the west is also referred to as working in the Sea Temple. Many beginner magical books will simply say the cup is in the west and it represents love. But the west is so much more than that, and people forget to look beyond the beginner presentation: they do not realize it is less than 1% of what is actually there.

The west is primarily about life and death, genetics, bloodlines, and the generations and waves of humanity, other species. It is about vessels that contain power, whether that power is to regenerate or kill. It is also the home of the moon, creativity, insanity, and visions.

Work in the magical west can take a few different forms. One inner structure that is worked with is the Sea Temple that I mentioned earlier. This can be approached in a number of ways, either working directly in vision with the sea or reaching this ancient temple through the Great Library. There is no ritual way of working with the Sea Temple that I am currently aware of, other than nature-based, almost 'shamanic' ways of working at the sea's edge with cup/blood etc. The west is a vision-oriented direction, and because it does not have an outer temple manifestation in our world, vision is the best way to work with it.[1]

Work in the Sea Temple focuses mainly on global weather or the bloodline of races. The deep sea is where our weather comes from, so if a magician wanted to be of service to the climate, for example, she would work in the Sea Temple to help restore balance. Her work would be done in vision and would be unconditional: when working with something as powerful as the climate, you have to be really careful to not try and consciously 'fix' it.

There are two reasons for this: one is that if you work in this deep temple with a fixed agenda, then you will be working alone and will achieve nothing: it will be like a gnat pissing in the wind. The second reason is that our limited understanding of the weather would drive us to calm the weather down, which is not necessarily what it actually needs. The weather has its own way of rebalancing itself: we only need to add energy to that process.

If you approach the Sea Temple with an unconditional willingness to work, then you will be working with vast numbers of contacts, adding your small fraction of work as a contribution. We as a species have caused so much damage, therefore we must give of our strength and power to assist in rebalancing all of that. The best way to do this as magicians is to turn up in the deep Sea Temple and offer to help. You will be put to work but you most likely will have no clue about what you are doing or why. And you don't *need* to have a clue.

6.8 Springs and fresh water

Working with fresh water is another way of working with the magical west. Not only are springs about healing or guarding the land, they also carry information through the land, both on its surface and underground. Working ritually at the west altar with some water which is then returned to some river or waterway can be a powerful way of working. Again, because the power of water is so vast and beyond our understanding, it is best to work unconditionally, to affect the water *in whatever way is necessary* for the land and the springs.

Water also holds memory and information. This quality can also be used to mediate magical knowledge from the Great Library or the inner temples to the outer world so that people in the future can access it. The information is carried out of the Inner Worlds, mediated through water which is then poured into the rivers. The knowledge will stay within the water, wherever the

---

[1]For example we still have temples to Ra, the sun god in Egypt, so that outer manifestation can be worked with ritually.

water goes, and any magician in the future who is capable of extracting that information will be able to work with it.

6.9   The Vessel

Working magically with cups can be interesting. Not only are they containers, but they are also mediators. In a ritual, the cup can contain the power worked on, and the water, wine, or blood within the cup can be used to mediate the power. It is the cup, not the fluid, which is the doorway to the power: the water simply carries the power of the cup. The cup can be used empty, as a mediator of power from the west. So for example if there is an imbalance of power—for instance too much fire power coming through—then placing the magical cup within the midst of that power will moderate it.

This is where you begin to learn how the different directions work together to offset each other. You can see some of this cooperation and modifying power working between the directions in myths and legends. Swords placed in stones, swords in relation to cups, fire over water, and so forth.

Working in ritual with the cup/vessel teaches the magician the mechanism of how substance can hold power, how the shaping of substance dictates its ability to hold power, and how that power can affect the elements which affect magic. The vessel can also hold fire, which is another old combination with the west: the fires of Brigh, who is a goddess of springs, warriors, and smith-craft, among other things. A magical fire in a consecrated cauldron will allow the magician to work with modified fire, fire that is contained within a vessel that holds the inner power of water.

This modified power can work on shaping and forging the magician and bringing magical patterns into form safely. This is also the direction and magical tool of the alchemist: this is where the transmutation of substance, the enlivening of inert substance, and the marriage of elements all come together to create something new and wonderful.

6.10   North: the power of earth and rock

The North as an elemental magical direction is probably the oldest magical direction, because it is the threshold that takes us back to our early ancestors and the first temples (that we know of), which developed in the Mesolithic era.

North is an interesting and often widely misunderstood direction. Similarly, the element of earth is also widely misunderstood in magic. It is taken simply as a shield, a protection, when it is far more than that. This magical direction is where the magician would learn about the depths of death, the Underworld, ancient Sleepers, faery beings, and early ancestors. The magician would learn to work with rock, earth, and sand in magical construction, i.e. golem making. Here north is worked with in conjunction with the east, for instance in the form of utterance with dust cast to the wind. The north also teaches the magician about disease, destruction, sending consciousness through substance, and working with mountains and fault lines through caves deep within the earth.

6.11 The Underworld and Abyss

Using the north temple of earth as an access point, we can gain entry into the ancient Underworld temples that were scattered around the world in our distant past. By doing so we can learn about the destroying powers of certain deities—Sekhmet, for example—how they operate, and why. We can also reach deep into the Underworld, where truly ancient deities sleep, and access their temples to learn about the powers they wielded, their function in the surface world, and what led them to retire deep into the land.

Those sleeping ancients eventually pass into the Abyss as they become far removed from our consciousness. For a certain amount of time we can still access them as they sleep in their tunnel/cave in the Abyss, so long as it still has a doorway from the Underworld to the Abyss. Eventually that Underworld doorway is closed and sealed, so that there is no way to reach an ancient being other than to go down the Abyss.

The Abyss can be reached by working in the vision of the Desert—the inner landscape of the Tree of Life—standing at the edge of the Abyss. The magician can either ask the guardian of the Abyss to grant her access, or alternatively they can access the Abyss through old Underworld temples that still have unsealed doors. Such an action can be a strain on the body, as the magician must work deep in vision to reach the depths of such a place. The Abyss is where powers that no longer have a place in our world go to sleep until the world is no longer manifest. Then they will release and return to source. You can reach some of these ancient powers to work with them, but you would have to have a good reason, as the impact on your body will be a high price to pay.

It is better to work within the Underworld temples if you can, as they are less dangerous and create less of an impact on your body. You can still reach some interesting and old powers in these forgotten temples, and it is possible to learn a great deal from them. But once their power passes deep into the Abyss, their consciousnesses become far removed from humanity, and so becomes both dangerous and incomprehensible.

There are also natural magical places deep within the consciousness of the planet that the magician can access to work with the land, the weather, and ancient Sleepers. By accessing these places—which appear to us as deep caves that connect to various mountains and fault lines—through the north threshold, the magician can build a series of deep workings that connect vision and ritual. Once the cave has been worked with sufficiently in vision, then the magician begins to open up the north threshold to enable it to lead directly to the cave. Once that is completed, the ritual work done at the north altar will be fed directly into the deep cave: it will be as if you were working ritually at the threshold of the cave itself. This is a method of working that is used when the span of work will take months, and is a deeply involved piece of magic.

So for example if the magician wants to disperse the inner impact of toxic nuclear waste being dumped in a mountain, then they would first work in the deep cave that connects to that mountain. The magician would need to keep all the other connected mountains that stem from that cave in equal balance throughout the work, so this is not an easy job. The work would begin in vision deep in the cave, and would be a matter of dealing with whatever was made apparent by the inner contacts within that space.

When this visionary aspect of the work is done, then restructuring and reenergizing needs to happen. This is done in contacted ritual, where the inner contact is brought back in the room through the north threshold and works with the magician at the altar. The threshold of the north altar becomes a threshold to the cave and the beings, and the magician and the ritual patterns flow back and forth over the threshold.

The cave itself can be found by working in the north parent temple, with the intention of finding the deep 'root' cave of the mountain in question. Its entrance usually presents as a long, twisting, deep passageway that goes deep underground and eventually turns into a tunnel that you have to climb or jump down. Another way of finding the 'root' cave is to go in vision to the mountain in question and begin exploring the cave system beneath it. You keep going down and down until you find yourself in the 'root' cave. The key is holding the intention of where you are going: this will help the beings who guard the mountain to see where you want to go and why, so they can decide if they will help you find it. If you hold the intention of direction, they will lead you.

6.12 Working with earth, sand, and stone

Magically working with rock, earth, and sand is an interesting experiment which can be done for various purposes. The basic magical use of rock/earth in the north is for protection/to shield. But it can also be used as storage, to pass on information, to connect with deep faery beings/land beings, and to hold stillness.

Rock can hold vast amounts of power and consciousness with ease, and is the most stable of the elements for us as humans. Rocks can hold many different types of beings. Smaller rocks tend to be inhabited by faery beings. These are not little giggly Victorian little girls in wee dresses, or large-breasted, scantily clad women with wings: those are fantasy constructs which have no place in magic. Faery beings tend to be strange-looking, often animal-like; they can be big, and are certainly not cute by any stretch of the imagination. These beings often inhabit certain rock outcrops. If you are respectful enough and give them sustenance like food and drink, they will often agree to work with you in vision and to guard you if you need it. In return, though, you must keep to anything you agreed to do for them. Pissing off faery beings can make your home really uncomfortable to live in.

Rock can also hold dragon power if it is in an area that the Romans never had access to. They were good at locking dragon power down, and in the UK you have to go to the Highlands and Islands, or parts of Devon and Cornwall, to reach the ancient power that still breathes within the granite. If you have a power or a being that needs putting somewhere, somewhere it will agree to go, then rock is a good place to put them. Many different types of beings are happy to live in rock for long periods of time because it is so stable and so connected to the different elements.

Dust and sand can be used to send power, energy, and consciousness if used in conjunction with the wind. Charging dust or sand with a power and a purpose, and blowing it out into the wind of a storm that is blowing in the right direction, can be a powerful way to send magic to a place or a person. It can also be used to create a smokescreen around a specific area to hide it from the inner vision of other magicians.

Larger rocks can be communed with and their consciousness accessed to ask them to be guardians. They will watch over an area and guard it, and the beings that live within the rock will inform you if there is trouble coming.

The smallest form of rocks—dirt and sand—can be charged with an energetic frequency that spreads from particle to particle. So for example taking a handful of sand or dirt and tuning it to stillness and silence, then putting it back where you took it from and mixing it into the surrounding sand and dirt will create an area of stillness and silence within the land that you can then work with. This method of work needs the magician to have the power and skill of total focus, and the ability to mediate power into substance. That comes from learning how to work in vision, how to work with ritual intent, and how to hold total focus.

6.13 Elemental combinations

Once you have learned in depth how to work with the different elements magically and have worked with the various powers that flow through the directions, you will begin to notice the crossovers and combinations of the powers and elements that work together. Basically, every element is in each direction, and the dominant element of a direction modifies or strengthens the other elements to create interesting power combinations.

We see some of these combinations in our myths and legends, like the sword in the stone, warrior goddesses who operate through springs, swords of fire, and so on. The combined power of the elemental directions is where magic really comes into its own: you learn to work the powers like an orchestra conductor. It is truly a form of magical alchemy, and the deeper your working knowledge of the elemental powers and their expressions becomes, the deeper you will be able to operate as a magician in the Inner Worlds. Your work truly becomes an action of gathering formless powers and mediating them through the elemental directions into being.

This deep work cannot be done if you do not truly understand the powers, their outer and inner manifestations, and how the elements work together. It is not a matter of book learning; rather it is learned from direct experience, inner observation, and outer ritual experimentation. This is why the training of the magician cannot be rushed: you cannot speed up understanding and experience, no matter what someone promises you.

On a practical level, you can engage this learning experience by working with the different tools in a ritual context in directions that are not their natural home. By working with, say, fire and the sword in the north, or earth and the wand in the west, you will begin to learn how the tools work with different elemental powers flowing through them. The next step would be working in ritual and vision with the different combinations, and learning how the power of different directions affects the tools in different ways.

Keep a tight record of all that you do in these combination experiments, so that you can go back over the notes years later to see how the learning curve unfolded for you. It is also interesting, once you have done some of that work, to look again at magical texts, or historical and religious texts, to see how fragments of magical power combinations manifest through those traditions. This will give you a deeper understanding of what those writers and artists were trying to quietly convey. This does not really work if you do the reading first, then experiment, as you become loaded with preconceptions and misapprehensions, which can shape and narrow your inner experiences. You come to expect something, so the inner connections narrow to fit in that expectation. Your consciousness filters the inner experience and lessens your learning ability. So work first, then read up on the subject matter.

6.14   The Four Temples

The Four Temples are the founding structure of many types of magical, ritual, and visionary work. They have many names; the four chapels, the four gates, the four cities,, and they appear in Hindu sacred texts along with many other ancient writings. They can appear in many forms depending on the culture they are flowing through but they all lead back to the same principle; each outer sacred place flows from an inner sacred place which flows from a parent structure that has developed naturally through the inner actions of humanity over millennia. The Four Temples are the 'parent' structures, inner gateways created by humanity over thousands of years that act as an interface with inner powers, inner contacts etc.

The four elemental temples are thresholds or templates that are the result of generations of priesthoods from many different cultures who reached in the Inner Worlds. Over thousands of years, different priesthoods have worked with these elemental thresholds, and have built their own temples that draw on these parent structures. Hence, you can access virtually any inner, and outer temple in our world by working through these four parent directional temples: they are gateways, and contact points for all the inner priesthoods, and temples.

The Four Temples are the formalized expression of the four elements. To us it appears that they all cluster around a central flame out of which all things come: this is a version of the Void.

The Temple of the East is associated with learning, formalization, recitation, and religions that use a book or text, or the Word. At a deeper level this temple is the source of all sacred utterances and patterns; it is the direction of heralding angels, the direction of magical swords, blades, and spears. At its deepest level it is the whirlwind which dismantles and creates.

The Temple of the South is associated with fire, volcanoes, healing, cursing, ceremonies, and bright, hot power. It is the direction of the wand or staff, and it is connected to electricity, explosions, and war. It is the direction of male power and life, of the power of the Sun, and of underground fire.

The Temple of the West is associated with the Moon, the fall, the ocean, the sea temples, genetics, waves of humanity, madness, emotion, sex, and death. It is the polarized partner of the temple of the east, the east being of the intellect and the west being of the emotions. The older Christian churches were balanced around this polarization with the altar and priest in the East (knowledge and recitation) and the people in the West (generations and emotions). The waves of humanity flow into and out of the Sea Temple of the West.

The Temple of the North is the temple of the depths of death, the Underworld, the Dark Goddess, and the ancestors. It is the temple of time, of opening doors to the past and future, thus making it the temple of prophecy. It is the temple of the planet, gravity, stone, and substance. It is the polar opposite to the temple of the Sun, and in ceremonies the priest will sit or stand in the south, and the priestess will stand or sit in the north: the God and Goddess facing each other.

Throughout the life of an esoteric student, they will, in phases, work within the temples. It may not be in a clockwise rotation, but through time they will begin to learn the Mysteries of each temple and how they work. Each temple, each element, has a whole lifetime of learning within it to do with how our universe operates, and where we belong within it.

The following four visions are old visionary patterns that will take you into the temples so that you can observe and learn. They will also teach you a little more about the contacts in those directions and what to expect from them. These are the 'parent' temples from which the elemental powers flow.

These visions can be intense, and the best way to work with them, until you get used to the pathway, is to record the visions in your voice, then let the recording guide you. Before you record them, read through the text of the vision and identify places where you need a short silence to enable you, when deep in vision, to pause, experience, and commune with the powers you will be meeting. Putting those pauses into the recordings will really strengthen the contactedness of the vision.

Once you have worked with the recordings for a while and have become accustomed to the vision, stop using the recording and work from the memory of how to get there. Once you know how to get there on your own in vision, then you will truly begin to work with the contacts. The vision will change over time: you will find different details, different people, and other areas over the thresholds.

The initial vision is not a dogmatic path; it is a map to help you learn how to access these inner places safely. The more you work in these temples, the less detail and 'dressing' you will see. Eventually you will simply pass into an inner space that is filled with the power of the element, and the consciousness that flows from it.

But to get to that stage safely, it is important to work slowly through a visionary interface using the imagination, so that your body and consciousness can slowly adjust to the ever-deepening powers that flow through these thresholds. The visionary interface known as the Four Temples is an old one and encompasses millennia of magical work: it is a well-trodden path that leads the magician into the inner realms.

6.15   The vision of the Temple of the East

Light a candle, and be aware of the direction in which you are seated. Close you eyes, and see the candle flame with your inner vision. As you look at the candle flame it grows bigger and bigger until it becomes a column of fire. You step through the fire and find yourself in a large hall full of priests and priestesses who are circling a central flame.

You join them in their meditations and walks, finding yourself walking slowly around the central flame and reflecting on your life. You begin to notice four gates, one in each direction. Each gate has a pair of guardians on either side of the entrances.

A priest or priestess comes to you and places a hand on your shoulder. They tell you that they will be your sponsor in this place of gathering, and they will help you learn about the temples. The contact guides you around the circling of the flame, and stops you at the entrance in the East. The angelic guardians look intently at you: you can feel them probing you in great depth. Things that you have done wrong in your life begin to bubble up in your memory, and they watch how you react. You look at your memories and see where you could have acted differently. And yet, as you ponder on the things you have learned through your mistakes, you realize that they have brought you wisdom and understanding.

On that realization the angels step aside, the great doors to the temple of the east swing open, and you enter. You step into a building that has a large archway opposite you, and you can see that the archway leads to a deeper part of the building. You find yourself surrounded by hooded or veiled priests and priestesses who wish to greet you. As you look around you can see that they are scribes, working on manuscripts, parchments, and blocks of stone. They are preparing books for the Library. One of the contacts holds out a book for you to look at. You carefully take the beautifully bound and tooled leather book and look at it. The inscriptions are in a language you do not understand.

The contact shakes his head and shows you how to hold the book against your heart. You do as he asks, and you begin to feel a stream of emotion flow through you. You feel many emotions at once, and you also begin to feel how those emotions can be turned into power.

The contact takes the book from you, and you are led deeper in the temple to a long high ceiling tunnel. The contact stays at the entrance to the tunnel and tells you that he can go no further, that you must continue alone.

As you step into the tunnel, a high wind comes from nowhere and tries to blow you back. You lean into the wind and push as hard as you can against it. You inch your way forward through the tunnel until you come to a large, elaborate door. Pushing the door open you are faced with a hurricane that tries to blow you back down the tunnel, but somehow you manage to crawl forward to the centre of the small cave. Then the air is sucked out of your lungs, and you feel as if your life might be in danger.

Just as you are about to give up, the wind suddenly stops, and you stand up. You are in a small circular cave with a large hole in the centre. A tornado twister is raging in the centre, coming down from above and up from below. You tentatively step forward, drawn to the power of the twisting wind.

As you look into the wind you see many eyes looking back at you, and you are shocked. Something makes you turn away from the eyes, and as you turn your back on the wind, you immediately feel a power building up behind you. Your lungs begin to hurt, as though they are straining, and you feel something touch you at the back of your neck. Instinctively you open your mouth, and something blows through the back of your neck: the breath comes out through your mouth and turns into words and sounds which transform into shapes.

The shapes travel out of the cave and down the tunnel towards the outside world. The sounds continue to come from your mouth until your body begins to collapse from exhaustion. Instinct tells you to close you mouth and fall forward. Someone picks you up and carries you down the tunnel towards the outer level of the temple.

You are unaware of the contacts around you until you come to the threshold of the temple. When you reach the threshold you open you eyes, and look at the large angel who is carrying you carefully. His wings have many eyes, and his hair blows in all directions. He breaths gently over you and whispers a word in your ear.

A feeling of great power passes through you and changes you. He carefully puts you down and allows you to step forward over the threshold and back into the main gathering hall. You walk straight towards the central flame and step into it.

Bathing in the flame revives you, and when you are ready, step out of the flame and find yourself back in your body, seated before the candle. Sit for a while in silence before carefully opening your eyes.

⋆ ⋆ ⋆

The vision of the Temple of the East puts you in direct contact with the stream of consciousness within the Inner Worlds that deals with the recording of knowledge and the Mysteries of air. It has no cultural overlay as it is a template place, and versions of this place will appear in many different cultural, religious, and magical streams.

The deeper part of the vision connects the magician to the deeper power of utterance and air as it passes across the Abyss and expresses itself down the Tree of Life. In this vision the magician is on the receiving end of that utterance, and acts as a mediator to bridge that utterance out into the world. It teaches you at a deep level how to mediate the power of air and how to work with the angelic beings who operate around that power, and it gives you a solid structure to work with as an interface for that power. Once you have become used to working with the power of air, you can take the knowledge that you have absorbed and work with utterance in more depth within the Tree of Life in vision, and then, work ritually with the power at the altar. The final unfolding of that power would be to work outside, uttering into the wind.

6.16 The vision of the Temple of the South (the Temple of the Sun)

Light a candle, and be aware of the direction in which you are seated. Close your eyes, and see the candle flame with your inner vision. As you look at the candle flame it grows bigger and bigger until it becomes a column of fire. Stepping through the fire, you find yourself in a great hall filled with priests and priestesses who are circling a central flame.

You join them in their meditations and walks, finding yourself walking slowly around the central flame and reflecting on your life. You begin to notice four gates, one in each direction. Each gate has a pair of guardians on either side of its entrance.

As you walk around the central flame, something draws you to the threshold of the south gate. The angelic guardians look intently at you as they probe you in great depth. The angels look to see your intent, and when they are happy with what they see they part, letting you pass over the threshold into the Temple of the South.

The sunshine is almost blinding as you step into a bright, sunny courtyard with many flowers and plants. Before you is a gathering of people who seem to be watching something that you cannot see. You edge closer to see what is happening, and as you break through the crowd you begin to see a life-sized game of chess in progress.

The chessboard is painted onto the courtyard's flagstones, and the chess pieces are being moved by two helpers. The two players, both elderly men, sit in deep thought as they ponder their next move. One of the old men looks up and spots you in the crowd. He beckons to you to join him. He asks if you would like to take his next move for him. You look at the chessboard but you don't recognize many of the pieces. The old men both laugh, and one tells you that *this* is the real chess, and that you should try it once so that you understand it.

They tell you to wander around the pieces until you know by instinct which one to move. Stepping onto the chessboard you immediately feel the difference: it is like walking on water. Your hands trail over the pieces, and with each one you touch, you have a deep knowing that they are not ready to be moved.

One piece seems to begin to glow as you get nearer to it. As your hands touch this piece, a strong feeling comes across you that the piece no longer belongs where it is, and it has to be moved. Carefully you push the piece across the board into a new position. Suddenly, everything changes: the weather, the board, and the feeling that is flowing through you.

This action triggers the strong realization that the piece you moved was connected to someone's life, and the action you have taken has changed their life forever. You turn in panic to the old man, but he just smiles. The understanding of the power of the Sun Temple begins to reveal itself to you, and you begin to understand how they use power to manipulate things for good or bad. The power of this courtyard is the power of conditional change: moulding the world from a particular viewpoint.

Step back from the chessboard with the intention of going deeper into the temple. In the distance you see an old dilapidated rock entrance, almost like a crack; but you can see it has been worked to make it into an entrance. It draws you in. The entrance leads to a long, dark tunnel that seems to slope downward, and you begin to walk down it, deeper and deeper underground. The smell of sulphur begins to rise, and it burns your eyes and lips.

The tunnel opens out into a vast rock chamber with volcanic fire in the centre. The fire draws you closer, and though you can feel its heat, it does not burn you. A strong impulse overwhelms you to step right up to the fire, and you lift out your arms as if to embrace its flames. The fire responds, and a loud rushing sound builds up around you. Power builds and builds, and there is intense pressure around your ears, until suddenly a loud sound pierces your brain.

All at once the pressure drops, the sound stops, and many bright spinning wheels of fire dart out from the volcanic flames. They spin around you at high speed, their brightness dazzling you. It is then you notice the Wheels have many eyes which look back at you. One of the Wheels passes right through you, and a feeling of immense power rushes from your feet to your head and back, like a surge of electricity. As it leaves your hands tingle and throb. Carefully you put your hands together, and the feeling of power subsides.

Someone comes up behind you and puts a blanket around you. He scoops you up in his arms and you lie like a child, held by a man with the face of the Sun. His brightness dazzles you, and his warmth flows through you, energizing you. He walks back through the temple and carries you to the threshold of the central great hall filled with priests and priestesses. Carefully he puts you down over the threshold, and before he leaves he hangs a medallion around your neck. You look down at the medallion: it is the golden image of a man's face that glows with the sun.

The man withdraws back into the temple, and the guardians close ranks to protect the Temple of the Sun. Walk straight back into the central flame. Bathe in the flame: it will revive you. When you are ready, step back out to where you are seated before the candle. Sit for a while in silence before carefully opening your eyes.

* * *

Experiencing the Temple of the South will put you into direct contact with a specific quality of solar priesthood. This will give you a better understanding of the power dynamics that played out through priest-king states. It will also introduces you to the power of angelic beings that work with fire which, will broaden your inner ability to sense such angelic power when it is time to work through the Tree of Life.

The above vision only touches on a small section of the power that flows through the south: there are many fire, and solar lines of priesthood and power: far too many to list. But once you have connected with one priesthood in a direction, it becomes much easier to reach for connections to the other strands. If you are working in a specific line of magic with roots in an ancient system or culture, then the solar line will be apparent within that line. For example if you are working with, or learning about, the inner aspects of Egyptian magic, then working in vision in the South temple will let you reach for a connection with the priesthood of Ra. From that work, you will learn how to turn your face to the sun and connect deeply to its power.

6.17   The vision of the Temple of the West (the Sea Temple)

Light a candle, and be aware of the direction in which you are seated. Close your eyes, and see the candle flame with your inner vision. As you look at the candle flame it grows bigger and bigger until it becomes a column of fire. Step through the fire and into the great hall where priests and priestesses circle the central flame.

Joining them in their meditations and walks, you find yourself walking slowly around the central flame and reflecting on your life. You begin to notice four gates, one in each direction, and each gate has a pair of guardians on either side of the entrances.

Circle the flame, and stop at the entrance in the West. The angelic guardians look intently at you, and you can feel them probing you in great depth. One of them sniffs you, and the other one tastes you: they are reading you to make sure they know who you are. When they are satisfied with what they have found, they let you pass over the threshold and into the Temple of the West.

A woman greets you as you step over the threshold. She is tall with long red hair, and many tattoos adorn her arms and shoulders. She escorts you into the Temple of the West, where many priestesses are gathered around something. Looking closer, you see that they are weaving what looks like a giant web. One of the priestesses offers to show you what she is doing, and hands you a piece of thread. As soon as that thread falls into your hands, you see all your family. You see your ancestors, your extended family: everyone who is connected to you through blood.

The priestesses gather different threads and tie them together, creating beautiful patterns that form a web stretching as far as you can see. You realize that you are part of that weave: you can feel yourself within it, and yet it is hard to grasp exactly what it is. One of the priestesses has been watching you with amusement, and when you have seen everything of the weave that you need to see, she takes you hand and leads you down a dark tunnel that smells like the sea. You can hear the ocean all around you, and water laps around your feet. The two of you emerge through the back of a long cave that opens out onto the beach. The priestess leads you up to the water's edge.

She washes her face in the ocean and motions for you to do likewise. A wonderful feeling of cleansing washes over you with the sea water, and as you dry your face and look up, the light of the full moon falls on your face. You begin to cry, and your tears merge with the ocean. The woman places her hands on your shoulders, and you sob as all the pain and suffering that is in your family flows through you and is emptied into the sea.

The woman holds out your hand and gives you a knife. "Give of your blood to the ocean, and offer your honour to the temple of the sea." With one swift movement, you draw a cut across your hand and throw the blood into the sea.

The sea begins to swell, and the waves crash over you, but they do not pull you off your feet. The moonlight becomes stronger and the sound of the whales calling lulls you into a deep state of peace. You fall down into the sand and allow the water to wash over you. The moonlight dances over your body, changing and triggering the deepest part of your immune system.

Sleep pulls at you, and you vanish into a dark, deep, peaceful sleep full of dreams that are wild and full of prophecy.

Nothing disturbs you as you drift until a flicker of a flame awakens you. You find yourself back before the candle flame where you first started. When you are ready, open your eyes.

★ ★ ★

Working in the Sea Temple exposes you to deep and ancient lines of magic that ebb and flow through our species. This is the place to explore and work if you wish to develop your innate psychic abilities, learn about the lines of consciousness that runs through your bloodline, and work in service with the priestesshoods there.

It is a fluid (ha!) temple, and best worked with in a mutable way. Do not try to organize yourself or the powers, or ritualize, formalize, or quantify their powers: you will hit a stone wall if you do.

Working in the Sea Temple is instinctive, creative, and dreamlike; and when you allow such qualities to guide you, the contact will become strong. It will flow through your outer life and affect everything around you. Work at the edge of the sea, and work in the depths of the sea. When you have connected deeply with the sea, then do the same with fresh water springs, lakes, and rivers. The fresh water contacts are different, but they work in the same way, and can be approached in the same way.

6.18 The vision of the Temple of the North (the Temple of the Dark Goddess)

Light a candle, and be aware of the direction in which you are seated. Close your eyes, and see the candle flame with your inner vision. As you look at the candle flame it grows bigger and bigger until it becomes a column of fire. You step through the fire, and find yourself in the great hall where priests and priestesses circle the central flame.

You join them in their meditations, and walks, finding yourself walking slowly around the central flame, and reflecting on your life. You begin to notice

four gates, one in each direction, and each gate has a pair of guardians on
either side of its entrance.

A priest or priestess comes to you and places a hand on your shoulder.
They tell you that they will be your sponsor, and they will help you learn about
the temples. They guide you around the circling of the flame, and you stop at
the entrance in the North. The angelic Guardians look intently at you, and you
feel them probing you in great depth. One of the angels places a hand on your
chest, and you feel the angel asking the organs of your body many questions.
When the angel is happy with what he discovers, the two guardians part and
allow you to step over the threshold of the Temple of the North.

You find yourself in a dark cave with a pool of water in the centre. Many
priestesses and priests are gathered here, and are tending to sleeping animals,
birds, humans, and plants. As you look around the cave, you notice in the
shadows the outline of an old lady sitting on a stone chair. Her hair has grown
down into the rock, and her arms hold many sleeping animals. She is watching
you as you look at her. She nods to acknowledge you, and in a strange, almost
whispered voice, she tells you to come closer.

The closer you get to her, the more creatures you see hidden in her clothing,
in her hair, and in her arms. Her long cloak, which lies in layers across the
floor beyond her, has humans curled up asleep in the folds of its dark fabric.
Something compels you to touch her feet in reverence: her skin is cold, like
death. She feels your fear and smiles with compassion. There is something
about her smile that triggers long-forgotten memories within you, and as those
memories begin to surface in your mind, the fear within you falls away.

She tells you to come often and visit her. She will teach you about the land,
the rocks, and old magic. In return she asks you for a gift. Give her whatever
appears in your hands. If it is something you own in life, then you must bury
it for her.

One of the priestesses places a hand on your shoulder and leads you to the
back of the cave, behind the goddess, where there is a tunnel cut out of the
hard rock. Together you pass down this tunnel, which has many strange and
beautiful images painted on its stone walls. In the distance is a large doorway
that is carved out of the stone. Many fabrics hang over the entrance, and above
the entrance is the face of a demon, her eyes glowing red in the darkness.

You pass through the doors and find yourself in a small, dark cave that
smells of sulphur. There is little light, and you stumble around until your foot
hits something. Kneeling down, you find your hands on a large, smooth stone.
The stone breathes beneath your touch, and the power of the Goddess in her
rawest form passes through you. This is the Goddess in her truest form: the
earth, the stone, the planet. You can feel all life in your hands, all existence,
and the potential of birth.

Instinctively you place your forehead to the earth and rest your head on the
breast of Mother Earth. She moves under you, and you hear a heartbeat. You

merge with her, becoming one with the rock, and together you sleep through time as the planet turns around the seasons.

You drift in the stillness and silence, losing all sense of body, time, and identity. In your slumber you merge with the rock and feel the passage of the planet through space, the turning of the earth, the warmth of the sun, the pull of the moon. You feel as if you have come home, that this is where you belong. You relax deeply in the stillness and drift.

Something, somewhere calls to you. Lifting your head, you see a doorway. Through the doorway you can see a candle burning brightly. You lift your hand to your eyes to shield them from the unaccustomed light, and you edge nearer to have a better look. You see a human sitting before a candle flame. With a shock, you realize that it is you. You go and sit down and merge with yourself, becoming one. When you are ready, you open your eyes and blow out the candle.

★ ★ ★

Working in vision with the goddess in the cave is a fundamental cornerstone of magic. She is the key contact that anchors magic in the physical world, and she also helps you learn to connect with the land around you. Working with this vision gives your inner self 'roots,' it grounds your power while confronting your fear of death.

Don't fall into the trap of trying to name or identify this goddess. She is a deep filter that earth and Underworld goddesses flow from. If you reach for the power behind Cybele, then you would reach this ancient goddess in the cave.

When you have worked for a while with this deep power in vision, you will find that the need for a visionary interface falls away, and the contact is strongest when you are simply out in nature. She flows all around you, and once you have communed with her in vision, the land itself, all around you, will begin to commune with you. The same holds true for all the elemental/directional visions. The visions are merely steps, not final destinations. Through working in depth with them your mind and body will change, and the connections between you and the powers will deepen until the visionary interfaces are no longer necessary.

There is no shortcut to this level of communion with power: it has to come slowly over time through vision, contact, and ritual. But if you persevere, there will come a day when the contacts and powers flow all around you, all the time. Because you have spent so much time working consciously through interfaces (visions and contacts) you will instantly recognize the 'signature feel' of a specific power, deity, or line of consciousness.

Chapter Seven

Divine power and its containers

With the net, the gift of Anu, held close to his side, he
himself raised up IMHULLU the atrocious wind, the tempest,
the whirlwind, the hurricane, the wind of four and the wind of
seven, the tumid wind worst of all. All seven winds were created
and released to savage the guts of Tiamat, they towered behind
him. Then the tornado ABUBA his last great ally, the signal for
assault, he lifted up. He mounted the storm, his terrible chariot,
reins hitched to the side, yoked four in hand the appalling team,
sharp poisoned teeth, the Killer, the Pitiless, Trampler, Haste, they
knew arts of plunder, skills of murder.

— The battle between Marduk and Tiamat. From the translation
of the *Enuma Elish* by N. K. Sandars.

7.1 Through the eyes of the wind

One of the predominant streams of religion and magic in our world today is
one that comes out of the magical direction of the East, and is dominated
by recitation or 'air.' Seeing as we have looked in depth at the elemental
expressions and how they flow through magic, I thought it would be interesting
to look at the concept of the Sephiroth and the Qliphoth through the magical
element of air. The Sephiroth is a Divine Power, and the Qliphoth is the shell
that contains the power and acts as a filter between a specific resonance of
Divine Power and physical manifestation.

Because the magical direction and power of air is so predominant in
Western religions and magic, the Sephiroth and Qliphoth are good examples
to demonstrate how the power behind certain deities, beings, and elemental
powers flows through our lands.

Clues about how this 'air' power rose in dominance can be found in ancient
texts, and with careful study and deep inner work it is possible to track the
foundations of certain religions to the release and expression of this air/east
power.

While it is interesting to go deep into the ancient creation myths of Sumer,
Canaan, Babylon, and Egypt, my focus is more on the inner and magical

visionary expressions of this power than its historical context. However, working from an inner magical visionary aspect to observe these powers certainly brings the ancient texts to life, and they begin to make far more sense. As always, my constant mantra is to do and experience first, *then* go away and read the ancient texts.

Ancient texts tell us repeatedly of the powers of storm gods, the ones who bring terrible winds, storms that bring chaos, storms that destroy. Often one storm god supplants another, as was the case when Marduk supplanted Enlil, an earlier form of the Wind power. The same patterns repeat in various ways across North Africa and the Near/Middle East. We find smattered references to storm gods connected with blades and serpents. Of course, writings can be changed, misinterpreted, supplanted, or manipulated to make a point. But the inner experience of these powers is direct: through observing and interacting with them we can discover the inner source of these stories.

On the surface they appear to be stories that attempt to explain the creation of the world and man's struggle to understand his environment. But as you magically interact with the environment, you will begin to identify a deeper aspect of these stories, and recognize keys that will tell you a different story, a story about how to communicate with these primal powers.

7.2   The magical path to the elemental forces

These powers are not particularly friendly to humans or human consciousness, so the path towards their core can take some time to tread. My treading towards the core container—Qliphoth—of the Wind in the East was not a conscious one, it sort of happened despite myself. I do not know if there is a defined ritualized inner path to the threshold and container of these vast powers: if there is, I have never found it. But that does not mean it does not exist. I was sort of funnelled, channelled, and occasionally dragged into magical and visionary situations that brought me into various layers of contact with the East Wind power.

Looking back, it was a clear and defined path that I walked down, a path that brought me deeper and deeper into the Mysteries of this power. Yet at the time I had no clue, no idea what was really happening. I thought I was in control: I thought I was making definite magical choices, connecting with specific inner beings in a way that gave me a broad outlook. In reality, I was being marched like a squirming child down a corridor towards the Head Sister's office (I went to convent school). Now, in my fiftieth year, I stand before that Head Sister's door, and I can remember exactly what it feels like to be seven years old and in trouble... and boy do I know I'm in trouble...

So it is worth bearing in mind that the magical path and development towards working with these powers can often be haphazard and born out of spontaneous experiences. The more we try to control our progression, the more we will end up locking ourselves down. So before we look at the pattern of what a path of development might look like, let's look at the formation of the power itself.

7.3 The primal force: divine power and its expressions

One of the things I discovered, when I eventually figured out what I was really working with, is that these primal elemental powers have various expressions that we can perceive and interact with. The source of these primal forces is a Qliphoth or container that holds, and gives form to, a specific expression of Divine power. The deities and externalised forms flow or 'echo' from this container. The closer you get to the container and its contents—Qliphoth and Sephiroth—the stronger and more powerful the contact is, and the more elemental and natural its expression becomes.

The Qliphoth emanate lower octaves of the power of the Sephiroth, and some of those lower octaves can be worked with, as they express as primal powers which are used to form a deity. When the deity is formed or adjusted by humans using ritual techniques, it takes on a filter of humanity with all its inherent imbalances. These imbalances can be unhealthy, and this probably led to the mystics' view of the Qliphoth as demons: they are not, but their 'echoes' can be.

7.4 Qliphoths

Let's take some time to look at the Qliphoths, moving away from the views of Regardie, Crowley, *et al.*, and going back to the source to look more closely at what is going on from a magical perspective. The word means 'shells' or 'husks,' which is exactly what they are: they are containers that act as filters or skins for Divine Primal Power. They can manifest as forces of nature, which give us the forms we recognize as deities, demonic beings, Titans, and so forth.

To observe this process we must go back to the Tree of Life and see how Divine Power emanates down the Tree to finally manifest. Once it has crossed the Abyss and begun to take on a patterned structure,[1] the power begins to express itself through various qualities. These are the Sephiroth, which bring the specific positive and negative qualities of the Divine power into orbit. The Sephiroth are pure expressions of Divine power potential, but in our imbalanced human form, we cannot directly connect with it.

The Qliphoth, or shell, surrounds and contains the Divine Power potential, slowing it down in its expression and allowing it to express through a manifest form. Remember, for power to take form it has to have polar opposites: positive

---

[1]This is the point of Daat, which is the mirror of Kether.

and negative. There must be tension between the two poles, and the two expressions of power must be constantly of, and within, one another.

At this stage of the game, the orbit of the negative/positive power inside its shell expresses out through our world as an elemental force that we can begin to interact with. That interaction and mediation creates a conversation, and through that conversation the container of the power creates an echo or form that we can communicate with and understand better: a primal deity.

Then come the deities who are 'created' through magical action. Through long-term ritualized interactions with the primal deity, we create interfaces that are easier for us to commune with, interfaces or substations which have more human qualities: the deities.

The option that Judaism took was to steer as far away from these emanations as possible, and work only with the Divine Power itself. This is why it has no filters such as deities. This grew the religion into a pattern containing no image of Divine Being, no deities, no filters: there is only the Utterance, and its outer expression as a sacred alphabet. Its lack of filters makes its pattern easy to corrupt, which can cause terrible problems since we are imperfect beings. To commune with such pure power there must be absolute internal discipline and balance—and no emotion.

Unfortunately, we are inherently imbalanced as spiritual beings due to our physical manifestation. Therefore pure Divine Power, unfiltered and unchallenged, will hit our imperfections and spin us out of control. The slightest imbalance will be magnified as the power reaches us, because that is what power does. We try to channel and control that power by using recitation, prayer, self-control, self-denial, and ultimately trying to control everything and everyone around us...

The Abrahamic religions thus go to great lengths, through laws, to teach us how to be balanced; but ultimately lesson of balance must be learned through experience, not through laws. Humanity generally learns best through hardship and bitter experience. Just like cells, we humans like to take the easiest route possible, expending the least possible energy. The combination of receiving great deal of power, then only budging if we absolutely have to, does not always make the greatest mix.

The key to working with the Qliphoth is to use the singular or least complex forms of deity when at all possible, and to have a balance of the Qliphoth without allowing for too much subdivision. Good practical examples of this can be seen in the more ancient and early classical religions. For example in Ancient Egypt, in the Old Kingdom, you had a smallish group of major deities, linked to elemental powers and the flow of life and death. These deities balanced each other out and kept the dance of creation and destruction under a Divine system called Ma'at—who was also the goddess who oversaw the whole system.

Magical priests slowly discovered that you could mirror the act of creation and create a man-made Qliphoth as a filter and container, then breathe Divine breath into it to create a deity. They also learned the key to subdividing deities, creating narrow filters that would only allow certain aspects of a deity through, thus learning how to split the power of the deity into subsections or multiple deities.

This had two results. Firstly, the imbalance of humanity passed into the constructed Qliphoth: we cannot play at being Divine, not matter how much we think we can. I suspect that this is the source of the destructive, imbalanced Qliphoth so many magicians tap into.

Secondly, by subdividing the deity powers they were weakened, which gave the priesthoods more control over them: their smaller, constructed Qliphoth did not hold as much Divine power. (Think of pouring a large jug of water into little egg cups.) The human need for control overtook the earlier wisdom of *sharing* power with the Inner Worlds in order to mediate more power overall. It may be hard to lift, and control, one enormous bucket of water if you want to fill something, but it gets the job done. Whereas trying to fill a bath with an eggcup gives you much more control, and the eggcup is far easier to lift, but it is far less effective: really the eggcup is almost useless for the task.

In the Roman pantheon, they had a god for just about anything and everything. When they figured out that they had subdivided too much and were now under threat, they brought in Magna Mater, Cybele: the Great Mother. As a deity she is one of the expressions of primal power: difficult to control, hard to please, and powerful. Unfortunately for the Romans, though she did save their ass, they did not really understand what was happening to them, and so it all eventually went horribly wrong.

The same pattern of behaviour repeated again and again in the ancient world: we connected with a primal power, built a relationship with it as a deity, and learned to control and subdivide its power, which then led to powerlessness and collapse. We can also see aspects of it today in India, which still has the mass of subdivided deities in its religions.

7.5 Ritual and magical orbits

With the Qliphoth, the basic natural relationship between humanity and these powers is one of survival, respect, and 'listening.' We evolved beyond this and wished to interact more actively with it, taking on some control and bargaining, manipulating, and exploring.

Staying with the element of air, let's look at how this relationship works. As the temple cultures began to evolve, their priesthood developed their skills as they worked closely with the angelic mediators/filters. The priesthoods learned how to form their own Qliphoths or containers for Divine power in the form of human deities, and using the power of the angelic filters they mediated this power into outer created forms which were then interacted with.

At this stage, the deities were windows for elemental power, with the angelic filters keeping the balance. Usually the deities held both sides of the power, negative and positive, and angelic/demonic beings made sure that the power flowed out to the manifest world as it should. The deities would warn their priests or priestesses if a major surge of creation or destruction was on its way: a more formal and verbalized version of the tribal relationship with nature. It was at this stage that offerings could be made, covenants struck, etc. to change the course or expression of the power to suit humanity or the land in general.

This brought about a major shift in the thinking of priesthoods and humanity in general. The temptation to offset danger and destruction, and encourage creation and growth instead, was great indeed. Sometimes this bargaining worked, unless the elemental force had a major job to do, in which case the filters still gave a warning but the disaster could not be averted: the power had to sweep across the land, as that was its nature, that was its function.

Such failures to control the deity's force in full flow encouraged priesthoods to develop methods of filtering and subdividing power in an attempt to fully control it. Powers were split into two deities or more, and priests learned how to change the power expression of a deity by changing its man-made outer material form and attributes. They also learned to manipulate the filters/mediators that worked with the deities by binding the angelic/demonic beings into certain forms that would limit their functions.

This can be seen in some of the ancient temple cultures in which the primal deities have been supplanted by more human deities that take on more 'useful' attributes, and where the angelic/demonic filters have been bound into service as guardians, deliverers, etc. This is where the guardian spirits and angelic/demonic beings are given names, attributes, functions, etc. all within a temple service.

The more these powers are contained, bound, and controlled as the filter/window through which they flow is subdivided and diluted, the weaker they become. Later on in history we see a complete degeneration of this system, with deity containers created with intent but without any proper knowledge, resulting in empty containers available for any degenerate, weak being to occupy. The human gives it a voice, food, and lodging, and the parasitical being enters in a relationship with the human.

What we are seeing with this dynamic is the octave of the creation of the world as it goes through its various levels. The Divine Consciousness is housed in a container or shell that is the world/Malkuth. The container is constantly reshaping itself as it interacts with a species. The container is further shaped or patterned (emergence of deities) when a specific species—us—engages in direct communion and subsequent relationship. The species then attempts to subvert the process by creating its own containers in an attempt to mimic Divine Consciousness: we try to be God, and we believe we can create deities. That is the stage we are at now.

One of the ways our forebears tried to step away from this degeneration was to try and build a relationship with Divine Being that was not dependent on deities, filters, and suchlike. This is monotheism. Unfortunately, this approach, too, quickly became degenerate. Maybe the answer lies not in the method, but within ourselves. In Kabbalah this whole process would be the lesson of Hod with the consequence of Geburah behind it: give people enough rope to hang themselves.

7.6 Pathways and parasites

Let's stay with the element of air. The most common way that humans have attempted to create pathways to the Qliphoth, and elicit interactions with the Sephiroth through the Qliphoth, is by the use of magical incantations and spoken rituals. This can be good or bad: much depends on the spiritual integrity and purity of the intent of the ritual, and your ability to form and manipulate power. If a religious recitation or magical incantation/ritual is focused on the supremacy of a single 'deity'—not Divinity—at the expense of all others, and reaffirming its power expression in our world, then invariably this will bring disharmony, imbalance, and destruction. We can see this played out with elements of Christianity. If the filter is heavily littered with controlling dogmas, particularly ones that evoke strong emotions, then there is a good chance that a parasitical being has moved in and is operating the filter/religion through the priesthood.

Parasitical beings are beings within their own right. They have certain mediation powers, are often conditional, and can be elementals, demons, deities, or even thought forms. *Parasites can be any type of being.* The common denominator is that they step into a man-made container for their own agenda, which is usually a search for a source of energy. The real (natural) Qliphoths (containers) are immune to parasitical infestation: they are a much higher octave, and whatever they emanate, for good or bad, is the power of Divine Consciousness.

A man-made Qliphoth, however, is as flawed as its creator; and even if one of these containers survives for thousands of years, it will still carry the inherent imbalance of humanity. This imbalance not only attracts parasitical beings, it also enables them to move into the container and operate it indefinitely.

The way to avoid ending up with a parasitic Qliphothic creation is to make sure that you are working with a real deity that has firm roots in the elemental powers, has established positive and negative powers, and is a 'known' image or identity that can be traced back for a long time. There are many parasitic containers around these days, particularly in the magical community in the form of 'edgy' deities like 'Babalon,' 'Lilith,' and 'Baphomet.' These 'deities' were constructed out of glamour, ego, and misread history and theology: they have no inner connections. There is nothing 'evil' or 'bad' about these containers, they are merely man-made structures that can only mediate limited flows of powers with the parasitic beings that have stepped into them to do business.

These more modern containers developed as a result of human focus, repeated use, and a cooperative parasite willing to help construct a new source of dinner for itself. They are quite different from the highly-crafted, man-made Qliphoth and deities that emerged in the ancient world: those are in a magical class all their own. To spot them, look at a culture, and look at its early deities. Then look at the subsequent generations of deities and their subdivision of power: that is usually the junction point for created containers. Their creation will also correlated with a time of instability for the nation and its rulers. Whether this was the direct result of subdivision, or the instability spurred a priesthood to attempt to acquire more control, who knows? Either way, what we know from history is that when humanity attempts to interfere with the Qliphoth or tries to create its own containers, it all goes horribly wrong.

Now it becomes clearer why Qliphoth were, and are, considered demonic or 'bad.' The shells themselves are not bad: it is a natural dynamic that once power begins to takes form and become externalized and moulded, the potential for interference and corruption is vastly increased. Add humanity into the mixture and the potential for corruption is overwhelming. That is the nature of power manifest and externalized: if it is 'born' out in the manifest world, it also has to 'die' and withdraw from the manifest world.

The *true* Qliphoth protect the pure balance of Divinity from the imbalance of humanity, and *vice versa*: they keep Divinity and humanity apart in a constant magnetic orbit.

7.7 Deities, the Qliphoth, and lots of wind

The wind is only balanced when it is expressing itself naturally. A developing primal deity is in balance and with, and remains within the context of, all the other deities that mirror the various forces of nature. However, once one of these deities demands singular worship above all others, and that demand is adhered to, then the balance will spin out of control. Its negative powers are expressed through religion that becomes 'supreme.' In the case of the East Wind, this power manifests as dogmatic control, aggression, and destruction.

This unfortunate progression can be seen happening again and again in ancient religions. There is an initial contact and communion with some society. Later a covenant is sealed with blood sacrifice. Subsequently the relationship spins out of balance and there appears dogma, books of laws, prophecies, and eventually war.

Often the original elemental nature deity gets supplanted, and perhaps also subdivided, by an artificial container or containers made by its priesthood. The cult then becomes more aggressive, which leads me to suspect that this is the point where another, more parasitical being, has stepped into the frame with a promise: you do this for me, and I will do that for you. So it goes from a relationship of understanding and mutual respect to one of control and supplication.

We can see this repeated in various Near Eastern religions. In the early Sumerian pantheon Enlil, the storm god who visited the storms of nature on the land, was balanced out by Ninlil the wind goddess—who is probably the root of the later demon Lilith. Their relationship was one of balance and counterbalance, and their union created other deities.[1]

Eventually Enlil was supplanted by Marduk, another god 'who controlled the winds.' He was a storm deity, the son of the sun, who became the patron god of Babylon. He had titles like 'Lord of Lords' and 'Supreme Lord.' He was a warrior, a leader, and a magician, and most definitely a force to be reckoned with.

Similarly in ancient Egypt, at first we have Shu, the wind god, in balance with his sister Tefnut, the moisture. Later she faded into the background, and by the New Kingdom another god of wind was rising in prominence. Amun supplanted Shu as the god to talk to about the wind and weather. He became more prominent than the other gods, and was considered the saviour of Egypt after 'his' line of kings successfully expelled Hyksos.

One stele calls Amun "Lord of truth, father of the gods, maker of men, creator of all animals, Lord of things that are, and creator of the staff of life." Uttering his name could appease storms: "The tempest moves aside for the sailor who remembers the name of Amun. The storm becomes a sweet breeze for he who invokes His name." As can be seen, the relationship between man and deity had moved from one of warning a society and exhorting it to act, into one of supplication and control.

Ba'al Hadad/Adad, a storm-god in the North Semitic/ Babylonian pantheon, again is a close echo of Marduk, and a possible root of the Semitic god Yahweh, who some scholars now connect with the attributes of a storm god. The shift from communion with Divinity through natural, primal deities, to bargaining with subdivided deities was becoming apparent.

These storm deities, which had wider useful attributes (bulls, sun, war, kingship, land requisition, etc.) successfully supplanted earlier, less controllable primal wind/storm gods. But they demanded total obedience and exclusivity. From this we see the development, both religiously and magically, of systems

---

[1]From what I have come across magically, there often seems to be a connection between the power of the wind and the descent into, and emergence from, the Underworld.

that mediate a wide variety of watered-down powers that often bring war and conflict. Lots of smiting, battles, covenants, and promises of power!

7.8 Working with the Qliphoths

In essence, working with the Qliphoth is working with the formed nature power that flows through a primal deity, and approaching it from an understanding of its shell, makeup, function, and abilities, as opposed to mindlessly worshipping it or seeking to control it through magic. The Qliphoths are the powers behind the deities: they are the bridges that connect raw Divine Power in a first filtered form —Sephiroth—with deity expressions and physical manifestations. The Qliphoths are the gates to the Divine Sparks which are steps towards the threshold of Divine Universal Power.

With the birth of psychology and the breakup of the Victorian moralistic, sexually repressed society, magic was looked at, theorized over, and experimented with as a vehicle to break away from the tight bonds of an uptight society. Throw in a fashion for the 'exotic, deep and mystical' East, and you have a cooking pot that is potentially disastrous for magic.

I am not saying that the exploration of the darker side of humanity was not fruitful: those pioneers forged new paths in how we think and how we approach power. But at the same time, in their glee of being dark and edgy, they created a system of working within Kabbalah—The Tree of Death and the Demonic Qliphoth—that, while it was exciting, diverted attention away from the real depth of these powers. Choosing that system of working is like choosing a greasy, cheap burger over a finely cooked sirloin steak.

When considering working with a deity, the most important thing ensure is that it has two sides to all its attributes: a good creative side, and a darker destructive side. This tells us that the access route to the Qliphoth—and the Sephiroth contained within it—is healthy. If it can access and express the positive and negative powers of the Sephiroth, then it is balanced. The Qliphoth is also a complete expression, being both creative and destructive, so it too is balanced; and this will express through a deity that has both opposing powers within it.

If the darker or lighter side has been fragmented into a separate deity, then so long as they work together as a team to keep each other in check, the power can still be contained and balanced. If, however, only one side of the equation is expressed, then there is a huge potential for imbalanced power, and the Qliphoth expression is probably a human construct. This can happen if the primal deity expression of the Qliphoth has been magically manipulated to suppress one end of its power spectrum. The result would be deities emanating from this Qliphoth threshold that are one-sided, imbalanced, and therefore destructive, even if their emanations are creative. They will mediate *destructive overgrowth*, having no balancing destructive power.

The other thing to look at is whether the natural primal forces have been filtered down in controlled use for human consumption. For example, let's go back to the Primal Wind—a Qliphoth expression. If we look at this through the deity Enlil, then we will see that he is primarily a storm god, specifically the god of the north wind, sometimes also connected to the east wind. He is presented as male, and as a potentially destructive wind. His partner is Ninlil, the goddess of the north wind, known as the Lady of the Breezes. They are both connected to agriculture, with Enlil providing the tools and Ninlil providing the seeds.

Though the Qliphoth expression of primal force has been split into two deities, their power is still focused: it is complementary and they work in orbit around one another. They are two opposing forces that are of one another, and which work in harmony as a combined force. They reflect the duality of the Divine Power of the Sephiroth. That is a important point. The primal force of the wind manifests as two deities, Enlil and Ninlil, but they are still only of one Qliphoth. If those deities are subdivided again and again, it will still be only one Qliphoth that is expressing through a multitude of deities. The power echo of the Qliphoth will merely be diluted over and over until its ability to express the power of the Sephiroth within it is too dispersed to work with.

Where this all went terribly wrong, in human terms, is the supplanting of this primal force of wind/air through further human tinkering. Enlil and Ninlil as deities were too powerful to manipulate, even when divided into their two opposing forces. Eventually the priesthood understood how to tinker with the containers to subdivide or supplant the deity forms: Enlil was over taken by Marduk, storm god and warrior with many different dispersed attributes (sun, bull, kingship, etc.) who immediately demanded that only he be worshipped and worked with as the god. You start to see the process spinning out of balance, and breaking down.

Once you have found a balanced deity to work with, and its attendant beings, then it is time to begin to work in vision and ritual to step through the deity to the Qliphoth beyond. Don't forget, a window or threshold is a two-way street. To do this safely, it is advisable to first work in depth with the deity so that you really understand the power dynamics that it mediates. This would be done first by working in ritual with the deity, then in vision within the confines of the human realm, and finally in vision in the inner temple of the deity.

Now you can start to see why it is so important that the deity you work with is in fact a true deity, and not a human created shell. For this passage deep into the power of the Qliphoth, it is important to pass through the inner patterns of the inner temple of that deity. Such interactions with an inner structure will help you form a safe path to the seat of power, and will also provide you with the necessary beings to facilitate such a connection. You cannot just wander up to a Qliphoth, a real container of Divine Power: not only would you not find it, but you would not be able to communicate with it without filters.

The inner temple of the deity provides filters, paths, and safeguards. In return you are, of course, expected to mediate that Qliphoth power into the inner temple and out into the world. There are no free rides: you work for your supper.

7.9   Approaching the Qliphoth through the Inner Temple

When working in the Inner Temple of a deity, there are a few different ways that you can approach the Qliphoth behind them. The first route would be through the knowledge of those who have served the deity in the past, plus the knowledge of those who shaped the deity and first interacted with it. That collective knowledge is expressed as a Library. Working in the Library in vision, you would hold the intent to connect with the powers behind the deity, and with that intention you would build or clear a path through the Library in increments.

Once you are at the end of that path, you would probably find yourself standing before what appears to be nothing, but which feels like it is filled with everything. That is the threshold of the Qliphoth. Beyond that is the spark of Divine Being taking form (Sephiroth) which for us as humans is unapproachable. The threshold of the Qliphoth is held in place by two opposing archangelic forces whose job it is to stop you crossing that threshold. Rather than force the issue and get catapulted out, it is a good idea simply to come to this place with the intention of going no further, and simply being there, on that threshold, in a state of silence and peace.

This simplicity achieves a couple of things. It allows your body to normalize to the level of power there, and it allows the threshold to normalize towards you. You could spend the rest of your life standing at that threshold in vision, and it would be time well spent. Why? Because you would be in orbit around the Qliphoth, and therefore in orbit along with the deities: you would be taking your place in the pattern of orbits that start with Divine Consciousness and end with humanity.

Being at peace and in stillness means there can be no agenda, no 'container' of wants or needs to fill. This allows you, eventually, to become a mediator of the power emanating from the Qliphoth, allowing it to flow through you into the inner temple. As you leave the inner temple, you can take that power out with you and let it flow through you out into the world. Once this has been done, you become an open door for this power flow.

There is no shut off valve, and no moving on: it will constantly ebb and flow through you. Being in the orbit of the Qliphoth will cause the Sephiroth within you to resonate with the Sephiroth within the Qliphoth. We are all octaves of the same power: we are all expressions of Divinity within substance, and we are all, in reality, Qliphoths that contain a spark of Divine Being.

Chapter Eight

The dead, the living, and the living dead

When old friends come to visit

In *Magical Knowledge Book Two*, I talk about the death process from a visionary/inner perspective, and about how to work in vision with someone who has just died. In this chapter I will talk about the dead from an outer perspective, in terms of how they interact with the world of the living through presence and haunting, and how we can live magically with the dead living alongside us.

Not every person who dies goes straight onto the path of deep death to emerge into another life. Some stay around the living, some sink deep into the land to wait, and some, depending on their culture, will intentionally stay within the land to act as an interface with the living. As magicians, the dead who choose to stay in our world can be contacts we can work with, or they can be part of our service as we care for them and give them shelter. This is not a popular branch of magic in the Western tradition: many societies and religions today tend to view the dead with suspicion and fear. This is a sad degeneration, and something which has generally fuelled a fear of death which has become deeply embedded in our psyche.

There is a fragment of wisdom in such fear, for clinging to the dead is unhealthy for all concerned. Forcing the dead to stay and work is definitely an unhealthy way to work magic. But like everything else in life, the truth of a situation is often quite complex with many variables, and no one rule will work for everything.

8.1 Working with the dead

Working with the dead who present themselves to you is a major part of the ancient path of magic. It is an opportunity for great learning, necessary service, and establishing bonds with the past.

This much-ignored area of magic can give us a deeper understanding of the nature of life and death, and it can help us work with a sense of our own death, so that we will die in a more fulfilled, balanced way. Death work in all its forms has always been a major part of the Mysteries, and it is something that really needs bringing back to the fore.

125

Working with the newly dead is a form of magical service: you make sure everyone goes where they need to go, and that no other beings, particularly parasitical beings, are hitching a ride with the dead person. Often when the newly dead make their presence known, they just need it acknowledging that they still exist, a bit of help getting any unsettled business out of the way, then pointing in the right direction on their journey.

Work with the longer-term dead and the ancestral dead tends to be more about making connections with land spirits, and bridging information back and forth between the living and the dead. It is a chance to learn lost skills, and to work with the long-term dead who are still in the land (Sleepers) by assisting them in the service they are performing. These contacts also tend to warn you of impending major danger, especially intense weather and earthquakes, so that you can act accordingly. They can also act as advisors and guardians—but treat their advice as you would advice from any human. Just because someone is dead does not mean they are all-knowing. They will see things you do not, but you will also have perspectives that they do not. You must use your common sense when working with this type of consciousness.

8.2 The dead

When we die, if we have a strong spiritual or religious pattern that has a clear path through death, we will tend to follow that path without question until we get to the point where we no longer need that pattern: the veils part when the time is right, and we are able to move forward through death.

So if you were an active Christian Baptist, then after the initial shock of your death your consciousness will begin to emerge again, and your spirit will 'see,' and 'be' within the Christian setting. This will continue until you begin the process of letting go. First you will let go of exterior things: loved ones, belongings, etc.; then comes the shedding of your personal identity. Once that identity begins to break up, there is no need for the religious structure to give your spirit a vocabulary, and your spirit can begin to engage directly with the powers and beings that work within death.

Then your spirit will choose either to rest, to merge with Divinity, or to go in a new life. If you were a magical/spiritual adept, however, then you will stay in the Inner Worlds as an inner contact, guide, and teacher. This is not the same as the dead hanging around the land. Some of the dead stay in a phase of death which enables them to stay within the land and keep communion with the living. The Catholics call this purgatory—God's waiting room—a place within death where life can still be reached.

In this state, the spirit of the person can flow back and forth between the living and the dead, and they are usually still connected to the body they left behind. So if their body was buried as opposed to cremated, then they will still have a connection to that body. When a spirit is in this phase it can be communed with in inner vision through the death vision, or they can be communicated with in the physical place where they have chosen to hang out. This situation is also what lies behind most hauntings.

Then there are those who are still very much locked within their bodies and bones. Sometimes this locking-in is a result of ritual or binding; sometimes it is the result of the dead person's culture. This can be perceived magically by working with the burial or bones in ritual and in vision, and with the outer manifestations that express themselves in areas close to the body in question.

After working with burials for a long time I have discovered that a strange dynamic sometimes happens with long-term burials, in which the spirit of the dead person begins to interact, then merge, with the consciousness of a land spirit: they then commune together with the living as a hive being. The symbiotic relationship of two different types of consciousness—for example an ancient Sleeper, and a faery being—enables the spirit of the dead and the spirit of the land to communicate with the surrounding humans in order to pass on information regarding upcoming events that would threaten the tribe.

Though these close-knit tribal communities living closely with Sleepers have long since gone from many areas around the world, these contacts can still be worked with, which is something we will discuss later in this chapter.

8.3 The newly dead

People who have recently died often get an urge to tell their loved ones that they still exist. The success of this largely depends on the culture, beliefs, and ritual actions of the living family members; it also depends on the natural capacity of the living to pick up on the 'cues' attempted by the dead.

Some cultures do not encourage communion with the dead, and a small number of cultures will actively shut down any chance for the dead to make a connection. This manifests itself as the covering or removing of all pictures of the dead person, the refusal to utter the name of the dead, and the keeping up of prayers or religious rituals to move the dead on quickly, whether they like it or not.

Another barrier for the newly dead to communicate is the aggressive refusal to acknowledge life after death, so that any phenomena the dead person may manage to produce can be ignored or explained away. This can be somewhat healthy, as it encourages the dead person to let go of the living and recognize that their connections in life are now over: the living loved ones can no longer exist for them. This spurs the newly dead on quickly into death.

In my younger days, I felt that this was always the best way forward for the dead, but over the years various experiences have taught me that the process is not so cut and dried. I now think that people need to go through the different stages of death in their own time: those who stay behind often have good reasons for doing so.

The attempt to make contact often—but not always—comes within a few days of death, and takes on many different forms depending on the state of mind and abilities of both the dead and the living. It is worth bearing in mind that previous cultures which had a good relationship with death would often have stories that outlined how a spirit could communicate, and what cues to look for. Learning these stories in life embedded the strongest methods of communication deep in a person's consciousness, so that it would be knowledge available on death: it would be second nature. Modern thinking and dogmatic religions have wiped a lot of this from our consciousness as individuals, and as a community, so really we have stepped backwards in a sense.

It takes time for a dead person to work out how to affect something in the physical world, and for some it takes longer than others. Some never figure it out at all, and some do not feel the need for it, so not every dead person will try and communicate. The first attempts usually involve something that has a high energy source, something that can be energetically triggered easily. In a house, that would normally manifest as the dead person working out how to affect electricity, and the objects that electricity flows through.

For us in our house that has manifested as all the light bulbs blowing, the TV going nuts, the computers going haywire, etc. My mother was a natural but undeveloped psychic. When she died, she visited our house within a few days. She managed to blow every light bulb in the house, and made the TV commit suicide. She also visited my daughter's and niece's houses, where she managed to blow the light bulbs again. Finally she backed off her light-bulb Armageddon when I told her that she was welcome for as long as she wanted to stay, and that we were proud of her. She hung around and worked with me until her funeral, after which she moved deeper into death.

My cousin died a few months later... and again, we had to replace all the light bulbs. But this time he hung around a lot longer, and would emit bursts of armpit smell in the hallway. He had been slowly dying from a terrible illness, and had suffered a great deal of pain: he was frightened, traumatised, and needed shelter. It took me a little while to figure out that it was still him, once he moved away from blowing light bulbs and began his armpit routine. The shift was probably brought about by him relaxing—and therefore not blowing things—and allowing the trauma of his last year of life to surface. The smell he emitted—along with the scent of alcohol—was a bitter smell of illness: he was still in that place, and was struggling to get away from it.

I let him hang out with us, and he even came on a day-trip with us. That was a bit weird, but slowly the hallway smell changed from sick man smell to his own natural presence. He was an interesting man, also psychic but again undeveloped, and his ability never had any outlet in life. It was a pleasure to share our space with him and give him shelter.

Smell is another cue used by the newly dead. Smell is a strong sense in us, deeply embedded in our brains, and is one of the last senses to go when we die. It also seems to be the sense that is easiest to trigger in the living by the dead: it is a quick and easy way to say "I'm still here." When my maternal grandmother died I was at my mother's house, and halfway down the stairs my grandmother's individual perfume wafted all around me. Again this stopped after the funeral and she went on her way. She was just saying goodbye to her family.

And that is what most visits from newly dead are about: they want to let you know they still exist, and to say goodbye. A simple acknowledgement of them, both out loud and in your mind, is often all that is needed. Sometimes they do wish to stay around for a little longer, and sometimes, when you are a magician, it is for magical reasons.

The dead are not all-knowing, but they do see things that we do not, just as we can see and do things they cannot. When you are working magically at any reasonable power level, you will be exposed now and then to dangers, and these dangers are often sensed by the dead. They will try to warn you, protect you, and even deal with things for you. This has happened to me a few times, when I had asked a newly dead friend or family member if they wanted me to escort them through death, and the answer was a resounding no. They wanted to work alongside me or protect my back as I worked for a time. Once the threat was over, they would withdraw.

Once when this happened to me, and the dead person—a dear friend, and magician—withdrew, I assumed they had moved deeper into death. In my linear time, they had worked with me for a couple of months, and then they had vanished. But ten years later they suddenly appeared again, and worked intensively to protect me in a difficult situation. I worked in vision to communicate with them, and asked why they had not moved on. The answer I got back was that they were about to move on, they just had a few jobs to do first.

After a rather confusing conversation, I realized that they were not existing in time: there *was* no time for them. They were seeing situations that they felt they needed to be part of, and once those was done with, they would walk into death and back into life.

Those two incidents in my life—one just after their death, then another ten years later—were both happening at the same time for them. They were not hanging around for years; rather they were popping into the flow of life as they saw need to, and that flow was at different stages of time in the physical world. I found this fascinating: they were not aware of the lapses of time in my life. It changed dramatically how I perceived the dead and how time worked for them. It also answered many questions I had struggled with.

For example, a priestess friend of mine who died had appeared to me shortly after death, then again a few months later. I had worked with her in the death vision for two weeks and slowly walked her through death and beyond. But years later they appeared to me again at a time of need, and I could not understand how they had come back after going into death so deeply. What had happened was that when they had died, they saw 'lights' go on in friends who really needed help, and they attended to those lights as any priestess would. Once that work was done, they walked deeper into death to sleep, ready to be reborn.

To us, those 'lights' would have been scattered over decades, but to the dead it all happens at once. Our living concept of time is only really applicable to substance, not to spirit or consciousness.

So if you get a visit from the newly dead, and your microwave blows up or your lights all die, just tell them well done, you are proud of them, and they are welcome to be with you until they are ready to move on—which often is not long at all. It is worth remembering, however, that most magical homes will house magical tools and deities, many of which will block out the dead. It is compassionate to have one area or room of your home that does not have anything magical in it that would block out the dead, so that they have a place of sanctuary.

Fear of the dead is unwarranted, and has no place in a magician's world. That is the product of Hollywood, cheap novels, and dogmatic, decaying religions.

8.4 Living with the dead

Our current cultural model of the dead considers them unclean zombies who want to eat our faces off, who should be avoided at all costs. People raised with a fear of the dead and an ignorance of the dying process have that fear embedded within them from a early age, and it can be a terrible struggle to overcome it. But really, the dead that hang around are more frightened and confused than you are a lot of the time. As a magician it is important to confront and dissolve your irrational fears that stop you from doing your work.

The dead seek out those who can hear, see, or feel them, and they seek out people whom they hope will not ignore them. Often they want something specific. Sometimes they want to be around you for a short while, particularly if they are family members, or they may want to guard you, or stay a while to bathe in magical energy. Their reasons for staying somewhere are as numerous as living humans' are, and some reasons are good, and some are bad.

If you choose to let a ghost stay in your house, keep a constant awareness of them when you do magic so that you do not accidently catapult them out of the house. Do not give them offerings, as this would encourage parasites to come along for the ride. This can result in the dead person having to try and fight off a parasite that wants to use their spirit to interface through and demand more 'food.' A normal dead person will not ask for substances: they will want songs, and they will want you to remember them and acknowledge them. If they start asking for food, drink, tobacco, etc., then you have either a composite being (dead person plus land spirit) or something masquerading as the dead which is hoping for an energetic meal. Know what you are letting live in your home!

The resident dead will come, and go, sometimes vanishing for months before returning. Just let them do their thing, and you do yours: you really begin to forget they are there until they try to catch your attention. As a working magician, they can be helpful in letting you know what is coming, if there is danger around you, etc. This is kind of a modern version of the ancient Sleepers (see below). You learn to work together by close observation of the cues that they put out, and finding ways to communicate productively.

I use a mixture of tarot, listening, dreaming, smells, sounds, and occasionally having a phone thrown at me—a desperate attempt by a ghost to say "talk to me!" But your work must not become reliant on the dead, just as they must learn not to rely on the living. They will vanish when they are ready, and when that happens, you know you have done a good job for them.

8.5   Longer-term hauntings

This can be interesting and complicated, depending on when in time the ghost was alive. If you are actively seeking a magical connection with the dead around you, and wish to work with them magically, then there are a few things you need to consider. One important point is that the cultural, magical, and religious ideas of the long-term dead can often be different from ours. This can cause a great deal of misunderstanding on both sides, so it is wise to tread carefully and take nothing for granted.

Usually, long-term dead—those dead for hundreds of years or more—tend to be tied to a particular place, and are there for a good reason. If you wish to work with them magically, then you need to understand what it is they are doing so that you do not inadvertently damage their work or block it in any way. To understand what they are doing you need to understand the social, religious, and cultural aspects of their time. In the UK, if someone was alive a few hundred years ago, then chances are their reason for staying is family or property based: they will be guarding or trying to interact with a family who most likely are no longer there. The culture in England over the last thousand years has been broadly Christian, and that has to be taken in account: very rarely are Christian ghosts willing to work with magicians.

Older ghosts—Saxons, Romans, Celts, and Picts—are more likely to be still around because they are guarding something, usually a sacred burial or other special place. Again, you have to take this into account: realize that they will be more or less limited to working in that area, and in a limited capacity.

8.6 Working with the ancient dead, or Sleepers

In the UK, once you get back to pre-Celtic tribal societies, things change dramatically in terms of magical communication. In Britain, you are probably talking Bronze age, Neolithic, or earlier. In countries like the US you only have to reach back a few hundred years: it really depends on the land, its history, and the people who have lived there.

These older societies worked differently from ours, and their dead also work differently from our recent dead. Ancient burials have Sleepers, watchers, and guardians, all of whom played an important role in the upkeep and general well being of the tribe. Some tribes would have special burials around them or in key places, and these would act as 'Sleepers.' Sometimes the bones of certain dead would be carried around as a working member of the tribe, and would provide advice and protection.

As magicians we can work with these burials if they are willing to work with us. However, the methods of approach, communion, and interaction with these ancient burials are different from working with the more recent dead. With the ancient dead, you have to automatically presume that there is a land spirit interwoven with the consciousness of the ancestor. While this may not always be the case, it is a pretty safe assumption that the burial will house a composite being, and treating it accordingly will get the communion going a lot quicker.

When the consciousness of a person has been deep in the land for a long time, it begins to connect with and interact with the spirits of the land around the burial. Over time the two merge, at least from our perspective. When you go and talk to an ancient burial, if they agree to talk back to you, you are potentially accessing wisdom, and information from both the dead *and* the consciousness of the land spirits in that area.

There are a multitude of faery tales, myths, and legends of princesses, warriors, queens, kings, and even whole armies sleeping in the depths of a hill, who will come alive when they are needed most by the nation or tribe. These tales can be found all over the world. Careful study of these old myths and stories can tell you a great deal about the power of the land around them. This is an echo of the old wisdom of these burials, and as magicians we can tap into them, if they wish to commune with us. Sometimes they just tell you to piss off. Sometimes there are human remains, but no spirit or soul.

8.7 Working with burials or bones

There are a few different ways of working with the long dead who are still around. The first thing to think about is why they are still around. Sometimes they are angry, and are waiting for revenge: this is something to be aware of, and a good reason to tread carefully. Sometimes they are ritually trapped because of some crime they committed in their own culture, or they were cast out for reasons that we may not understand. Not every ancient burial is good to connect with: let caution be a byword.

Often an ancient soul is still within the land because of a sense of service to the people living on the land. Some cultures call such souls Sleepers. While populations and cultures do shift and change, burials will rarely care about this so long as key elements of communion are activated.

Those keys depend largely on the cultural framework and spiritual system of the burial. However, the longer they sleep in the land, the more the Sleeper's surface cultural interface will dissolve and the broader their understanding will become. So certain elements of communion with the living will be loosened, but the underlying sense of service will still be there.

For example, a Sleeper in the British Isles will be concerned with the health of the land and its people, and will protect against invasion and warn of coming weather or natural disasters. Roots of this can be found in the story of Bran in British mythology, as well as the later stories scattered throughout the European landscape of warriors sleeping in hills and mountains.

In India, and Pakistan there are Sufi saints from the fourteenth and fifteenth centuries whose tombs are a focal point for both Muslims and Hindus searching for spiritual peace, a sense of balance, and harmony within the mixed population. These saints remain within the tombs and act as interfaces to guide those who visit them, connecting to the pilgrims through their dreams, prayers, and experiences.

We also see this within Catholicism: saints are visited for help with specific things, usually illness and disaster. What is interesting with this presentation is that often the bones of the saints are the focal point rather than a burial itself. Often the bones were not of particular people—there was a lot of dodgy relic business going on in times past—but the tuned focus of people's prayers over hundreds of years has created a spiritual interface or threshold that beings can operate quite well through.

The burial of Tin Hinan, matriarch of the Berber tribes, was a focal point for the people. They would go to sleep on her burial mound, and interact with her through their dreams. Similarly the Sleeper in the high Altai region of Mongolia, known popularly as the Ice Maiden, was considered the keeper of the tribes on that land. Today the tribal authorities are in conflict with the Russian Government over the return of her body, which was removed by archaeologists.

These ancient burials are important for us magically, as they are a direct magical link between the past, present, and future of the land and its tribes. Magically it is important to continue that generational interaction with them in a way that is acceptable to the Sleeper.

The first rule of thumb is to throw out any New Age ideas of connecting through leaving crystals, polyester ribbons, and other such mindless trash.

Each regional burial will have generated stories among the people that guide a person on the right approach to a burial. I spoke in *Magical Knowledge Book Two* about visionary methods for working with Sleepers, so here I will concentrate on the outer methods.

If you are not certain about how to approach a burial, there are two methods that are simple and are universally understood. The first is to give the sort of gifts that every tribe around the world would appreciate; the second is to make a connection through blood and utterance.

Honey is a universal commodity that breaks down barriers. It is full of magical energy, it harms nothing if it is left out in the environment, and it has always been a valuable commodity. Give good quality honey as a gift to the ancestors by placing it directly on the land—don't leave it in its jar! Smear it on a rock or pour it on top of the burial: this gives energy to the spirits and feeds the land and its creatures, which always scores points with ancestors. It breaks the ice, and is a 'good manners' gift to help open lines of communication. The only burial this would not be given to is one still within a specific religious or cultural framework like the Sufi burials, where an imam would overlook your interactions, telling you what gifts to give and where to pray.

When trying to connect to a tribal burial, once the honey is given, a song or poem would be the next step. In times past, when the skill of music was displayed only on rare visits by wandering musicians or poets, such an offering had a high status. By singing or reciting, you catch the deeper attention of the burial guardians and show that you have respect for the person buried there: you are taking the time to connect with them. The next step would be to prick your finger and leave a drop of your blood on the burial: you are giving of yourself, and all your ancestors before you, to honour and connect with the bloodlines.

Magically this is all a gentle yet powerful way of building a relationship with a Sleeper. Once the blood is dropped, sit quietly on the mound and just be still. How do you feel? Have your emotions shifted? The emotions are a good gauge of power interactions with spirits. If you feel still, or happy, or comfortable, then you have settled the guardians and will be able to build a connection with the Sleeper. If you feel anxious, afraid, or uncomfortable, chances are the guardians want you to leave, for whatever reason. If this happens, then leave the burial alone.

The next step is to find the way that the Sleeper interacts. It could be through dreams, vision, or outer keys. If it is through direct vision, then you will have an almost overwhelming desire to go in vision to talk to the Sleeper. See yourself either go down into the mound, or stand in vision on the land, and connect with them.

If they work through dreams, then you will be prompted to pick up a bit of earth or a small stone, and take it home to put under your pillow or leave in your bedroom. Or you could do what I do, which is to lie down on the mound and promptly fall asleep. Dream work with Sleepers can be difficult where there are cultural barriers to understanding: the visual and emotional keys given by Sleepers can be heavily misunderstood if you do not know the mythological patterns of their culture. I have often found that when I sleep on sacred burials, I go into a deep, strange sleep but have no memories of dreams other than snatched images. But the contact unfolds itself slowly, and over the following week or two I will start to get nudges of contact.

Sleepers or ancient burials work within their own framework from the time when they lived, so they may talk in dreams through creatures, birds, patterns, or land presentations. If that happens, and you do not understand what is being shown to you, then try to research further into the myths and stories of that culture.

If the Sleeper is powerful then they may try to connect with you through external cues or keys. This could be the appearance of a specific bird, insect, or animal at times of importance. Again you would need to read those keys in the context of the tribal stories of that person.

A lot of this work is experimental. We have lost so much knowledge of this phenomenon, and we can only regain ground through trial and error. Success will also depend on your own culture and your ability to be open-minded, yet able to differentiate between fantasy and reality. The older the Sleeper or ancient ancestor, the more mythological their presentations will be in terms of keys and visual language.

One thing that can be a major help is to make sure that you try as much as possible to see the world from their perspective. Try to go with what they would find acceptable: don't enforce what you feel they should want, or what you feel you need or wish to do. Approaching some of these powerful Sleepers with an egocentric "heal me, teach me, empower me" attitude can result in a hard slap. Or you may simply be ignored.

Another important thing to think about: where is the burial in relation to you? Sleepers often only operate within a small radius of their burial. So dream work will often only work if you sleep on, or near the burial. Though there are exceptions: certain burials have long-reaching action across the land. You really have to figure this out as you work. Some burials are meant to be only occasionally visited: these tend to be ones that offer help, advice, and guidance, like the Sufi saints. That is where the concept of pilgrimage came from.

If you live close to the burial that you wish to work with, then a much deeper relationship can be built over time. But this again comes with its downsides. Unless you have clear magical boundaries of what you are willing and able to offer the burial, you can end up with the spirit of the Sleeper trying to take up your whole life, demanding attention, work, and dictating

135

what kinds of magic you can and cannot do. You need to think long and hard about what level of communion, and what services, you are willing to offer.

8.8 Working with bones

As I write, Vodou and similar paths are the height of fashion in the magical community. These paths work directly with bones in various ways, sometimes very successfully, but a lot of thought needs to go in what effect you are having on the spirit connected to the bones, and how that relates in a wider sense to the land and the spirits around you.

At the moment there is a brisk market for buying bones from around the world and working with them. When you do this, you have no idea of the culture or the spiritual interface of the person who was connected to the bones, what type of person they were, or what they intentions are. This can open a huge bag of worms. You are using a magical interface without knowing all the parameters: you have no idea what you are working with.

In our internet age, cultural appropriation is big business. People have been told if their intentions are okay, then all will be okay. That is not necessarily true: magical dynamics do not work that way. Bones can just be bones, with no spirit connection within them, or they can be still heavily connected to the person who was once constructed with those bones. There is no way to tell until you have the bones in your home... and by then it can be too late! So many magicians these days are attracted to the old custom of working with a skull, for example; but they often do not think about how this process originally came about. In today's world you can simply buy a skull: this circumvents the whole magical filtering process, and places you in a different line of power which can be unhealthy at worst, and useless at best.

There are some easy magical ways to circumvent these problems. The first way to avoid such a mess is to be thoughtful about how the bones come to you. If you are at a magical phase, regardless of what magical path you are walking, and it is time for you to work with the long-term dead, then bones will find a way to come to you. They will either be given as an unexpected gift, or you will find them.

Instead of getting excited and acting like a kid with a new toy, it is better to tread cautiously, and find out as much about the bones as you can magically. This can be done using a divination vocabulary like tarot (or whatever works best for you). Ask questions like: "Is there still a spirit connected to the bone?" "Are they ritually bound there?" "Who is this person: male or female, elder, magician, priest or priestess, mother, criminal, father?" "What do they need from me?" And most importantly: "Are they willing to work with me?"

If bones, and particularly skulls, come to you through magical ways, as gifts or finds, then there is probably a job to be done, for them and for you. This is how inner magical filters work. You will come to a stage in your magical life when it is important to learn a specific magical skill, and the tools to enable you to learn it will turn up on your doorstep. Bear in mind, if this happens, that the learning will come about through you being prompted to do a job: that is how this form of learning works.

Just be willing to work with what crosses your path and stay open-minded. This will help the inner flows of power work with, and through you. So what comes to you is meant to be with you. The other dynamic to be aware of is that sometimes bones will wish to be with you only for a limited time. You have to be willing, and able, to let go of them when the time comes.

This is harder if you have spent hundreds of dollars, and taken ages to find, 'your skull,' only to have to bury it or pass it on. It is also about taking magic out of the toy box mentality. A real magician is able to accept and let go of power as it flows in and out of their life.

Working with bones and skulls can take various forms. How it works will depend on the power or spirit within the bones, what they need, and what you are trying to achieve. Sometimes they become prophetic tools, or voices of warning, or teachers that operate through your visions and dreams. Sometimes they are more outward tools in that they simply live alongside you and slowly drip-feed you information. Or they may guard your work or living space, or open gates within it. The key, as with all powerful magical things, is to be open-minded, clear, and watchful. Make sure you spot the method of interaction that the bones are using, be it dreams, visions, nudging your emotions, being present at workings, or something else. If you are observant both of your space and your mind, then the working method will become apparent, and that method will be far more powerful than any method dictated by a current magical trend.

The exception to this rule is when you are still living within the culture that the bones came from, and you are still operating within a traditional path of magic that the spirit of the bones recognizes. That is rare these days, but it still does exist. In such a case, the shared spiritual and cultural context between you and the bones will dictate how best to work with them. But for most of us, that lovely option is no longer available.

I have the skull of a Bronze Age ancestor who lived and died in the land on which I now live. She and I have similar genetic lines, and she came to me unexpectedly. She worked with me for a while and taught me a great deal about the powers in the land around me. Then one day she impressed on me the need for her to go to sleep, so she was placed in a casket and hidden away. It is important to respect the wishes of the spirits within bones.

It is a sad reality of modern life that we have to relearn so much, and that is best done through direct experience and paying attention! Often the ancient bones that have spirit connections will also contain intermingled land beings, so it is wise to bear that in mind as a possibility. In such cases, it is often possible to directly connect with the land being beyond the bones, and the bones act almost as an introduction. This will become apparent if the signs and connections that flow from the bones affect you out on the land away from the bones. It is not that the spirit of the ancestor is following you around; it is more likely that the land being who connected to you through the bones has a sufficient connection to you that they can commune with you at will.

If this is the case, then you will be able to slowly ascertain the 'territory' of the land being by being aware of when the contact fades as you travel further from home. The beings I connected to through the skull fade off within a couple of miles of my home, so the land spirit entwined within the skull/spirit of the dead is specific to the land around my village. The skull came from farmland around the village, and the contact is much about specific land beings and power contained within the land. It connects with me through external signs and dreams.

8.9 Your own death

One of the major cornerstones of the Mysteries is learning to die properly. This is approached in a magician's training by learning to work in death in vision, by going through the full death visionary process in life, and by learning to interact with the beings who work within death in all its stages.

The death vision itself that Western Mystery magicians work with is ancient. It allows us, through the controlled use of our imaginations in structured vision, to interact with the powers, energies, and beings within death, and to learn the various stages that the spirit goes through. First we work in vision to learn the processes of death; later we then work in service with the newly dead, which prepares us on a deep level for an important step that all souls must go through.

The difference between dying as a magician and dying as a non-magician or mystic is that you will know, at the deepest level of your being, what to do. You will know how to react and how to interact with death, so that your transition is conscious and deliberate. Different cultures and Mysteries around the world have their own versions of the inner passage through death. Some have interesting similarities.

However, the visionary interface that we use is for the living: it allows us to form boundaries and images so deepest selves can interact, communicate, and learn. The images themselves are not that important: they are merely a vocabulary for our brains to decipher what is happening at an energetic level. With long-term practice, the interface images fall away, and we move into a deeper energetic pattern where we learn to be with such power in gnosis.

Alongside your visionary training, there are outer details that you also need to understand, practicalities that stand alongside the inner wisdom of death. Together they make sure that at your death you can move forward unfettered, calmly, and with deliberate intent towards your next step of existence. The inner visionary process is dealt with in *Magical Knowledge Book Two*, so here we will look only at the outer practicalities.

Death can be slow and expected or sudden and out of the blue. If the death is sudden then certain preparations cannot be done, but there are many others that can. Preparing for death is not something that should be put off until you are old; it is a process that should stretch through your life and be an integral part of your magical life.

8.10 Letting go

The first hurdle that needs to be overcome in life is the ability to let go. This is a major sticking point for many in both life and death, as our culture these days encourages people to cling to everything and everyone.

Letting go covers everything in our lives, and it is important, when something comes to an end—be it a job, a relationship, a house, an object, or a person—that we understand that everything is temporary and has a limited lifespan. Learning to accept change and loss, and to pick yourself up and move, marks a major maturation within magic and life itself. People cling to lovers that wish to move on just as they hoard or cling to objects they have no further use for, and they morn the death of someone to the point of destruction and refuse to accept change. This creates stagnation in power and in life.

There are simple ways to teach oneself how to move on, let go, and grow. The first is letting go of objects of desire that serve no real purpose with you but will help someone else. Practise giving things you really love to other people so that they can give them pleasure. Practice sharing: if you have two coats and need only one, then give the second coat to someone who has none. It's not rocket science, and it is not a new concept: it is part of the outer Mysteries.

If you lose the dream job of your life, then instead of descending into depression, look forward to the future: when the door slams shut, climb out of the window. If someone you love dies, mourn them, then move on. They no longer exist in that form, and though you may have wonderful memories, you must not pull them back with your pain. Let go of the grudges: in general, do not hang onto things. This can all sound New Age, but it is not: it is a true dynamic of how power flows in and out of your life. I have been through it all: I have lost jobs, homes, loved ones, all my belongings, and everything that I cared about on more than one occasion. But I survived and grew from these experiences because I was willing to let go and move on to find new horizons, forge new paths, and find interesting new things to clog my home up with after everything was taken from me.

On an inner level, this ability to let go develops an interesting dynamic, and allows you to be more fluid with power: it will stop you stagnating and ending up in emotional paralysis, which is something that hits many people when they die.

8.11 Knowing what death looks like

It is also important to know about the processes of death so that they do not catch you unawares. Dying can be a peaceful process or it can get messy, it depends how you are dying. I have been at many bedsides and roadsides as people have died, and the process can vary enormously. If you have a large family or if you work in a hospital or emergency services then you will probably see this for yourself. You can volunteer to sit with people who are alone and dying: a magical service that will teach you a lot about the human spirit and the processes it goes through.

Do be aware, though, that dying can be painful. It can be accompanied by the vomiting of blood, the voiding of one's bowels and bladder, choking, and fits; or it can be a slow drifting in and out, or a journey taken while asleep or in a coma. Either way, from a magician's perspective, the most important thing is stillness and connection.

This takes us back to the first thing that should be learned as a student magician: the skill of stillness and going into the Void. If that has been learned and worked with over a long period of time, then it will have become a deep second nature that follows intention. It can also kick in automatically in times of stress, danger, and death. The more it is worked with, the deeper the experience and the skill level becomes, until it is like breathing. I have been close to the death threshold physically a couple of times, as have many of us, and the deep stillness that the Void brings allows us to view the prospect of death without emotion, but simply as a process. As the beings appear, we recognize them, understand them, and we do not panic.

There is no one point in life that is your death time; rather there are a few points of contact scattered throughout your life. One will take you, whereas the others may take you close, giving you a preview of what is to come. Some people will have many of these points in their life, and some may have only one or two. Either way, the more you work with death, the more you will recognize it and learn to deal with it.

A major skill to learn in life that will have major bearing on your death as a magician is the discipline of controlling your wants and needs. For a non-magician this is not so important, but for a magician it is a major tool. As your spirit begins to go through the death process, it will still reflect the image, feelings, wants, and needs of the body it has just left. Part of the death process consists of wiping out your memory, culling your life's connections, loves, needs, and passions so that you can walk forward unfettered. This process is triggered by an urge which can become unbearable. Whatever your culture or beliefs, the same urge will present itself: the visionary interface used by the living to recognize this urge differs from culture to culture, but the underlying dynamic is the same.

In the Western Mysteries we understand it as a terrible thirst that grips your spirit as you travel across the Desert towards the River of Death and the mountains beyond (the Plain of Lethe). This is an ancient pattern used within the Mysteries—it is described the descent of Aeneas into the Underworld, for example—and though non-magicians generally view it as an allegory, it is not. It is a magical narrative interface that the spirit remembers so that it knows what to do. The ancients hid the patterns of the Mysteries in the myths and stories of the time.

As the spirit reaches the river, a non-initiate will drink to slake their thirst. An initiate of the Mysteries will simply wash their face to rid themselves of their previous identity: they will not drink. This enables them to retain their memories, and their magical training will make sure that they are not affected by them. This is achieved by developing a strong internal discipline within life, by not giving the body everything it desires but only what it needs, and only when it needs it. This internal discipline remains deeply embedded within your psyche so that on death, your spirit has the instinct of self-control.

By working as an initiate in the death vision in life, and learning to control and temper your basic instincts, you learn to act from a deep place of understanding rather than be driven by your impulses. This in turn allows you to make informed and controlled decisions about whether you want to continue in the cycle of life and death, or step out of that cycle and work as an inner contact. Or, if your work in life is finished, then you may wish to move deeper into the Inner Worlds, beyond life altogether. It is a major step in your deeper development not to be driven purely by instinct, but to engage the powers of existence consciously: it is the step into true gnosis.

8.12 What to do magically when you know you are dying

However the act of dying occurs, so long as you are conscious there are things you can engage, if it is possible, to smooth the passing both for yourself and for those to whom you are connected. If you die while unconscious, then it is the deeper training of your spirit that will take over, hence the importance of actively learning about death in life until such knowledge becomes second nature.

If you know you are right at the point of going into death, then it is really important to withdraw emotionally and intellectually from everyone and everything around you. Don't worry about any loved ones who are around you, nor about their emotional or physical wellbeing. It is important to focus on *your* process: the rest of the world can take care of itself. This is a simple but important dynamic: it is the first stage of letting go of everything and everyone, both for yourself and for their sake.

As an initiate, be still. Forget your memories and emotions, even if you are in pain. There is a threshold within the stillness that will let you step aside from your pain so that it is still there, but it washes through you rather than grips you. Focus on the stillness and the sense of stepping forward into the Void. Keep a sense of moving forward, going into something. This will enable your spirit, on the point of death, to immediately step forward into its journey. This is an energy dynamic of birth and death, not an actual 'movement': the vibration/energy of our pattern shifts, which to us is perceived as a movement: there is a *turning* into life, and a *forward* movement into death.

The other important thing to remember on the point of your death is to drop your fear. There is no need to fear death: this is why, again, it is important as a magician to work in death while in life. You get to see for yourself how it works and what it is like, first from a visionary interface in meditation, and later by spontaneous experiences. The spontaneous experiences of death begin to happen after you have worked through the visionary interface of death for a while. You cannot predict when these will happen, only that they will.

Such spontaneous experiences arrive in a couple of forms. One is as vivid and powerful dreams, usually at key times; the other is through being taken to the threshold of death by illness or accident. The experience of death can come to you in both forms, or in one of them. When it presents in dream form, you will know what it is. I will not describe it, as it is important that you experience it for yourself, and that you experience the confirmation of it from outer sources. You will dream various forms of death in vivid ways as is necessary for you, and it will be clear afterwards that it is a magically contacted dream. Shortly afterwards you will come across a text or a painting that describes exactly what you experienced. It is really important that these happen as genuine experiences, not ones coloured by my or anyone else's descriptions beforehand.

I had two vivid dreams, years apart, which showed me various stages of death. Each time, within weeks, I was given a book or a picture, randomly, and out of the blue that depicted exactly what I had seen, and was an ancient description of the death Mysteries from two different cultures. I mentioned this to a magical elder I respect, who explained that the same had happened to him and to his teacher. It is just something that happens within the Mysteries as you work through their layers.

Tasting death's threshold can also happen physically, where you nearly die but do not. If this happens then you will be given a glimpse of death as it literally gets in your face. You will not meet Death as a tunnel of light, as your auntie May, or as Jesus; nor will you see landscapes of happy virgins. But you may see the pattern of death, or the being that bridges you from life to death—in the Western Mysteries this is an angel of death.

Either or both of these experiences will teach you a lot at a deep level about what the process of death will be like for you, so when you do stand on the threshold of death when it is your time, you can step forward in full knowledge and confidence. Death is a major transition yes, it can be a difficult one; but it is also an amazing, powerful, and magical transition. It is not an end; you as a being do survive, and you will be aware of that survival, just in a non-physical form. That understanding does away with the fear of the unknown—which is important so that you can transition intelligently.

The other fear that grips people is unfinished business or the protection of their dependents and children. If you do have unfinished business in physical world, then you just have to let go of it: there is basically nothing you can do about it. If you have some emotional needs connected with the world of the living then basically the same rule applies, but you do get some leeway. There is a period of time after death and before burial during which you can say goodbye, visit people, etc. You can also use this time to intervene magically—if it is necessary—if you see one of your close family or friends is in a dangerous magical situation and is out of their depth. It may not correlate to the time between your death and burial in terrestrial terms, as there is no time within death. But it is a time when if you are focused, you can look at the wider patterns that were connected to your life, and see if there is an absolute need for intervention for someone. You will perceive it at that time, just after death, but in material world terms, it could be happening at any time.

I have had help in certain situations which has come from family members just after their death. But usually the help came at that material time, before their burial, when I was in sore need of magical guidance and help with a difficult situation.

The more you look into death from an esoteric point of view, the more you will begin to see how and why it is important that you go into death with gnosis, wisdom, and stillness, so that you can actively engage with the process and be consciously aware of what is happening to you.

Over the years, I have had enough startling experiences, while working with the dead, to begin to understand the process—and to have extinguished my doubts, though questioning yourself is always important. I have realized how powerful, complex, and beautiful the whole process is. The only real way to learn about death is to work from within it magically, and hopefully the fragments of information in this chapter will help others find their own magical feet within death, and take their work further.

Chapter Nine

Weaving power into form

Chatting with the Three Fates

When you really start to dig deep into the power of magic and use the combination of inner and outer patterns of ritual/vision to instigate a magical action, then something interesting starts to happen. You become aware of the waves and frequencies of power that are constantly flowing in and out of our physical world.

In the visionary pattern of the Tree of Life, or what I call the Desert landscape, we observe in vision formless power flowing to us from Divinity across the Abyss, passing through a complex pattern at the point of Da'at: the Metatron Cube. This is a focused collection of thresholds and filters, in magic perceived as angelic beings. Da'at starts the process of forming Divine power into manifestation, a process which completes as it passes over the threshold of Malkuth. The completed power expresses itself out in the world as a vibrating energy which eventually becomes physical matter. This can be perceived as the waves of power/frequency/vibration that underpin physical expression, but also underpin or at least affect non-physical expression, like thought, emotion, magic, etc. We can observe this energy wave if we stand in vision on the threshold of Malkuth. Once our minds have been introduced to the phenomenon in vision it becomes much easier to perceive it in the world around us.

When we are conducting magic at a level of frequency that corresponds to one of these 'waves' of expressed power, we tap into that wave briefly. This gives our magic a massive boost—have you ever done a small magical working, and it had a massive effect way beyond what you expected? In turn, our conscious magical action when in harmony with the wave adds to the stream of energy, giving it a small boost for a second or altering it slightly.

I have found these waves to be far more powerful than we can currently comprehend. They seem to be the power source, or tide, for changes in many things, including consciousness, weather, civilizations, and physical matter. Some of these expressions, in human terms, are vast, and though we can tap into them briefly we will probably never understand their eventual externalized results. As the wave slows its frequency or organizes itself into a discernable outer pattern, it manifests in something, be this a huge change in consciousness or a physical expression like a natural event.

As magicians we can—and often do without realizing it—tap into and interact with these power streams as we conduct a magical act. But to tap into them consciously for a specific purpose we need to understand what frequency of power the wave is, how its frequency eventually manifests, and how it will affect what we do. That is currently beyond my understanding, and it raises many questions concerning cause and effect and responsibility.

I think this is where the concept of taking a conditional action with an unconditional intent comes in. So for example, we can be aware of a particular wave of power building up and consciously engage it (ritual, vision, weaving), but without a specific intent other than being a link in the chain. This particular action changes the human action from magical to priestly, from manipulative to serving.

It can be used intentionally for a conditional purpose: you certainly can ride the wave, if it is a power compatible with what you are trying to achieve, by tapping into its power to drive whatever magical pattern you are working with. Personally I would be wary of doing this before I had a really good understanding of what I was interacting with. You might accidentally be using a nuclear reactor to light one light bulb.

To intentionally work with this source of power needs a certain level of plasticity in your thinking and working method. You need an ability to work in more abstract ways than usual in ritual and vision. This plasticity comes from being able to think outside the box while having a solid foundation of magical understanding and experience to draw on. You start with what you know works, and develop your experimentation from that foundation.

If the dogmatic patterns of a magical path—like the Golden Dawn, for example—are strictly adhered to, then such abstract work is virtually impossible. Equally, if you have little foundational training and experience—as is frequently the case for Chaos magicians—then your consciousness will be too feral to sustain the complex and disciplined actions needed to interact with these powers. Studying the Mysteries of Kabbalah can potentially prepare you to work with these power patterns, but such study must not be weighed down by religious overlays, Hermetic abstractions, or hazy New Age feelgood thinking.

Working in ritual and vision, using a method in which the patterns of power, their elemental expressions, and their physical manifestations are acknowledged without dressing them in belief structures allows you to first learn to recognize power at work, then to engage actively with that power.

It is not within the capabilities of every magician to pick up on these power fluctuations. But for those who can, it can be a very interesting experience to move beyond the simple recognition that there is something powerful going on, and to consciously, actively engage with it. I developed my own method of working with these waves of power, using vision and outer action: I experimented with engaging the power then painting, writing, or weaving energy 'blind' in ritual. By that I mean standing in vision and seeing these waves of power, then using hand movements to weave it into a substance, be it rock, paper, fabric, or something else.

This active engagement of power/energy can also be used in group ritual, tapping into the waves in walking vision, bringing them through in the ritual action, and working with them as a group. It can be used to effect necessary change within the land if it is woven/mediated into the land beneath you as you work. The conscious use of the power to effect change using focused thought and action certainly does seem to engage this power and tune it to specific effect.

What are the long-term consequences of engaging with this power? I have no idea, as I have not been experimenting in this way long enough to know. This is where keeping tight diaries and records is important, so that every step discovered is recorded, and any long-term effects can be referred back to the original working method. This is how we learn what to do, what not to do, and what to adjust in our working practice, intent, and preparation.

Around the same time that I discovered this phenomenon (maybe I have reinvented a wheel that everyone except me knows about?) I began to come across pictures, writings, and temples of ancient weaving goddesses, and finally understood the deeper mechanics behind their power. They started showing up everywhere all a sudden as if to say, "did you get that?"

It then occurred to me to experiment in many different ways with this wave of power both a power source and as it relates to building, dismantling, and maintaining things.

9.1 Using weaving skills in magical defence

Once you have understood the dynamics of power/wave/pattern forming, you will begin to realize that all magic is really constructed by manipulating power in patterns then launching them.

It does not matter what deity, spirit, sigil or utterance is used in a magical attack: for it to take form and work it must have power and that power must have form. The patterns are formed by the type of magic used and the beings involved. The intent fires it, and off it goes.

Usually to dismantle a magical attack, curse, or binding that has been formed and sent, you would work within the tradition of the sender, or work with the same type of beings to take the attack apart. If the attack is simple, then that is all that is required. But if the attack is dangerous, large, and fuelled by a group of people, then you need to reach underneath the surface presentation and take the living structure apart or reform it. Reforming and reusing it is an interesting way to work through these problems, as it tends to kill more birds with one stone, so to speak.

The technique itself is simple, but it relies heavily on your mental focus, discipline, and visionary skills. The first step is to identify what elemental fuel has been used in the attack: fire, water, earth, or air. If it was fire, then the first step would be to light a flame. You focus on the flame, seeing it in your inner vision and simultaneously with your physical eyes.

Once that focus is there, you begin to tune into the feel of the attack, and who or what has been attacked. Looking at the flame, you use your imagination to see the attack as a three-dimensional pattern within the flame. That image is built up until you become aware of the beings involved within the attack. Once the inner pattern is exposed within the element, it becomes easier to discern what beings are also part of the attack.

You then ask the beings to 'pull the pattern out tight,' like stretching chewing gum. This breaks up the outer presentation of the attack without losing the power or contacts that drive it. You imagine the power pattern changing from a three-dimensional pattern in the flame to a pulled-out two-dimensional image, similar to a loom weave or long threads pulled tight. This is the beginning of working with the wave pattern of power and learning to manipulate and change it, albeit in a small way.

Once the pattern has been pulled tight—which basically wipes clean the structure of the attack—then it is time to use its raw materials to build a proactive protection. Instead of using the power to weave a protection around yourself, which has many inherent problems, weave a protection that filters the magic *at source*. Working with the beings involved with the pattern, ask the beings to reform the pattern with you, to create a filter to be placed over the attacker like a badly-knitted sweater. The filter is to be designed to filter out all references, contacts, connections, and images of the person on the receiving end of the attack so that their attacker can no longer see them or connect with them energetically: as a result, the person on the receiving end of the attack simply energetically vanishes.

The directions given to the working beings need to be specific: "create this filter to filter out anything to do with the victim, so that when the attacker has this filter placed over them, they will no longer perceive the victim magically or through their readings or perceptions, and they will not be able to energetically connect in any way, so that the victim will simply vanish from the reach of the attacker."

All this is uttered into the flame with the stretched-out pattern, and you observe as the beings reform the pattern into a new shape. Once that new shape is ready, and you are sure that the instructions are correct, then it is time to engage the filter. This is done by once more focusing on the pattern in the flame, and focusing on the intent to send it back to whomever sent the magic in the first place. You tell the flame, the pattern, and the beings that the filter is to completely surround the original attacker so that they can no longer see, perceive, or connect in any way with the attack's victim. Upon that declaration, the flame is blown out and the power is sent off to go and do its job.

This must be done a couple of times a day until the curse, bindings, or attack begins to dismantle and fade away. Usually it just takes a few days, and then it is up to you to keep an eye out to make sure everything stays calm. If the attacker is clever or has a deep understanding of magic, then they will eventually discover the filter and find a way to take it off. So it is important to stay alert and learn to adapt and change your protection methods.

This method, besides being effective, will also teach you about how power can be woven, and how to see weaves of power. This in turn prepares you for deeper engagement with the waves of power that flow from Malkuth.

9.2 Pattern recycling

Once you grasp the enormity of the revelation that everything around you is fuelled and shaped by energy with its own wave pattern, a pattern that can be restructured using magic, then the magical doors will really start to open. It is this fundamental understanding of the patterning of power that underpins all magic. It does not matter what system, path, religion, or philosophy you use; the pattern of power is where magic flows from. All the rest of the dressing is just that. That is not to say that systems and paths are not important: they are, very much so. Magical paths and systems enable you to grasp concepts, learn skills, and develop boundaries, and they facilitate your first interactions with power through (hopefully) sensible filters.

Over time you will begin to understand that your path is only a lens or a filter for you to look through: actual magic is power and energy, and how that power and energy is interacted with. When you reach this stage, it is a good idea to work on perceiving this power and its natural waves in your everyday life. Everything has a natural pattern within it that can be not only perceived, but can be interacted with and manipulated. I began to experiment using a flame: I would look through the flame to help me see the energetic pattern of whatever was behind it. I used the flame as a lens to see the world around me in a different way.

Using this method takes time and practice: your brain needs to learn how to interpret the data it receives so that your mind can build an understanding of what you are observing. My first observation was that natural things like trees, plants, and rocks had a certain quality of pattern that was harmonious. The patterns themselves were different, but they all had a defined quality of 'neatness' about them. Man-made objects were a different matter. Their patterns were diffuse in some cases and complex or excessively structured in others. Some patterns were clumsy and dense, others haphazard. I was fascinated. It took me a little while to realize what I was seeing in this exercise.

The man-made objects were created from different substances that each had their own pattern. The different patterns had been squished together, and it kind of worked with some objects, and was rather chaotic with others. I then began to experiment with trying to alter the inner patterns of various man-made objects, and something began to feel familiar: I realized I was looking at a deeper method of enlivening sacred objects and creating magic with substance.

When a statue or image is enlivened, or a deity is mediated in substance, the pattern of the substance itself changes to accommodate the power shift. I knew this intellectually, but I had never seen it happen so directly. By experimenting and observing I was able to discern the changes to the energetic power and frequency of a substance when I worked on it magically. By recognizing that change, and recognizing what it changed into, I was able to identify the signature of a specific energy change. So for example, when enlivening a statue with the power of a deity, I experienced a specific change in the energy pattern of the structure of the substance. It harmonized the slightly chaotic pattern of the man-made statue and changed it into a beautiful harmonic pattern that shone with power. Cool!

I have found the flame to be the easiest elemental form to use for such power observations. Water comes a close second. It did take me a while to build the capacity to perceive and work with these waves and patterns: I achieved it simply through perseverance and practice. You have to train your imagination to work in a specific way, to imagine seeing patterns in a flame while also looking at the flame with your eyes open. It does take time to get used to that. But once your brain gets the idea of what you are trying to achieve, it will all start to click into place.

Don't worry about the age-old magical dilemma of imagination versus reality. With practice you will begin to notice the difference. The one thing I will say about these methods is that they will not work for a beginner: the methods of weaving power need total focus, an already-developed ability to mediate power, and the ability to hold an inner contact while working. But once that training is in place, then these methods of weaving energy can become powerful.

9.3 Working with weaver goddesses

Once you have worked with basic power weaving, then you should look in depth at weaver goddesses, as it will give you a much deeper understanding of their power. Historians generally look at these goddesses as weavers of cloth and connect them to early agriculture. Nothing could be further from the magical truth of their power.

When you work with these deities, the first thing you realize is that these goddesses are not only ancient and powerful, but they also preside over war, death, and fate. Neith, Frigg, and the Greek Moirai are examples of the many Northern Hemisphere goddesses who preside over fate, weaving things into existence. When this is related to weaving the outcomes of wars, they are presented as warrior goddesses.

Using the knowledge and experience gained by working magically with power weaving, we can work closely with these deities to repair damage done to fate patterns by magical attacks. To try to interfere with a fate path or war outcome for our own agenda would be folly, but we can work unconditionally with these goddesses to try and understand the long-term impact of fate on a nation, a people, or a bloodline. We can also assist or partake of the action by working as assistants with these powers, following their path of action and agenda, not our own. It is important, when you are working with such ancient and powerful goddesses, to understand when it is safe to be involved actively with fate weaving, and when it is not.

If a human has constructed magic that is interfering with a fate path, then it is acceptable for a human to intervene to alter that interference with the help of these goddesses. If we appeal to these powers for help, say in times of severe conflict, and they agree to help, then assisting them by working in vision or ritual with them is also okay. But it is important that you follow their lead, their action, and their agenda, not your own: *they know what they are doing, you do not.*

If, however, you are simply curious or you have a specific agenda, and you try to work through these deities to weave the power yourself, then you are most likely to get an unpleasant backlash. It would be akin to a child going into an industrial carpet-weaving factory and sticking their hands in the mechanised looms.

However, if you are wishing to work on yourself, or you wish to work on something small, particularly if it is a problem caused by magic, then working with and through these goddesses is fine—but ask them first. Tell the deities what you are trying to achieve, ask them if it is wise to do what you are trying to do, and if all is okay, then work through them or have them work through you to achieve what you are trying to do.

So for example if you wished to work on someone or something whose pattern had been damaged by magical actions, then you would start the action from externalization. Firstly you would tune the altar you are working with to the weaver goddess that you work with, and ask her if she would be willing to work with you on the task. Some people commune with the deities using vision; others use a conversation interface through tarot readings. Experiment with what works best for you.

9.4 Magical weaving

You will need a candle, an altar or table as a focus, and a bowl to burn paper in. You will also need paper and a pen.

The first action of externalization would be to draw out a pattern that externalizes the inner pattern of the person or object to be worked on. This is very much an act of creation and intuition: follow your instincts and learn to work freely without the need to follow strict steps and rules. The name of the person or place would be around and within the pattern, and the drawing out of the pattern would include the areas of damage. Do not express these areas of damage intellectually: let your imagination guide you. This way, the deity can begin to work through you from the start of the action.

The finished pattern may or may not resemble the shape of the person, which is not really a major requirement. What is a major requirement is that your mental focus of intent is directed towards the fact that what you are drawing is the energy grid of the recipient of the work. The full name of the person in the pattern helps with that, but your use of imagination and your intent matters more. Let your hand guide you: the source of the damage may be different from what you think it is. As you are drawing out the patterns, you will be nudged to express the damage in certain areas. Trust that instinct and let it strengthen.

The next stage is ritual. This is simple but important: name the pattern formally. Voice your acknowledgement of the presence of the goddess you are working with, name the pattern—"I name thee X"—then ask the goddess, and the beings that work with and through her, to work on the pattern with you.

Once that is done, then comes the visionary work. Standing before the altar, close your eyes and see the drawing in your imagination. See the goddess standing on the other side of the altar, and see the power flowing through the pattern, and where the pattern is broken. The use of your imagination to trigger the work tells the beings and deity what you are trying to achieve. Ask the goddess for beings to work through you, to assist and teach you in your work. You will get the sense of beings building up behind you ready to work. Take your time with this: for some people the act of triggering magical interactions using their imagination is easy, but for others it can be hard. Give yourself time to build the power and intent.

Once you feel the presence behind you, look at the pattern on the altar, and notice that it has become bigger and is no longer just a drawing: it has become the living pattern there on the altar with you. You will see broken patterns and weak areas. See yourself pick up the broken threads. The moment you touch them, you will feel arms passing through your arms and working through you. When you feel that, surrender your logic and just let your arms work.

You will find yourself weaving the damaged threads back together and reconstructing the original pattern. You will know when the job is done because the sense of beings working through you will come to an end and they will withdraw. Upon that withdrawal, open your eyes, place the drawing in a bowl, and burn it while seeing the whole pattern as a pattern of light still remaining on the altar.

Ask the beings who were working with you to bridge the pattern of light into the person or object that is being worked on. Look into the candle burning before you, and imagine that completed pattern held in the flame. Take your time with this step, and let the image of the pattern build in the flame. Once it is strong in your mind's eye, blow the flame out and voice out loud that you are sending the pattern to its owner. Ask the beings to make sure that it is properly delivered and absorbed by the person or place. If the pattern was for yourself, then as you blow out the flame imagine it flowing into you and settling within you.

Leave the candle burning on the altar, and offer the weaver goddess bread, wine, water, and salt in thanks for her work. If she asks for anything else then give it to her without question or hesitation. The sending of the altered inner pattern will be absorbed by the person or object, and will slowly unfold in its own time. Keep a watch on events, the healing of the person, etc. so that you can learn how it works in action. If the damage was extensive then it will take time to unfold and heal, but you will see more immediate, subtle shifts as the healing process is catalysed.

9.5 Weaving by utterance

This form of magical weaving is far less ritualized. It is free-flowing and more 'shamanic,' for want of a better word. It would be used primarily on a patch of land that had been damaged or magically pinned or interfered with.

The tool for this work is simply your voice. What matters is repetition, focus of intent, and using your imagination to allow the weaver goddess or fates to work through you. The key is visiting the land or site in person every day for a certain length of time, and the rest of the day, tuning into the space to work from a distance. So really, this technique will only work if you are living or staying close to the space.

Every day that you walk towards the space, be aware of the deity you are working with as you walk. See them building up alongside you and their attendant beings all around you. As you arrive at the space, land, or rock, simply utter over the earth a simple single sentence of declaration. It would need to be tailored to the individual circumstance, but would be something like, "you are rewoven," or "you are whole," "you are strong and healthy." Note that the declaration is a positive one, not a negative one. This is of paramount importance: you need to instruct the pattern, the substance, and the attending beings what needs to happen.

For the rest of the day, every thirty minutes, stop what you are doing and see the place in your mind's eye. Utter the declaration, then continue with your ordinary tasks. Do this all day every day for the set length of time that you have dedicated to the task. This works like a dripping tap, putting focus and instruction on a particular thing to happen. Your focus directs the power, and your declaration instructs the beings what to do. All this is overseen by the deity. At the end of each day thank the deity for their assistance, and when the job is finished, leave her a gift by the space being worked on.

This method of working does not directly engage waves of energy or a pattern: you are not working directly in vision with the energy structures to bring change. Rather you are tuning into the deity that oversees an energy weave and focusing an intent, a request, for the deity and beings to actively engage the energy pattern. You act as a link in the chain by your intentional request and by bridging the action by the use of utterance with intent.

As with all magical weaving, you will often not see an immediate dramatic result—though that can happen—but you will see powerful results nonetheless. Magic takes time to filter through into a physical space, as it works through the natural tides of the land. But you will see results. I have had immediate dramatic results, and other times I have had results that were powerful and defined, but took a full four seasons to manifest.

One particular patch of land I worked on was a massacre site that still had all the fear, rage, and mental imbalance churning within the land. The area was renowned for being devoid of birds, and creatures: nothing would go there. Firstly I opened the gates to death to shepherd through the remaining spirits still trapped on the land. Next I worked to reweave the pattern of that patch of land, and to unhook the pattern of death/disaster from the substance of the land. I did that by working with utterance, then more directly in vision, using a weaving action in collaboration with the weaver goddess I was working with. Finally I opened the gates again and called in the directional elements to reset the land. So you see that in practical application, a variety of methods and techniques can be used as appropriate, layered one on top of the other.

Within days of finishing the work the birds returned, deer were spotted, and the trees started to look healthier energetically. It was a joy to see. Within a year the place was totally transformed, and had gone from a place that local people shunned to a place where children went to play and flocks of birds sat and chattered. Wild flowers were springing up all over the place. No 'magical power' of mine, or anything egotistical like that, had anything to do with this success. What brought about the success was simple magical dynamics: it was the right time, the right weaver goddess, and the right intent. It was like popping a boil. We are minor players, simple catalysts that come along at just the right time. Nature, and the Inner Worlds had already done their part; what was needed was a human catalyst who had the intent to bring about rebalance. When the damage is caused by humans, it is humans who must instigate the healing process.

9.6 Water

Similar types of work can be done with water. One can utter over water, then return the water to the river or stream so that it can spread out and work on the land as well as the waterways. This is a diffuse way of working, and can be used to heal vast tracks of land. And because water often goes underground, it can also effect change at a deep level not only for the land but also for the ancestral consciousness of the land.

Again the techniques are simple: the keys are still intent, picking the right deity, and repeating the utterance or sound. Just remember that water is immensely powerful, and that once something is poured into the river it will replicate over and over again until its pattern has spread out across the whole landmass that the river touches. As such it is important that the intention for healing be kept simple and to the point. It would also be good to commune with the consciousness or deity of the river first, to ask if they actually need or want your help. Often what we see as being a toxic, damaged river is already under some natural process of change or repair. So check first before you dive in to save the world. It might not want saving!

9.7 Summary

The magical action of weaving has endless applications and possibilities, from externalized action to deep and formless inner action. The more you work with it, the more you will recognize it in magical texts, mythical stories, and cultural applications. Old songs passed down from generation to generation that are about protection are a form of magical weaving: through the pattern that the song produces, a weave of ancestral protection is developed, which is passed on from mother to child.

Songs sung while women literally weave, particularly traditional songs about the family, the children, and the land, are woven into the fabric as they weave. That fabric would then make up the marriage bedding for a new family, and the song would be embedded within the fabric.

At the other end of the magical spectrum, kabbalists working in vision within the Tree of Life, particularly at the edge of the Abyss, often work to weave power and consciousness within the angelic patterns of physical manifestation. This is a key element of magical work, and one that is sadly overlooked.

The examples I have given you are just the tip of the iceberg for this form of magical work: most forms of magical weaving have to be individually discovered and developed. It is not a technique that can be easily passed along through text, as much depends on the traits and abilities of the individual, their culture, the strength of their imagination, and the weaver goddess who flows through their land.

You will have to experiment: find ways to work that are appropriate for you. The main step is to find the right deity to work with. There are many weaver goddesses, and various cultural expressions of the fates, but you will need to work with the ones who work strongly through your land. Every land has a version: find yours. Don't choose by fashion: don't decide you want to work with Ariadne because you love all Greek stuff! Look at the cultural, religious, and mythical patterns within your land and bloodlines, and see what comes up. Look at myth and legend, and also reach in vision into the land to see what presents. You can often be surprised by what emerges. *That* will work the strongest for you.

As magicians it is always important for us to push boundaries, experiment, stay curious, and be constantly willing to learn, to be surprised, and to be humbled.

Appendix A

Nature visions

Here are a couple of nature visions for you to work with if you wish to do magical service for the land, the forest, etc. You can record them and follow along while working in vision, but if you use this method, make sure you leave silences so that your deeper self has time to interact directly with the beings with whom you may cross paths.

This appendix also has a short story based around a stone circle in Northern Ireland that holds clues to working with stone circles.

A.1   Breathing with the forest

This is a simple vision to help you connect with nature and trees from an inner perspective. It is a more developed version of something I used to do as a child in the woodlands around where I lived. Where possible, it is best to do this vision outside on the land, sitting under a tree.

Seat yourself at the foot of a tree and lean against it. Close your eyes. Be aware of the flame of life housed deep within you in your centre. As you focus on your inner flame, feel yourself becoming still and silent. The everyday noise in your head slowly fades away as you breathe steadily and naturally, leaving you in a place of stillness, silence, and peace. With each breath you take, keep a focus on your inner flame and the stillness within. Bathe in that stillness, withdraw from intrusive thoughts and mental noise, and move deeper and deeper into the stillness.

As you become still, be aware of the tree that you are leaning against. Be aware of its size, strength, and life force, and feel your inner energy start to melt into the tree. Allow your hard barriers to soften so that you spirit can mingle with the spirit of the tree. Feel into the tree gently with your mind. Hold the thought of stillness as your mind slowly washes into the energy of the tree, and in that stillness, be aware of the energy of the tree, how it feels, and how it reacts to you. Be aware of any birds or sounds of nature around you as you melt your boundary, and allow the tree to feel into you. Feel yourself becoming part of the energy of the nature around you. Be aware of how your energy can spread out into the woodland or landscape, coming into silent energetic communion with everything around you.

The deeper into the stillness you go, the more aware you become of the tree's life force, and of the life force of everything around you. The rhythm of the tree is different from yours, and slowly you find yourself tuning into its pulse. Your breathing slows, and your consciousness starts to shift away from the human rhythm of life. You begin to tune deeper and deeper into the tree and the surrounding land. Your awareness of the outside world falls away as you join with the tree. All your awareness of your modern life has fallen away, and you sit in peace and stillness, breathing in the wind and air, and breathing out peace and silence.

You breathe as the tree breathes, slowly and peacefully. Your body rhythm slows right down, and the rhythm of your spirit slows even more. You merge deeper into the tree, feeling its age, its time, and how it moves so much more slowly through time than you do. You withdraw even further from your everyday self, feeling as if you are part of the tree. You feel the brightness of the life force of the tree, you feel your roots pushing deeper and deeper into the earth and your branches reaching up to the sky. You feel solid, silent, and connected. You feel all the forest around you, connected through your roots. You feel what the tree feels: you and the tree are one.

The days come and go, and you watch as the sun rises and falls. Leaves bud, push out, and bathe in the sunlight: you experience the joy as your leaves turn to the sun, drinking in the early morning goodness. Roots deep within the earth anchor you and the forest around you moves and breathes as one with you. Each individual tree is felt by you, yet they are all one being. As you breathe out, your breath passes through the forest; and as you breathe in, the power of the air nourishes each tree. You are truly at one with the forest.

The power of the land beneath you strengthens you, and the stars above you reach out their wisdom to you. With your head in the stars and your feet in the earth, all life passes through you as you become a bridge between the worlds. Humanity comes and goes, but the forest always remains.

Be aware of the stars above you and the Underworld beneath you. Be aware of yourself as a human who can bridge power from one place of being to another. Be aware of yourself as one who serves everything that needs service. Deep in your stillness, ask the forest what it needs. Be silent. Allow the answer to come back as a feeling, not as words. When you sense the feeling, hold that feeling.

Take in a deep breath and focus on the feeling that the trees communicated to you. With the intention of bridging whatever is necessary for the trees and forest, breathe out slowly. Feel yourself stretched between the stars and the Underworld, and allow whatever is necessary, whatever answers the forest's needs, to flow from these places, through you, and out through your breath. Take in another deep breath. Again, breathe out whatever is necessary. On the third deep breath, as you breathe out in the act of bridging whatever is necessary, finish the breath with a sound or word. Don't think about what that sound or word is, just let it flow through you and join with the air and wind around you. Externalize that power as an utterance: in the beginning was the Word. Do this as many times as you feel you need to for the catalyst needed by the forest to flow through you and reach where it needs to go.

When you have finished, be still, silent, and at one with the forest. Breathe with the forest and be still.

Something calls out to you through the stillness, and you become aware of yourself once more as a human. The forest slowly retreats from you, and yet the tree is still strong within you. Spend time just allowing you and the forest to slowly separate. Be aware, as you separate, that you and the forest are changed. Remember that feeling within you of change and connection. Whenever you walk among the trees again, you will feel them and they will feel you.

Slowly the everyday sounds around you filter back into your mind. You become more aware of the sounds of the birds and creatures around you, and more aware of your heart's rhythm and your breathing. Be aware of your connection with—and yet separateness from—the trees, and be aware of being surrounded by a family of trees.

When you are ready, open your eyes. For a moment, turn and lay your hand flat on the tree. This tree is your brother or sister, your kin: you have joined through the seasons together and breathed as one. Come back here often and sit with the tree if you can. Join with the tree, and leave offerings of food[1] for the plants and creatures that keep this tree strong. If the tree is near where you live, don't be surprised if the spirit of the tree enters your dreams when it is in danger or is stressed. If the trees need help, their collective consciousness can reach out to those who pay attention, just as they do through their roots to their fellow trees within the forest.

A.2 Carrying the forest through time

Sit comfortably and close your eyes. Using your imagination, see your inner flame burning brightly within you. The flame of life burns gently but brightly: stay with that image as you slowly deepen into silence and stillness. As you relax, you become aware that there are beings who are drawn by the brightness of your flame, and they inch closer to investigate.

In your inner vision, stand up and look around you. Out of the corner of your eye you see many beings hiding and trying to move closer to you. One of them steps before you, a being of the forest, and asks you if you are prepared to be of service. When you reply yes, they put their hands over your eyes and tell you to look.

---

[1] Any food left by trees or anywhere in nature must be unprocessed and not a risk to anything. Never leave heavily processed foods, meats, or chocolate, as they are poisonous to some creatures of the land. Honey is always a safe option, as is bread.

Looking through their hands, your vision changes, and you become aware of things you had not seen before. The building or landscape around you falls away, and you find yourself sitting out in nature with the rocks, trees, plants, and water. The stars are above you and the earth is below you.

The inner light of the plants and trees is dull, and they all seem to be covered in a dark heaviness. The animals are the same: their inner flames grow weak as they battle against the toxins in their bodies and environment.

The being, a faery who is working with you, tells you that there is something you can do for the future. They ask you to walk through the meadow or forest and let a plant choose you.

You set off walking, feeling the rich earth beneath your feet. You pass through tall grasses, bushes, trees, plants, and flowers. One plant in particular seems to stand out. As you get closer to it, you can see that the plant is struggling to breathe through the polluted air.

Gently and quietly, you scoop up the plant, being careful not to damage its roots, and hold it close to you. The inner power of the plant, its inner consciousness, surprises you with its vast power and beauty. The faery being comes up behind you and urges you to place the plant within you, next to your heart.

As the plant passes into you, a heavy tiredness creeps over you, and you lie down to sleep on the grass. The earth is warm and soft, moving gently as though you were lying on the body of a sleeping mother. The sleep pulls you deeper and deeper until you feel yourself sinking down into the earth, into the rock.

Deeper and deeper you fall, until you become still and silent. Now you sleep in the rock, deep below the surface of the planet. The seasons come and go, and you sleep. The years pass by, and still you sleep. Time has no meaning as you slumber within stone. Your body is getting heavier and heavier, becoming part of the rock itself. The mother curls around you as you sleep, singing her lullabies of the wind to you as you sleep.

Somewhere is the distance, someone calls your name. The sound echoes through your mind, and you struggle to regain your consciousness. The sound gets stronger and stronger until you are urged to move forward. Reaching up, you fight and climb back to the surface world, leaving the stillness of the rock behind you.

After a struggle, you emerge out of the darkness to find yourself on the surface. Everything looks strange. The world has moved on through time as you have slept, and now is the time to replant the children of the land—The Mother.

You look around for the best place to root the plant. Finding a good spot, you dig with your hands to create a space for the plant to root itself. Placing the plant carefully in the ground, you find yourself overwhelmed with a strange sadness.

Tears begin to fall from your eyes and moisten the ground around the plant. The more you cry, the more the plant is watered. The plant begins to glow with a powerful inner flame, growing beyond its physical boundary until it stretches in all directions.

The inner expression of the plant is a beauty you have not seen before, and you are overwhelmed as the inner consciousness of the plant reaches out to touch you. The earth around the plant changes as it begins to interact with the power of the plant, and you watch in wonder as the land springs to life.

The touch of the plant knocks you off balance and you fall backwards. You fall as though falling off a large cliff, your body tumbling through time as it twists around the directions. You fall and fall, becoming disorientated as your falling becomes ever faster.

Suddenly you stop, finding yourself sitting back in the patch of land where you first started. You can see all the beings within the plants and trees all around you as you slowly reorient yourself.

You remember your inner flame, the flame of all being at the edge of the Void. When you are ready, open your eyes.

A.3   Beaghmore: Secrets of the Stones

Beaghmore: Secrets of the Stones, is a fictional short story about one person's interactions with a stone circle complex in Northern Ireland. Embedded within it are signposts and keys to working with stone circles. It also touches on the experiences of the 'sight'—the inner seeing with the mind's eye and what a quiet voice it can be. The key to developing the sight is to pay attention.

The story also outlines the deep underlying relationship between the land, the Underworld, and the stars, which is a constant ladder of power and communion that a person can tap into to work in service to the land: the human acts as a bridge or axis between the dynamics. The story touches on working with storms at a deep level in vision, not to alter the weather but to join in communion with the vast powers of weather systems. The simple act of communion between a storm and a human becomes a catalyst, where the consciousness of the storm and the human become one.

★ ★ ★

A damp bitter wind blew mercilessly around the standing stones as Hillary, for the fourteenth time, circled them in curiosity. She had flown across the Atlantic to Northern Ireland, after saving her hard-earned dollars for three years, just so that she could stand here among the ancient stones of Beaghmore. She screwed up her eyes against the dull light and wind, looking at the many small standing stones, cairns, and stone circles.

They were not as impressive to look at as she thought they would be. Some unknown reason had pulled her to come here and sit among the stones. And now here she stood, dripping wet from the rain that never seemed to leave this place. The anticlimax almost drove her to tears. The stones seemed dead, lifeless in the face of her enthusiasm as she went from stone to stone, kneeling down to touch them with her forehead. Nothing.

A lone bird flew overhead, calling to her in her stupidity. This was the third day that she had ventured out of Cookstown, the local town, to stand in the peat bog and be with the ancient stone alignments. They were small stones, their height hidden beneath the depths of the peat, leaving only their heads showing. Somewhere in her mind she had imagined them to be tall, impressive, and mysterious. Rain dripped off the edge of her chin, taking all her hopes and longings with it as it fell to the ground, leaving her with nothing. What had she expected? She was not sure.

For years she had read books about Celtic stone circles, Celtic history, and Irish myths. The blood of her father's family had pulled at her to discover the island of Ireland for herself, to walk the paths that her ancestors had frequented. But now she was here, and the rain and incessant aroma of damp peat were the only things that impressed themselves on her.

Driving back into the town, she nodded to the old man sat outside the pub. He was always there regardless of the weather, and Hillary had concluded that he never went home but simply lived on that wet bench under the Guinness sign. He smiled as she drove past, and Hillary cringed. She was convinced that the whole town was laughing at her, the American who sits in the rain staring at stones.

The following morning, her last day in Cookstown, the sun graced the world with its presence and shone down on the stones of Beaghmore. Hillary went to the stones straight after breakfast. She parked her car and carried a blanket through the wet grass to the collection of stone circles and cairns. Standing to catch her breath, she covered her eyes from the sun and looked around the moor. In the mist and rain, she had not been able to see much. But now, in the sunshine, the vastness of the stone alignments became frighteningly clear: they went on seemingly for miles, mostly hidden except for the tips of the stones that peeked out of the wet peat.

The heavy blanket proved to be a good barrier against the damp as she sat in the center of the largest circle and began to sketch the alignments. The curlews called to her as sat in the weak sunshine trying to absorb as much as she could from this magical place before the long flight home.

Shielding her eyes from the sun, Hillary squinted as she systematically looked at the alignments in sections. Not only did she want to draw them, but she wanted to fix their appearance in her mind forever. There were three apparent clear circles among a jumble of other stone alignments, and beside the circles stood small collapsed cairns that could serve well as perches. Hillary had been tempted to sit on one rather than on the grass. But as she had approached the collapsed pile of stones, some instinct warned her off. What if it was a grave? she asked herself.

Beyond the clear circles, stretching out into the peat bog were numerous stones that lay half hidden beneath mud and grass. She was tempted to follow the stones and explore just how far the alignments stretched. But the voice of the local pub owner emerged in her head.

She had popped into the local pub the night before for a Guinness, and the barman had asked her why on earth she was in Cookstown of all places. When she told him that she was here to visit the stones, he had roared with laughter. When the laughter had finished, his face grew serious:

"Don't you be going beyond the circles now, de yar hear? Strange things happen out there and people vanish. Now you mind yerself and take care."

Hillary had smiled, but fear slid sideways in her previously confident thoughts and she nodded quietly. As she had drunk her Guinness, she had caught the old men in the pub looking at her and shaking their heads sadly. As each man got up to go home to his meal and his wife, they first stopped at Hillary as she sat at the bar and patted her shoulder solemnly while shaking their heads.

But sitting now in the midst of the stones and drinking in the view of the sparse terrain that stretched off as far as the eye could see, she did not feel any danger or fear. Taking their advice, she had not wandered off, but remained within the circle that drew her the most: the larger one at the far end of the alignment, on the edge of the bog.

After only a short time, her hand became heavy and her eyes struggled to stay open. The pencil she had been sketching with dropped from her hands, and her loose-leafed notebook slid down onto the wet grass, its thick papers instantly absorbing the moisture. She had only been awake a few hours and yet Hillary fought the sleep that crept on her, threatening to take away her precious last few hours with the stones. Rubbing her eyes, she began to sing in an attempt to wake up. Rabbits darted past and something, perhaps shadows in the low-hanging sunshine, moved around the edge of her vision as though watching her.

The battle waged until finally Hillary closed her eyes and lay back in the damp warmth. The sketches lifted from the grass and danced around the circle, carried by a strange wind that only blew within the stone circles. Hillary did not notice as she fell deeper and deeper into a dark sleep. The wind grew stronger, pulling at her hair as though to tease her and whispering a song in payment for Hillary's song.

The sound of the wind's song carried only to the edge of the stone circle and no further. Beyond the stones, all was stillness and calm. The song pulled Hillary from the depth of her sleep, keeping her on the edge of awareness, but not allowing her to open her eyes. While she was trapped in the twilight of half sleep, the wind carried words that moved around the stones:

Ringstone round, ringstone round,
bring rain and wind and thunder sound,
storms will dance when you do tarry
and only stones your heart will marry
Whatever shall it be, whatever shall it be...

Hillary drifted on the threshold of sleep. Whatever shall it be... the words circled around her head, digging for memories. Quite suddenly, without warning, Hillary was transported back through time to a memory of her childhood in California. At only eight years old, she had stood on top of a hill near her home town of Petaluma and held her arms up to the sky.

Hillary remembered the taste of the memory. She was playing out on the top of upside-down hill, her name for a towering hill where water was fabled to run uphill and where lanes vanished to confuse the drivers. Something had stopped her game of tag with the butterflies and caused her to stare into nothing. A rush of power formed a wind that blew only where Hillary stood, and the little girl held her arms up to the sky in wonder.

In that second, Hillary saw in her mind a terrible storm with flooding and mudslides. She watched as her Grandmother's house, on a steep hill by Tomales Bay, slid into the water with Grandmother trapped inside. In terror, Hillary screamed out for her Grandmother and looked up to shout at the storm. The powerful being that was the storm looked down in anger at Hillary, its rage centred on the humans who had desecrated sacred power lands. Suddenly the wind ceased and the vision faded, leaving the little girl shaking and crying on top of upside-down hill.

Hillary jerked awake, finding herself back on the damp blanket in the stone circle. She lay for a second trying to orientate herself. The dream of her childhood had been vivid, and she had forgotten about that incident until now. The wind had stopped, but her drawings were scattered all over the circles. It had left a strange scent in the air, a scent that she could almost taste, and a scent that she remembered from that childhood day on upside-down hill.

She sat up, pulling her knees under her arms and placing her chin on her knees: her thinking position, particularly when something had frightened her. The storm she had seen in that vision as a child had happened two weeks later. She had told her Grandmother about the vision, which had caused her mother to react angrily towards Hillary. Hillary's Grandmother and mother had argued for hours while Hillary lay outside on the lawn weeping. She always seemed to cause trouble, and she hated that. It was not as though she did it on purpose.

Two weeks later, when a storm whipped up and began moving into the bay, Grandmother put the cats in the car and headed inland to her daughters house, just to be on the safe side. The house did slide down into the bay, but Hillary was not allowed to talk about it. The day after, when her mother returned with

Grandmother to what was left of the house, Hillary's mother had spun around and pointed a finger in Hillary's face.

"Don't you ever speak of this to anyone, do you hear me? Not ever. You saw nothing and said nothing."

Hillary nodded dumbly, unable to understand what she had done wrong. Had she not saved Grandmother's life?

Some of the residual pain from that time now bubbled up in Hillary's eyes. Her mother had been distant with her from that moment, her father was always away, and only Grandmother seemed thankful for what Hillary had seen. Now, as a mature woman, she sat and wept for her mother and her lost childhood. All because of a strange day and a strange wind.

Slowly, she got herself up and started to pick up the drawings that were scattered untidily around the stones. But each time she reached out for one, a breeze picked it up and moved it. She chased the pictures around the circle until the breeze turned into a wind, carrying the drawings high up in the air before dropping them just out of her reach.

A laugh echoed from behind her, and Hillary spun around to see an old man and his large black dog leaning against one of the taller stones.

"I see they like you. Wind's... aye... a good un, means they've woken up. About time so it is."

His accent was deep and broad, causing Hillary to look blank as she tried to figure out what he just said.

"What do you mean, they have woken up?"

Hillary was excited, but she tried hard not to show it. The old man waved a hand around the stones as he spoke.

"This lot. When the wind blows around here and nowhere else, it means they want to work with whosevers in the circle. It's easy. Just walk round the circle til you're fit to drop, then go sit yerself down in the middle. They'll show you the rest. Have to go, mi dinners getting cold."

The wind blew Hillary's hair across her face and it took her a second or two to get the hair out of her eyes. She cleared her face and looked around, but the man had vanished. Hillary turned in all directions. It was impossible for him to vanish so quickly: the moor was flat for miles before it hit the rolling hills in the distance, and there was nowhere to vanish to. She should have been able to see him walk away for a least a mile in any direction. But he was nowhere to be seen. The hairs on the back of her neck stood up to attention in terror.

Her hands fumbled for the scattered pictures as her eyes kept watch for the disappearing man. Hillary was frightened and excited all at once. She had read about such encounters in her Celtic books. Of course! She slapped her forehead in recognition of her stupidity. The legend of the guardian with the black dog: the guardian of the stones. She must have read about such apparitions a hundred times, and when it happened to her, she did not recognize him.

There would have been so many things she could have asked him, so many things she could have learned. Swearing under her breath, she caught the last picture and weighed them all down with a stone. What an idiot, she thought to herself. And yet, did he not tell her something? Her mind filtered through the details of the conversation until she remembered what it was that he had said. Circle the stones until you are fit to drop. Then sit and let them do the rest.

Hillary looked around her, just to make sure there was no one to watch what she was doing. When she was sure that she was alone, Hillary began to walk clockwise around the stones. She had chosen the biggest circle, which was surrounded by small cairns. Around and around she circled, trying hard to concentrate on what she was doing.

An hour passed, and Hillary's legs were beginning to hurt. She had given up concentrating, and instead amused herself by mulling over her life in America. She had looked into the possibility of moving to Ireland, and she had been excited to find that she would be able to get an Irish passport on the strength of her Grandfather's birth in Cork. Maybe she would move to Cookstown and live on the edge of the bog. Then she would never have to leave the stones. Reality came crashing back with her footfalls when she admitted to herself that she could not afford to move and that there was no way for her to make a living out here in the middle of nowhere.

The resentment at her trapped life caused Hillary to walk faster. Why did life always do this to her? Why did things never work out? Why did she always lose things when she loved them? Her heart ached for permanence and love: she needed to belong and be loved. Unhappiness punctured every footfall as she marched around the circle, deep in thought.

Her legs started to tremble from the unaccustomed exercise, but Hillary pushed on, circling and circling as she thought of the time when she had lived in Manhattan for a while, the city where she had settled after college. Everything was fast, young, successful, and unhappy. Manhattan had hidden her from herself, allowing her to function in the world of frenzy. But here, among the stones and birds, Hillary could not hide.

It was the knees that buckled first. The pain shot through both her knees, bringing Hillary to an abrupt halt. She walked gingerly into the centre and lay down on her blanket, cushioned by the damp rough moorland grass underneath it. Exhausted, she allowed her body to slump as she lay watching the clouds scurry past overhead on an intent mission to rain on some poor unsuspecting soul. Her body lapped up the well-needed rest and her skin soaked up the moisture from the damp air and weak sunshine. She pulled the sides of the blanket around her and lay in wait for what was to come.

But nothing happened. She lay waiting patiently, not knowing what to expect. The minutes moved on, and Hillary was beginning to feel stupid. Maybe she had imagined the old man. Maybe she dreamed him? Her body was too tired to care, and Hillary drifted slowly to sleep, serenaded by the birds and the light wind.

Just as she tipped over the edge of sleep, her mind plummeted downwards at high speed through the land. The rush terrified her as she fought to awaken, but something held her firmly in the grip of unconsciousness. A whirlwind ripped at her as she fell, twisting and turning her until she could neither feel nor see anything except the wind. At that point, the wind ceased, but the falling continued. She looked down and saw the earth, the planet, beneath her. She was falling towards it at high speed.

Hillary tried to cry out, but nothing would move. The planet was getting closer and closer as she tried to pull away from the imminent impact. Breath froze in her throat as the ground rushed up to her face. Hillary closed her eyes in horror. But there was no impact: everything was still, and Hillary lay on the grass with her eyes still shut. She opened them slowly, sitting up so that she could look around her.

The damp blanket was still there, but everything else was different. The stones had gone, and bright lights had replaced them. Hillary sat unmoving as the lights pulsed brilliant colours that seeped up into the sky and joined with the sun. In among the lights where the stones had been, Hillary could see people, almost shadows, moving between the lights. The people appeared briefly before vanishing, their place being taken by another human shadow that moved as though unaware of its predecessor.

Some moved randomly and others seemed to be conducting a ritual. Hillary watched in awe. Something, maybe instinct, told her that she was seeing through time: the shadows were people who had visited and worked with the stones over the centuries. Moving slowly, Hillary got up and tried to approach one of the lights which, she now understood, were the stones. As her hand reached out and touched the light, a shadow moved swiftly around her. Her hand felt the cold stone beneath her touch, but all she could see was light and movement. Her eyes focused on the movement of the shadow, which transformed into the hazy image of a child. The child could see Hillary and was clearly frightened.

Hillary held her hand up to the child to tell her not to be afraid, but as she removed her hand from the stone, the child vanished, leaving only the bright light to blind her. This fascinated her. She touched the stone again, feeling its solidity through the light as its power coursed through her. Again she saw shadows move around her. A shadow approached the stone that Hillary was touching. As the shadow touched the stone, Hilary could see it was a young man. She touched him on the forehead, and the young man jumped back in terror, his face contorting as he clutched his head. She panicked: what if she had injured him?

She touched the stone again, this time closing her eyes from the distractions around her. As soon as her lids shut, the ground started to spin beneath her.

Hillary felt nauseous, but refused to let go of the stone. The spinning became faster and faster until the sensation became comfortable. She opened her eyes and looked up. Weather fronts passed over quickly and then vanished. Night and day moved rapidly, and the wind came and went.

She leaned into the stone, which supported her as she looked up. The deeper into the stone she leaned, the clearer her vision became. As the storm fronts passed over, Hillary became aware that they were conscious: she could feel the storm thinking and looking for something as it scurried on across the sky. She reached up towards one as it passed over, her mind searching for contact.

Immediately she was travelling with the storm as it passed over the land and sea. Its fury built within her as it sought to cleanse the land with its force. Rain was unleashed on the land, and Hillary fell with the raindrops, touching everything around her and sensing the conscious awareness of the storm scattered in every drop of water. The land breathed in response to the storm, creating a conversation that had Hillary in the middle. The land and the storm communed, and Hillary joined in. Her body felt the interaction, lapping up the life-giving water and enjoying the feel of release as the land gave power to the storm.

It stopped as suddenly as it started and Hillary was back leaning against the stone. Her body felt heavy from the exertion and she slumped harder against the standing stone which seemed to absorb her. The feeling of absorption became more intense until Hillary slipped fully into the stone and joined with the rock.

Her breathing slowed, her thoughts deepened, and her movements ceased as she joined in union with the sacred stone. All the other stones around her connected with her, communing together in their timeless vigil on the land. The endless journey of the earth moving from season to season, from year to year, became like breathing for her.

Her thoughts guided those who wished to commune with the sacred land, and her joy was immeasurable as the power of the Underworld flowed through her, reaching for the sky, while the power of the stars flowed down through her on its way into the Underworld. This was what she was born for, this was the purpose of her existence.

The breath came suddenly and a dull light crashed into Hillary's brain. Voices echoed all around her as someone called her name. She felt her body being moved, and sharp needle pricks in her wrist. Hillary tried to open her eyes. A voice shouted in her face, its noise deafening in its coarseness.

"Can you hear me, miss? Miss, can you hear me?"

Hillary tried to turn away from the noise as she sought the peaceful stillness of the stones. But she could not move her head. Reluctantly, she slowly opened her eyes and looked at a face peering into hers. Everything was dull. The sky, the face, everything. Nothing had light or colour. Hillary wanted to die. The face spoke to her again as she tried to focus on the intruder.

"We will put you in the ambulance now. Everything will be okay. It was a good piece of luck that Mr. Henry found you, eh?"

Hillary did not want putting in an ambulance; she wanted to be left with the stones. As they carried her out of the circle, Hillary felt the stones pull on her to stay. But there was nothing she could do but cry as she was driven off, away from where she belonged.

II

The male nurse bustled around her as Hillary stared out of the window. After a battery of tests that lasted many days, they had finally agreed to let her go. Words like 'epilepsy' and 'drugs' had been bandied about between the doctors, which had made Hillary angry. And yet she could offer no alternative explanation without exposing the secrets of the stones.

The male nurse watched Hillary closely as she packed her bags. He looked towards the door, then back at Hillary. He spoke to her in a low voice, keeping one eye on the door and one on Hillary.

"Miss, mi name's Fra. I was born near Beaghmore. It's a special place, isn't it."

He waited for Hillary's reaction. She sat down and looked at him more closely. There was something in his eyes that she had not noticed previously, a brilliant fragment of light. She nodded slowly in response to his comment.

"Did you work with the stones, then? Is that why you were there?"

He turned as he asked her the questions, making sure that no one could see him from the corridor. Hillary nodded, and Fra watched the nod in the room's mirror.

"Well," he continued, "if you want to work with them properly, there are ways of doing it without killing yourself. Call me, and my grandad will teach you."

Fra shoved a piece of torn paper with a scribbled telephone number on it into Hillary's hand, then darted down the corridor and out of sight before she could speak to him. She fingered the paper in her hand and looked back at her bag that contained her air ticket. Hillary reached into her bag and pulled out the wallet that held her passport and plane ticket. Without a second thought, she tore the ticket into bits and threw them in the bin.

The sky darkened, lowering the light in the room; Hillary got up and looked out of the window. Clouds were gathering: she could feel the power of the storm as it edged nearer, calling on her to join it.

She slung her bag over her shoulder and picked up her suitcase that had been dropped off by her hotel. On the threshold of the hospital, she looked again at the sky and breathed in its scent as she stepped out into a new world. There would be no going back now.

★ ★ ★

Note: Beaghmore is a large complex of Bronze age megalithic structures, circles, and cairns north of Cookstown in County Tyrone, Northern Ireland. It is a place I visited a few times in the early 1990s, and is one of the sites that really taught me how to work with stone circles and cairns using vision, utterance, sleep, and walking. Not all stone circles are magical: some are social. The 'switched-on ones' often have different powers or focuses. Some are places of communion, some are places of death, some are places of healing or fertility, some are tribal places of focus, and some are connected to the weather and the power of the storms.

If you are ever visiting a stone circle, always treat it with respect. They are not there for your baggage or agenda, or your rituals and beliefs. They are of themselves. If you want to take a gift, honey is a good one. But simply showing up, communing, and showing respect is enough. Do not leave candles, tealights, plastic ribbons, plastic figures, or chocolate: these are poisonous to most animals. Don't leave any other New Age bullshit stuff either. Do not paint or carve the stones, and take nothing away. The stones are not there for you; you are there for them.

The Magical Understanding of Good and Evil

When walking a magical path the practitioner soon comes up against issues of good v evil, duality of power, left hand/right hand path etc. which can bring to the surface a great many questions that we have to ask of ourselves and those involved in the particular magical path that we are walking. I feel it is important for us as magicians to step outside of the dogmas and beliefs inherent within our culture and society, which are often deep seated and not immediately apparent to us. By doing so it enables us to ascertain what is actually happening, why, and how to find a way to navigate through issues in a way that compliments who we are and what we are trying to achieve

What we perceive as good or evil largely depends on our system of beliefs, be they religious, cultural, philosophical etc., and our own emotional development. It also is deeply affected by our own needs both in personal development and everyday living.

Our systems of belief and the wider religious/cultural pattern in which we were born and raised in have a massive effect upon how we view the world. As children we accept such dogmas without question, particularly if raised in a religious household. As teens we rebel against such dogmas and begin the process of questioning. Often though, the questioning element of our personal development can become limited by a continued unconscious adherence to the dogmatic pattern which results in not a breaking away from the pattern, but a continuing rebellion against a dogma which in turn feeds and strengthens it.

We can see this for example in the work of Crowley. I am not an expert on Crowley by any means, and am commenting from the outside looking in. But it is an example that is known by most people in the magical arena. Crowley was raised in a very strict, and unhealthy Christian household that was mired in the sexually and behaviour repressed Victorian era. Crowley struck out to try and become the opposite of what he had been raised in. This eventually brought about a huge change in thinking, but his reasoning was still mired within the dogma of Christianity, just from an opposing point of view.

At that time, I think it would have been near on impossible for someone of his time, culture and background to have completely stepped out of that pattern. But in his struggle, whether we agree with it or not, he and others like him opened doors that our generation no longer has to bother with and yet many branches of magic still cling to that outworn pattern. And there in lies one of the problems: we have become so used to working and evolving within the pattern that we forget that we are now able to step outside of the pattern rather than being the antithesis of the pattern. We become stuck in the white magician, black magician, left hand and right hand path mentality.

So how do we operate? I think the first thing for a magician is to know their own personal limitations of what they are and are not willing to do and take responsibility for. On one hand, the more 'spiritually' inclined magician is likely to have a set of heroic ethics that they vigorously defend, often without direct experience, and postulate to others about. Over time, with the dedication of a magical path, the magician is then put into a variety of life situations that directly challenge not only the validity of those ethics, but also the ability of the individual to make more informed decisions regarding their ethics. Some are realized to be empty shells of dogmatic or fanciful beliefs, and some are discovered to be of vast importance. That distinction also strengthens the magician and enables them to uphold the important ethics in the face of extreme challenge.

Slowly, the ethics or concepts that may be considered admirable in many societies are put to the practical test and many fall by the wayside as the magician realizes their futility. Others prove to be difficult to uphold, but wonderful boundaries that bring out the best in someone. This is a filter mechanism that most of us have been through in one way or another, so that when we emerge battered and still standing a few decades later, we have a much more realistic idea of what we can and cannot do, and more importantly what were truly are willing or not willing to do to survive. The high ideals we started with are tested to the extreme until we are either destroyed, or we have learned to understand which ethics, boundaries and limitations are actually really necessary, and which are just egotistic vanity.

It is easy to stand in judgement of someone from a safe vantage point and feel good about ourselves. But once fate tosses us to the ravages of harsh life, then we begin to feel a lot more compassion and understanding for those whom we observe to be struggling against themselves or their society. We know, because we have been there - understanding the hardship involved in true survival becomes a lantern to light our path.

Similarly in the other direction, following a magical path of selfishness, of using power purely and unashamedly for the pursuit of wants and needs gives freedom to the magician who has lived in a stifling society. Self indulgence and self preservation give a person a sense of power, a sense of control over our own lives and destinies. We gain a sense of our own power and importance. Until it begins to go wrong—the dawning of how limited we are, and how wants and needs do not fill a greater sense of identity nor do they teach us truly about power. Our addictions begin to rule then destroy us, to weaken and expose the false sense of security that was gained. A magician walking this path will either begin to develop their own unique self containment, ethics and understanding, or they will implode.

For myself, I began my magical path as a teenager in the 1970s with a terrible sense of self righteousness. In my early twenties I asked the inner contacts for learning, for wisdom, for experience (not always such a great idea). I certainly got what I asked for and was thrown to the wolves. Every pedestal I took delight in standing upon was knocked over until I understood the dilemmas of those I had so arrogantly looked down upon in my youth. It is a terribly hard long and painful lesson, but that is what magic does. It confronts you. Eventually I learned and am still learning to look beyond the 'pattern' of what I personally consider 'ethical,' and to recognize my own weaknesses and failures in the cold hard light of day. I realize now this process will never end, which is good as it means we can constantly grow, evolve and learn.

Knowing our own personal limitations is a very important part of the development of magic within us and has great bearing upon how we wield that magic. The rules of engagement in life are the same for magic, from the small aspects to the greatest ones. So for example, eating meat. It is easy to buy a prepacked, chopped and ready to cook bit of meat. It is not so easy to look into the eyes of an animal and watch it die by your own hands. In rich first world countries, many people say, "I could not kill an animal, but I eat meat", or they will say 'I could not kill an animal therefore I am vegan". It is a statement that is easy to make in some first world countries where there is a financial social safety net, and also access to vegetarian protein sources—although some may go hungry from time to time, people in such countries do not die of starvation. We have that choice and often choose not to kill—our ethics are a product of our living circumstances.

But put in a situation in a country where there is no social safety net, and you are very hungry, your children are hungry and if you do not kill an animal you may starve, then it is a different matter. Your ethics change according to your circumstances. So they are not really ethics at all, but social and hierarchical expressions.

The will to survive is all encompassing. It does not make the killing any easier, but it makes it necessary: that is the reality, the true reality of nature that we are often protected from in modern society. That luxury enables us to be 'ethical': but magic begins when we know our true limitations, we know what we are really capable of doing, both for good and bad under extreme circumstances. Then and only then can we begin to understand power in a magical context: we learn about it through knowing our own true limitations, then we can learn how to navigate our way through the maze.

So it is back to good and evil. What do those words actually mean anyway? We bandy then around in religion, in spirituality and in magical paths. But do we really understand what they mean? What is evil? Is it evil to maim and kill?

Is it evil to destroy? It all depends on where you are in context to the power. As humans, we find genocide against other humans as intolerable, evil incarnate. But we commit such acts without thought on a regular basis against other creatures. Is mass murder evil? If someone kills a load of seals, or ponies or kittens, we consider that unacceptable. But if they are cows or pigs, then that serves our purpose and is therefore acceptable. So evil in reality is something we do not like to happen to us either as individuals or as a species. For us it is hard to differentiate between what is necessary destruction and unnecessary destruction. Necessary destruction is a part of nature, unnecessary destruction is the closest we can truly come to understanding the complexity of what is truly evil.

High or powerful magic is like wielding nuclear power; it can do great damage over a long period of time. The power itself is neither good nor evil, but its use can have devastating effects regardless of the intention behind it. It is a dangerous tool and the more power a magician is able to access the more damage or good they can potentially do with it. How that power is applied is directly related to how that magician perceives themselves and the world around them.

Because of that dynamic, what often happens is the more potential for power that a magician has, the greater their life experiences will be in order to bring them to a relative mature place, or to switch them off – a bit like blowing a fuse. Those who do not have the capacity for mediating large amounts of power tend to have a more stable constant life experience (unless of course they have already got their shit together). This dynamic seems to run in relation to the capacity of the person/path for power.

It is something that has happened to me and something I have also observed many times over in other magicians. There is no sense of any paternalistic teaching parent god/s in the dynamic; it is more a matter of power in, power out, in the weave of life. The trick is to recognize what is happening and engage the process for learning and strengthening, rather than flailing around in the dark and cursing the gods. (been there, done that)

When the dynamic first really kicked in for me, I was horrified that suddenly life was throwing me big balls of shit on a daily basis that was beyond silly. Luckily there was an elder magician around in my wider community that pointed out to me that every damn thing I was going through was directly challenging me on my stance of ethics, of understanding, and of limitations.

That was a major turning point not only in my coping strategy, but also in my magical understanding and development. I began to engage directly with each challenge in order to draw what I could from the situations and turn them in to learning curves, strengthening exercises and humble pie eating sessions. The more I engaged, the wider the door of magical contact became. I began to see the 'bad' side of life and magic as something that balanced out and polished the 'good' side. I began to see the dynamic of how creative magical power needed to exist in the presence of destructive magical power so instead of trying to get rid of the bad power, it is merely balanced out by a creative power and visa versa.

Like everything else, you can read about something or be taught about something until the cows come home, but the true deeper meanings and the visceral understanding of magic cannot really take seed and grow until it is a direct learning experience. So for example this article is not really written to teach, not even to burble about my own opinions/expressions, but to open the door as that elder did for me once and say, "hey its okay don't panic, this is what is happening and this is how you deal with it to survive". It is a path that thousands have trodden before us and knowing that it is a path that can not only be survived, but will bring you to a wonderful dawning of deep magic is a lifeline that can light your way in the darkest of times.

Appendix C

Understanding the Void and the Inner Worlds

There has been a lot of confusion in various magical discussions at conferences and online about what certain words mean when they are used in terms of magical visionary work. The two biggest questions that tend to arise repeatedly are "what is the Void?" and "what are the Inner Worlds?" Hopefully this appendix will clear such questions up!

C.1 What are the Inner Worlds?

The Inner Worlds are states of energy and consciousness that exist outside and independently of the human body. They are not a product of our collective imagination. However, our collective imagination over the millennia has created interfaces or images by which we can understand and interact with the various forces that exist all around us. These energies are the forces of the universe, the templates of creation and destruction, though some are energetic constructs that humanity has built and worked within throughout our history.

Through visionary work we can interact with various beings such as angelic beings, land spirits, deities, demonic beings, and the dead. We find these beings in various inner realms, for example in the realm of death, the Underworld, the angelic realm, the Desert/Tree of Life, and the inner temples.

We can also plunge deeper into the Inner Worlds to experience and interact with the forces of nature, of life and death, and of Divinity itself. This interaction is not new, and has been used in various ways by tribal magicians, ancient priests, mystics, and visionaries from various cultures throughout time.

In the West we have slowly become divorced from this method of working for a variety of reasons, including our cultural beliefs, religious dogma, and scientific rationalism. This divorce has had a massive impact on magical practice in the West, and we are only recently starting to recover from it.

Bear in mind that my terminology is not universal: other traditions still working in these areas use different names, but the place is the same. It is important to understand the place itself and its function rather than getting hung up on its name.

C.2 The Void

The Void itself is the most commonly misunderstood term used in visionary magic. Some think of it as the Biblical Abyss, some think of it as the 'astral realms,' and some think it describes their head the morning after a bottle of whisky.

The Void is a place of nothingness that holds the potential for everything: it is like the universe drawing breath before it breathes life into existence. Everything comes from the Void into manifestation. It is the raw power of potential, when the energy has gathered to create and is just on the threshold of the process of manifestation. For kabbalists, it is the power of Divine Utterance as it begins its parade down the Tree of Life, taking its form from interacting with the spheres of power before finally manifesting in Malkuth.

In visionary magical terms, the Void can be worked with in two ways. The first way to develop a method for working with the Void is to imagine it as a place of nothingness that lies beyond a threshold: we imagine a flame, we pass through the flame using the element of fire as a gateway, and we pass into a place where there is no time, no movement, nothing.

As the student gets used to being in a place where there is nothing, and being able to have a still and silent mind, then they will acquire the ability to work with the Void. Because the Void is full of all potential, it can be used as a stepping-through point, or threshold, to gain access to other places. It is also a good tool to use to slow the mind down so that clear work can begin. You can step through the Void, and you also experience the Void by having your mind totally still and silent.

The next phase of working with the Void is to bring the Void into yourself, or better said, to tune yourself to the Void. Instead of stepping over a threshold to the Void, simply sit and slowly silence your mind and body until you are nowhere and nothing. Within that silence you focus on the Void as the place that all potential and creation comes from. Your shift from being still and silent to having an awareness of the Void as the energy from which everything flows will move your consciousness from simple stillness to being 'within the Void.' This in turn prepares you to bridge and mediate power from unformed potential to manifest form.

That shift of awareness is a major tool in magic, and allows the deeper powers within you to rise to the surface while plugging you into the power frequency of creation: the power potential that is within everything physically manifest. Everything is constantly creating and destroying at an energetic level in some form or other, and the use of the Void shifts you into that stream of power and consciousness.

This is not an easy thing to learn. Some people take months to learn the technique, some take years, and others can master it in weeks. It is a individual experience, but it never stops deepening and developing. The power of the Void within you will deepen and grow throughout your working life as a magician until it becomes an extremely profound and powerful experience.

It really depends on your mind, the environment in which you live, and the external input your mind receives daily. For someone used to living in a simple way, getting into the Void is not too difficult. For someone raised around computers, fast bites of information, television, and mobile phones, it can be much harder for them to master the stillness. But it is not impossible. The longer your attention span, the easier it gets.

The Void can be used as a threshold; it can also be a place to work if you are working on a magical task that involves mediating a new power or energy into the manifest world. It is also an extremely useful bolthole if you are magically attacked by a powerful being: when you go into the Void, your boundaries loosen, which enables you spread out your consciousness to everything that is around you. You become like mist, which creates a situation where the being has nothing to grab onto. Comes in handy!

C.3 Stilling the monkey mind: why?

It is important, particularly with visionary magic, but really in all magic, that your mind can be properly stilled and silenced. Once that has been achieved, then you can learn to use your mind with absolute focus to achieve magical patterns, inner contact, and hold/mediate power without distraction. Your mind is your main tool, and a monkey mind is a disaster in magic.

Meditation, working with the Void, and learning focused, simple rituals are all ways that you can learn to harness your mind and imagination so that you can work with it effectively. Magic is about moving around energy and power, and interacting with other beings through consciousness, so a trained mind is absolutely essential. The longer-term magical training of the mind also begins the process of rewiring your brain so that it can learn magical skills in detail and recognize and work deeply with magical imagery and vocabulary, so that you as a magician can do your job.

It is exactly the same as learning any detailed craft such as a classical art, carpentry, or science at doctorate level. The brain has to adjust itself to develop specific skills that only long-term work and study develop. This is why instant magic manuals and ritual recipe books do not make a magician. Only constant practice and training in specific areas of inner and outer work make a magician.

Being aware of how much of a monkey your mind really is can be a bit of a shock. Just test it by sitting in a room with no stimuli: no noise, no people, nothing to look at. Sit in the silence and be aware of your thoughts. See how your mind jumps from one thing to the next, how much your body wants to move. It can be quite a revelation. Then shut your eyes and sit silently. Again be aware of the thoughts and movements that your body tries to make. We are rarely silent in our modern world.

Once you are aware of the level of monkey mind you possess, then you can slowly start to train it to settle and be quiet, and train your body to be still and not itch, move, or twitch. Don't try to force this too much: don't approach it in a determined "I am going to conquer myself" way. Just practice once or twice a day to be silent for a short while, and slowly let that time increase until you can sit in silence for a long time without realizing how much time has passed.

With that achieved, begin work with the two different levels of the Void visions to see how different the two states of silence feel. One is simple silence and stillness. The other is silence and stillness but with a huge sense of power behind it. That is the creative potential that is in the Void.

The next stage is to practise walking around the house and down the street in a state of inner silence. This exercise is harder, but it is the initial training for empowered ritual: ritual performed while the mind is in the Inner Worlds. You learn to be in two places at once, with your mind in the Inner Temple or in a specific inner realm while your body is conducting a ritual action. The power begins to flow from the Inner Worlds through you and out into the ritual. That ritual forming of power is then mediated out into the world in whatever form you are working on.

Quareia
A New, Free School of Magic
For The 21st Century

Advancing education in Mystical Magic
and the Western Esoteric Mysteries.

www.quareia.com
schooldirector@quareia.com

Quareia is a practical magical training course founded by Josephine McCarthy and Frater Acher. It is a complete and freely available course designed to develop a student from a complete beginner into an adept. There are no barriers to entry: the course is accessible regardless of income, race, gender, religion, or spiritual beliefs.

Quareia is aligned to no particular school or specific religious, mystical, or magical system; rather it looks at and works with various magical, religious, and mystical practices that have influenced magical thinking in the Near Eastern and Western world from the early Bronze Age to the present day.

The entire course is free and openly available on the Quareia website.

Printed in the USA
CPSIA information can be obtained
at www.ICGtesting.com
LVHW082037041123
762998LV00035B/1207/J